JAPANESE AMERICAN ETHNICITY

# Japanese American Ethnicity

*In Search of Heritage and Homeland
across Generations*

Takeyuki Tsuda

NEW YORK UNIVERSITY PRESS
New York

NEW YORK UNIVERSITY PRESS
New York
www.nyupress.org

References to Internet websites (URLs) were accurate at the time of writing. Neither the author nor New York University Press is responsible for URLs that may have expired or changed since the manuscript was prepared.

Library of Congress Cataloging-in-Publication Data
Names: Tsuda, Takeyuki, author.
Title: Japanese American ethnicity : in search of heritage and homeland across generations / Takeyuki Tsuda.
Description: New York : New York University Press, [2016] | Includes bibliographical references and index.
Identifiers: LCCN 2016011168| ISBN 978-1-4798-2178-5 (hbk. : alk. paper) | I SBN 978-1-4798-1079-6 (pbk. : alk. paper)
Subjects: LCSH: Japanese Americans—Ethnic identity. | Japanese Americans—Cultural assimilation. | Japanese Americans—Social life and customs. | Japanese Americans—Racial identity. | United States—Ethnic relations. | United States—Race relations. | Taiko (Drum ensemble)—United States—History. | Children of immigrants—United States. | Japan—Emigration and immigration. | United States—Emigration and immigration.
Classification: LCC E184.J3 T7873 2016 | DDC 973/.04956—dc23
LC record available at http://lccn.loc.gov/2016011168

New York University Press books are printed on acid-free paper, and their binding materials are chosen for strength and durability. We strive to use environmentally responsible suppliers and materials to the greatest extent possible in publishing our books.

Manufactured in the United States of America

10 9 8 7 6 5 4 3 2 1

Also available as an ebook

# CONTENTS

## ACKNOWLEDGMENTS

The fieldwork and writing for this book project have been long in the making. I have been sidetracked a few times by other research projects and opportunities, which led to edited book volumes. As a result, I did not initially embark on writing an entire book on contemporary Japanese Americans from scratch, but worked on independent papers on specific topics. The dominant theme and framework for this book therefore coalesced over a number of years.

This book would not have been possible without the supportive and collegial academic environment provided by the School of Human Evolution and Social Change at Arizona State University. A sabbatical that the school granted me during the spring semester of 2014 allowed me to finally finish the book manuscript.

The ideas and analyses contained in this book have benefited considerably from feedback I received at various conferences, workshops, and departmental colloquiums. I thank the individuals who invited me to these occasions and the audiences for their helpful comments and questions. I would especially like to acknowledge the comments and suggestions I received from James Eder, Lieba Faier, Jon Fox, Nelson Graburn, Harlan Koff, William Kelly, Sangmi Lee, Karen Leong, Wei Li, Cecilia Menjívar, Tariq Modood, Luis Plascencia, Claudia Sadowski-Smith, and Hung Thai, as well as Wisa Uemura and Franco Imperial (of San Jose Taiko) and two anonymous reviewers for New York University Press, who provided very thoughtful and extensive comments on the manuscript. Parts of the Introduction, Chapter 4, and Chapter 8 were previously published in *Anthropology Today*, *Ethnic and Racial Studies*, and the *Journal of Anthropological Research*. I thank the editors and reviewers at these journals for their helpful comments. As always, errors in fact and interpretation are the sole responsibility of the author. I would also like to gratefully acknowledge my editor at New York University Press,

Jennifer Hammer, for her enthusiasm and support for this project and for her effective and efficient work behind the scenes.

Most importantly, my heartfelt gratitude and deepest thanks go out to the many Japanese Americans in San Diego and Phoenix who so openly welcomed me to their communities and generously allowed me to share their lives and experiences through numerous conversations and interviews. I truly appreciate their willingness to talk to me for hours and their thoughtful comments and insightful observations about their lives, without which this book would not be possible.

# Introduction

*Ethnic Heritage across the Generations: Racialization, Transnationalism, and Homeland*

## Four Generations of Japanese Americans

Ruth Morita is a serious and soft-spoken second-generation Japanese American woman in her seventies. Although she can be quite engaging in conversation, she is not naturally talkative, and it took some coaxing during our interview to get her to elaborate on some of her experiences. Like other elderly *nisei* (second-generation Japanese Americans), she had been interned in a concentration camp during World War II. Because the internment is such an integral part of the Japanese American experience, Ruth assumed that I wanted to interview her about it. Although I had told her that I was mainly interested in the contemporary ethnic experiences of Japanese Americans, she brought a copy of a PBS documentary that had brief footage of her in an internment camp with other girls. "I couldn't believe it," she said. "I was watching this documentary one day and I see this child running around in camp. I was like, wait a minute, that's me!"

Because it is such an important part of her past, I asked Ruth in some detail about her internment experience. I was surprised that she actually characterized it as "fun" and "like a long summer camp." It was a safe environment, she was together with a lot of other Japanese American kids, and she was no longer under the control of her parents. She spent her days going to school and playing with the other girls and made some really good friends whom she continues to see today. She had no stories of misery and oppression to tell, which I had fully expected to hear. Nonetheless, Ruth spoke about how the interment had been a defining moment for Japanese American nisei:

Despite being American citizens, we were locked up just because of our Japanese ancestry. So the niseis had to show they were loyal Americans. That's why the men went off and fought in the 442nd [the Japanese American Regimental Combat Team that fought very bravely during World War II in Europe]. We stressed being American and assimilation, and didn't want the cultural baggage of our parents. It wasn't until after the war that we were gradually accepted and finally given opportunities to get ahead.

I then asked Ruth about her parents and their internment experiences. "It wasn't that bad for the kids, but it was really tough for my parents," Ruth recalled. "They lost everything, their business, the house, their possessions . . ." Her voice started to crack with emotion. "It devastated them. After camp, they had to restart their lives again with nothing. I don't think they ever completely recovered from it. I don't think the emotional scars ever healed."

\*\*\*

Steve Okura was a board member of the Nikkei Student Union (NSU), the Japanese American student organization at the University of California at San Diego. The first time I encountered Steve was in the hallway of the student center before one of NSU's meetings. He was speaking to a student from Japan in fluent Japanese. His Japanese sounded so native, I was not sure whether he was Japanese American since I had heard that some students from Japan are members of NSU. I asked Steve during the meeting, "Are you Japanese?"

"No," Steve replied. "I'm *shin-nisei*" (a "new nisei," whose parents emigrated to the United States from Japan *after* World War II).

"Oh really?" I was a bit surprised. "You know, I'm shin-nisei too!"

This was the first time during my fieldwork that I encountered another fellow shin-nisei. During my interview with Steve, I was repeatedly struck by how his experiences were very similar to mine. Our Japanese parents had immigrated to the United States as high-skilled professionals, we grew up speaking Japanese at home, we attended Japanese Saturday school with children from Japan for many years, and we were fully bilingual and bicultural. We had also lived transnational lives since our parents took us to Japan on numerous occasions to visit relatives and travel through the country. And we had both briefly considered applying to Japanese universities for our college education.

Another commonality we shared is that neither of us identified as "Japanese American" growing up. "I never thought of myself as Japanese American or even used that word," Steve remarked. "I always thought of myself as just Japanese, who was born in America." Like myself, Steve did not start identifying as Japanese American until college, when he became one of the large number of Asian American students on campus.

Steve confided in me that even today, he does not feel like an "authentic Japanese American." "It's because my family didn't go through the internment and all that," he explained. "So I don't share that history. In fact, I've always felt much more connected to Japan and its culture my entire life than to the Japanese American experience."

***

George Okamoto is a delightful person with an effusive personality. He seems to always be in a good mood with a perpetual smile on his face, and he loves to joke and tease, often releasing his big, engaging laugh. I first met him at the annual meeting of the Japanese American Historical Society of San Diego, where we had lunch together, and then encountered him again during a community event at the Buddhist Temple of San Diego.

George was a *sansei* (third-generation) and very much fit previous images I had of the "typical" Japanese American. Despite his Japanese appearance, he was completely Americanized, had never been to Japan and had no interest in the country, and did not speak a word of Japanese. "I'm a good example of a 'banana,'" he told me with a laugh when we first met. "I look yellow and Japanese on the outside, but if you peel me, I'm just like a white person inside." Like other Japanese Americans of his generation I interviewed, George felt he had lost touch with his Japanese heritage, which he directly attributed to his nisei parents' internment experiences. "They had to prove that they were loyal Americans, so they had to kind of push their cultural identity aside," he explained. "So we sanseis, we just weren't exposed to our heritage as kids and were raised just like whites. In fact, growing up, I thought of myself as white. It didn't always occur to me that I looked different from them!"

I finally had an opportunity to interview George and we agreed to meet at a local Starbucks. When George showed up, he greeted me warmly as always.

"So . . . you really want me to tell you everything about myself, huh?" he asked playfully.

"Yes, everything," I replied.

"Are you sure? I've done some crazy things in my life!" George laughed.

When we walked up to the counter to order our coffees, the barista instantly recognized George's Japanese last name on his credit card and decided to try out the Japanese he had learned, perhaps in college. "Anata nihonjin desu. Genki desuka?" (You are Japanese. How are you?).

In contrast to his usual, jovial demeanor, George's face suddenly took on a serious expression. He looked straight at the barista, his eyes almost confrontational. "I am *not* Japanese!" George said emphatically. The barista was taken aback.

"I'm American. I just look Japanese," George's expression suddenly eased, followed by his signature big laugh. We were all relieved. George was back to his normal self.

After we sat down at a table with our coffees to start the interview, George leaned over and asked, "So what the hell did he ask me in Japanese?"

\*\*\*

I was lucky enough to get tickets for a performance of "Camp Dance," a play about the Japanese American internment experience during World War II. The play was a big hit among Japanese American communities across the United States, and the traveling theatrical troupe had given a series of sold-out performances. I attended the San Diego performance with Cathy, one of my very first sansei interviewees, and her sister. When we entered the auditorium, the place was already packed. I was a bit surprised to find that the stage was set with a row of colorful, traditional Japanese *taiko* drums instead of props for the play. Before the play began, a group of young taiko players marched onto the stage dressed in *happi*, traditional Japanese festival costumes with *kanji* (Japanese characters). They immediately took their positions alongside the drums and raised their *bachi* (drumsticks) into the air in an elegant ready pose.

With a coordinated shout (*kiai*), they suddenly began drumming in unison, the thunderous beating reverberating throughout the auditorium.

This was not a taiko ensemble from Japan. These were *fourth-generation* Japanese American youth, the *yonsei*. Nor was their performance unusual. Taiko has become popular among the yonsei, and many events in the Japanese American community now begin with a taiko performance from a local ensemble (Ahlgren 2011; Konagaya 2001). The drumming was quite good, and the audience showed their appreciation with loud applause after the brief performance.

"It's kind of surreal to see Japanese American kids doing this today, wearing such old-fashioned Japanese costumes and playing such traditional drums," Cathy remarked. "It's like you are being transported back to old Japan. The yonsei have really gotten back in touch with their Japanese roots. It's something we sanseis lost and makes us feel good."

\*\*\*

This book explores the contemporary ethnic experiences of U.S.-born Japanese Americans from the second to the fourth generations and the extent to which they remain connected to their ancestral cultural heritage. As shown by the above vignettes, the strength of ethnic heritage among Japanese Americans varies considerably by generation. Therefore, my topical focus is not intended to imply that all (or even most) Japanese Americans are in search of their heritage and homeland. My interviews indicated that some of them, especially the third-generation sansei, clearly are not. However, many Japanese Americans continue to think of their ethnicity in terms of the relative importance of their Japanese ancestry and their ethnic homeland of Japan. Even the sansei continue to feel the impact of their Japanese ancestral culture on their personalities and ethnic identities. They also began the taiko movement, which has become the primary ethnic heritage activity among Japanese Americans today.

Therefore, ethnic heritage is a useful conceptual lens through which to understand the cultural experiences of Japanese Americans as well as differences among them in terms of generation, age, and history. The concept can also be used to interrogate issues related to assimilation, transnationalism, racialization, multiculturalism, and homeland, all of which influence how ancestral heritage has been experienced, constructed, and enacted by different generations of Japanese Americans.

Japanese Americans are one of the oldest Asian American groups in the United States. Although most Asian Americans are primarily the product of the mass immigration of Asians to the United States after 1965,[1] Japanese immigration occurred mainly between the 1880s and 1924, when the United States prohibited further Asian immigration until after World War II.[2] Because of the increasing postwar economic prosperity of Japan, Japanese immigration to the United States after World War II has been relatively limited. It initially consisted of war-brides,[3] followed after 1965 by students, professionals, and businessmen, many of whom are sojourners who eventually return to Japan.

Although Japanese Americans were concentrated predominantly on the West Coast and in Hawaii before World War II, those living on the mainland dispersed across the country after the internment experience in order to avoid the discriminatory environment in California. There continues to be significant internal migration of Japanese Americans within the United States today, for instance for educational and occupational reasons. As a result, contemporary Japanese Americans are much more geographically dispersed, with significant populations scattered across the western United States, as well as the Midwest and the East Coast. However, Hawaii and the West Coast, especially Los Angeles and the Bay Area, continue to have the largest populations of Japanese Americans.

Surprisingly, there has been a lack of recent work on the contemporary ethnic status of Japanese Americans, despite the continued expansion of Asian American Studies. Books about Japanese Americans in the last few decades have been primarily historical and often centered on their World War II internment (Azuma 2005; Fugita and O'Brien 1991; Fugita and Fernandez 2004; Harden 2003; Hayashi 2008; Kitano 1993; Kurashige 2002; Matsumoto 2014; Morimoto 1997; Nakano Glenn 1986; O'Brien and Fugita 1991; Robinson 2010; Spickard 1996; Takahashi 1982; Takezawa 1995; Tamura 1994; Yoo 2000). There are very few books (and hardly any journal articles) about their contemporary ethnic experiences,[4] although some of the historical studies do have brief overviews of their current status. Although Asian American Studies initially focused on the experiences of Japanese and Chinese Americans[5] when it first emerged from the Asian American movement in the 1960s, the field seems to be currently dominated by studies of Americans of Chinese, Korean, and Southeast Asian descent.

Undoubtedly, Japanese Americans constitute an increasingly smaller proportion of the total Asian American population because of the lack of large-scale Japanese immigration to the United States since 1965. According to the United States Census, the population of monoracial Japanese descendants peaked in 1990 at 847,562 and has been gradually declining since then and was at 759,056 in 2014. Nonetheless, the neglect of Japanese Americans by scholars studying contemporary Asian American populations is quite puzzling, especially since Japanese Americans still remain among the largest groups of Asian Americans. When multiracial Japanese Americans are considered, the population of Japanese descendants in the United States was 1,374,825 in 2014, which was only 449,517 less than the Korean-descent population.[6] Perhaps contemporary Japanese Americans are no longer being studied because they are an older Asian American group that is largely assimilated and well-to-do and does not face as much discrimination and marginalization as in the past. In addition, they are not as affected by current immigration nor are they as transnationally active or diasporic when compared to newer groups of Asian Americans. This does not mean, however, that their ethnic experiences have ceased to be interesting.

## Generations: Immigration and History

Because peoples of Japanese descent have been in the United States since the end of the nineteenth century, they have become a diverse ethnic minority group, not only in terms of geographical residence, but also in terms of generation. Because most Japanese Americans are descendants of Japanese immigrants who arrived in the United States before 1924, they are primarily of the third and fourth generations (sansei and yonsei) with a declining population of elderly second-generation nisei and a growing, but still limited number of young shin-nisei whose Japanese parents immigrated after 1965. In contrast, other Asian descent communities are predominantly of the first and second generations, with a majority consisting of foreign-born immigrants (Min 2006b:42–43). Therefore, the ethnic experiences of Japanese Americans and their relationship to their cultural heritage and homeland are perhaps more varied than they are among some of the newer Asian American groups.

When scholars analyze the internal diversity of an ethnic minority group, they may examine social class, gender, or age differences. I have chosen generation as my unit of analysis because I found generational differences in ethnic heritage to be the most pronounced. Not only do Japanese Americans often think of themselves in terms of specific generations; I was also repeatedly struck by the clear differences among the generations in terms of ethnic identity, historical experiences, levels of assimilation, experiences of racialization and discrimination, transnational connections and identifications with Japan, and of course, relative strength of their ancestral cultural heritage. In this sense, my work follows previous scholarship on Japanese Americans, which has often analyzed them in terms of generation (Kitano 1993; Matsumoto 2014; Montero 1980; Nakano Glenn 1986; Spickard 1996; Takahashi 1982; Takezawa 1995; Tamura 1994; Yanagisako 1985; Yoo 2000).

Social class is generally not a salient variable within the Japanese American community today, which has become well-educated, socioeconomically mobile, and predominantly middle class.[7] However, it *is* important *in general* for the ability of ethnic minorities to remain in touch with their ethnic heritage. As will be noted below (and discussed further in Chapters 2 and 5), socially integrated, middle-class minorities like Japanese Americans are encouraged by tolerant, multicultural ideologies to explore their positively regarded ethnic heritage and homeland. They also have the socioeconomic means to do so.

Although women are often regarded as embodying and reproducing cultural traditions, I did not detect any notable gendered differences between men and women in terms of attachment to ethnic heritage when I compared my coded ethnographic interview data from these two groups. Therefore, gender does not factor into my analysis as a significant variable, although I do note its importance when appropriate, such as in the gendered nature of racialization processes (Chapter 4) and the performance of ethnic heritage (Chapters 6 and 7).

Although the concept of generation may seem rather self-evident, it can actually be defined from both an immigration and historical perspective. For ethnic groups that are the product of immigration, generation is measured by distance from the country of ancestral origin based on genealogical birth order (Foner 2009:3; Kasinitz et al. 2008:400). The original immigrants, who are closest to their country of origin, are the first immigrant generation, and their children who are born in the host country and are farther removed from the country of origin are the second generation. The second generation's children are then the third generation, and so on.

Research on different generations of Japanese Americans follows this immigration-based understanding of generation, employing Japanese generational terminology of *issei* (first generation), nisei (second generation), sansei (third generation), yonsei (fourth generation), and *gosei* (fifth generation). These terms referring to immigrant generation are also frequently used by Japanese Americans to identify and classify themselves ("I'm nisei," "She's sansei," "Those children are yonsei," and so on).

However, according to Karl Mannheim's seminal work on the subject (1952: ch. 7), generations are not based solely on biology or genealogy, but are also age cohorts defined by common historical location. Therefore, generation can also refer to a specific age group that is a product of a certain historical period. Such "historical generations" were born and grew up around the same time and have similar historical experiences. Examples of generations that are historical age cohorts are the Greatest Generation, the Baby-Boomer Generation, Generation X, and the Millennial Generation.

In contrast to other Asian Americans, most Japanese Americans are descendants of immigrants who arrived in the United States during a limited historical period of about four decades, starting in the mid-1880s, when immigration of Japanese to Hawaii began, and ending in 1924, when the United States banned further Asian immigration. This means that the different immigrant generations of Japanese Americans correspond with distinctive historical cohorts (that is, historical generations) (Nakano Glenn 1986:8; O'Brien and Fugita 1991:14–15, Spickard 1996:68).[8] As a result, the nisei of the second immigrant generation were born between 1915 and the 1940s (Spickard 1996:68) and correspond with either the Greatest Generation who fought in World War II or what is called the "Silent Generation" (born between 1925 to 1942). Most elderly nisei who are alive today are of this latter historical generation. The sansei of the third immigrant generation were generally born in the first few decades after World War II and are of the Baby-Boomer historical generation. The yonsei of the fourth immigrant generation, born roughly between the 1970s and 1990s, are members of Generation X or of the Millennial Generation, which are the two historical generations that follow the Baby-Boomers.

Therefore, generation positions Japanese Americans not just in terms of immigration, but also in terms of history, since each immigrant generation is also a distinctive historical cohort that came of age during a specific period and experienced similar formative events. The second-generation nisei are not simply Japanese Americans whose parents are immigrants from Japan but a historical cohort of elderly who grew up during the World War II period and were incarcerated in internment camps. Third-generation sansei are not simply the grandchildren of immigrants; they came of age in the historical period after World War II when discrimination against Japanese Americans was declining and images of Japan were improving, but assimilationist ideologies were still prevalent and ethnic pluralism and multiculturalism had not yet fully taken hold. Likewise, the fourth-generation yonsei are the great-grandchildren of immigrants, but also youth who were raised in the contemporary ethnic diversity of an America that has fully embraced multiculturalism. Therefore, the concept of generation becomes an effective means of incorporating both immigration and history into the analysis of contemporary Japanese American ethnicity. In addition, because these three generations are still alive (the earlier historical cohort of nisei who were born well before World War II have now passed away), a contemporary ethnic analysis of different generations in the context of their historical experiences allows us to trace the development of Japanese Americans over time, in a kind of archeology of their ethnicity.

Most studies of immigrant-origin ethnic minorities in the United States do not go beyond the second immigrant generation (Espiritu 2003; Hurh 1998; Kasinitz, Mollenkopf, Waters, and Holdaway 2008; Kibria 2002a; Levitt and Waters 2002; Smith 2006), mainly because these groups are primarily the result of post-1965 immigration and do not yet have substantial numbers of third-generation individuals.[9] Therefore, Japanese Americans provide us with a unique opportunity to trace how an ethnic minority group was historically constituted over the *longue durée*.

Furthermore, even the members of one immigrant generation need to be properly historicized, especially if their immigrant ancestors arrived in the host country during different historical periods and faced different host country receptions (Berg 2011; Eckstein and Barberia 2002). As mentioned earlier, although most Japanese Americans are descendants of Japanese immigrants who arrived before World War II, there has been some postwar Japanese immigration to the United States. This means there are currently *two* separate *historical* generations of the second *immigrant* generation. They are the prewar nisei (whose immigrant parents arrived before 1924) and the "new" postwar shin-nisei, whose Japanese parents arrived primarily after 1965.

Although the shin-nisei are of the same second immigrant generation as the prewar nisei, many of them are actually of the same *historical* generation as the fourth-generation yonsei and grew up in the contemporary era of increasing multiculturalism, ethnic diversity, and globalization. As will be discussed in Part I of this book, their bicultural and transnational experiences and identities are quite different from the nationalist and assimilationist orientations of the prewar nisei, who were imprisoned in internment camps during World War II because of their Japanese ancestry and had to demonstrate their loyalties as Americans.

Therefore, as indicated by the ethnographic vignettes at the beginning of this chapter, U.S.-born Japanese Americans actually consist of four, instead of three distinct generations: the prewar nisei, the postwar shin-nisei, the sansei, and the yonsei, all of whom belong to both immigrant and historical generations. However, because of the dearth of contemporary research on Japanese Americans, there are almost no studies of the yonsei or the shin-nisei.[10] This book attempts to address this gap in the literature not only by historicizing contemporary Japanese American ethnicity, but also by bringing the story of their ethnic group up to date by closely examining the two most recent generations.

Because each generation of Japanese Americans corresponds with a specific historical age cohort, this also means that generation becomes a proxy for age differences as well, since those of the same generation are roughly of the same age group. Therefore, elderly Japanese Americans are predominantly prewar nisei (although some sansei are now elderly), middle-aged Japanese Americans are generally sansei, and young Japanese Americans are either yonsei or postwar shin-nisei.

In addition, the fact that the generations are also age cohorts means that most Japanese Americans (who have not intermarried) have married co-ethnics of the same generation of about the same age, in a type of generational ethnic endogamy. Few prewar nisei have married sansei, for instance, who are usually much younger. This means that there are relatively few Japanese Americans of mixed generations (that is, 2.5 or 3.5 generation).[11] For instance, only 9 percent of my interview sample consisted of individuals who are in between two generations and thus share some characteristics of both. Although it is conceivable for postwar shin-nisei to marry yonsei, since they are roughly around the same age, none of my interviewees had parents who were shin-nisei and yonsei. This type of generational ethnic endogamy in turn makes differences between the generations even more pronounced and significant among Japanese Americans.

As a result, the concept of generation has tremendous analytical power in the case of the Japanese Americans and other immigrant-descent groups whose ancestors immigrated during a limited historical period. To do a generational analysis of Japanese Americans therefore involves assessing their social distance or proximity to the original immigrants, while also encompassing varying historical experiences, age differences, and even marital status. This apparent alignment of immigration, history, and age is what has produced remarkable similarities among Japanese Americans of a specific generation and significant and consistent differences across the generations.

Because of the importance of generation to Japanese Americans, it is no surprise that the relative strength of ethnic heritage also varies considerably according to generation. In other words, each generation has responded to a confluence of varying historical and contemporary factors, leading to different experiences of ancestral heritage and relations with the ethnic homeland. Since this is the central focus of this book, we need to unpack what we mean by "ethnic heritage" and "ethnic homeland."

## Ethnic Heritage and Homeland

Heritage is a concept that is used mainly in the museum studies and cultural tourism literature (Chhabra, Healy, and Sills 2003; Dicks 2000; McIntosh and Prentice 1999; Smith 2006; Waitt 2000; Waterton and Watson 2011). Although some of this research is about attempts by states, museums, and local communities to preserve the cultural heritage of ethnic minorities, the concept has not been employed explicitly and extensively in the field of racial and ethnic studies. I am not aware of any research that has systematically analyzed immigrant-descent ethnic minorities in the United States from the standpoint of their ancestral heritage in the context of homeland.

In order to clarify my use of ethnic heritage, I must first address the multiple meanings and positionalities of "homeland." "Homeland" can be defined as a place of origin to which an individual feels personally and emotionally attached (Tsuda 2009c:5–6). However, immigrant-descent ethnic minorities such as Japanese Americans often have multiple homelands. The *ethnic* (or ancestral) homeland refers to the country from which such minorities originated (that is, where their immigrant ancestors are from). In contrast, the *natal* homeland is simply the "host country" where they were born.

For immigrant-descent minority groups, ethnic heritage consists of their traditional culture, which originates in and is derived from their ethnic/ancestral homeland. This ancestral cultural heritage can of course include language, food, artistic and musical forms, festivals and ceremonies, belief and symbolic systems, and other types of popular and traditional culture. Although almost all immigrant-descent minorities trace their ethnic heritage to their country of ancestral origin, this does not mean it has been inherited unaltered from the ethnic homeland. Instead, ancestral cultural forms, languages, and traditions are constantly remade, modified, and even reinvented as they are practiced and appropriated by local ethnic communities, families, and individuals. Nonetheless, they continue to be an integral part of the experience of ethnic roots and ancestry. In contrast, cultural forms that are adopted from the natal homeland by ethnic minorities are usually understood to be part of the assimilative process and not part of their ethnic heritage per se.

Therefore, for minorities such as the Japanese Americans who have generally become culturally assimilated over the generations, ancestral heritage is what technically makes them "ethnic"—that is, positioned as culturally distinctive from the majority population. Moreover, this distinctiveness is an integral part of the experience and practice of ethnic identity for any minority group.

Ethnic heritage can be a product of two different types of social processes. Cultural traditions, practices, and languages that the original immigrants brought from the ethnic homeland to the host country can be passed down to subsequent generations of descendants through ethnic communities, institutions, and families. In addition to this type of transmitted or inherited ethnic heritage, minority individuals, especially those from the later generations, can also make active efforts to retain or reconnect directly with their ancestral culture by establishing transnational relations with the ethnic homeland. Such maintenance and revival of heritage cultures through transnational homeland connections are becoming more prevalent in an increasingly globalized world characterized by cross-border flows of peoples, commodities, mass media, information, and cultures.

As a result, ancestral ethnic heritage not only is a local phenomenon, but also has a significant transnational dimension. This is especially true because the ancestral culture of the ethnic homeland is often positioned as more "authentic" than the apparently derivative heritage culture that is found and practiced in the local ethnic community, as will be discussed in Part III of this book. As a result, ethnic minorities often turn to the ethnic homeland for their ancestral culture instead of simply relying on local ethnic community activities. The construction of cultural heritage can often involve what I call *ethnic return migration*, which refers to minority individuals who migrate to their countries of ancestral origin after living outside their ethnic homelands for generations (Tsuda 2009a). Although much ethnic return migration among Japanese Americans consists of tourism, some have stayed and even lived in Japan for more extended periods, and some have a long-term, transnational engagement with the country.

Most ethnic return migration is from poorer, developing countries to richer ethnic homelands in the developed world. Because these migrants are often ethnically marginalized as cultural foreigners in their countries of ancestral origin, experience prejudice and discrimination, and are forced to work in low-status, unskilled (and even despised) jobs, they can have quite negative and alienating experiences (Fox 2007; Tsuda 2003, 2009a). However, ethnic return migrants from developed countries such as the United States generally have much more positive experiences in their ancestral homelands. Not only are their countries of birth more respected by the co-ethnic host population; they tend to work in high-status, professional jobs or are students (Tsuda 2009b,

2009c, 2009d:333–334). As a result, it is more likely that ethnic return migrants like Japanese Americans will have greater interest in exploring their ethnic roots and ancestry and develop an affinity for their heritage culture and a facility with the language during their sojourns in Japan.

This book will thus also examine the ethnic return migration experiences of Japanese Americans in Japan. The impact that their sojourns in Japan have on their sense of ethnic heritage again varies considerably according to generation. However, the literature on ethnic return migrants has generally ignored the importance of generational distance from the ancestral homeland (Capo Zmegac, Vob, and Roth 2010; Fox 2007; Münz and Ohliger 2003; Silbereisen, Titzmann, and Shavit 2014; Tsuda 2003, 2009a; King and Christou 2010). Despite the importance of generation for all Japanese Americans, the two major studies about their experiences living in Japan surprisingly do not analyze the clear generational differences among prewar nisei, shin-nisei, sansei, and yonsei (Takamori 2011; Yamashiro 2008).[12]

In addition to experiences in the ethnic homeland, a multitude of other cultural, racial, and historical factors account for the relative strength of ancestral ethnic heritage among different generations of Japanese Americans, as is true with other minority groups. Hence, we must outline the relevant variables that constitute Japanese American ethnicity and identity.

## Nonlinear Ethnicities and the Production of Heritage

Historical events and the ethnic climate during certain time periods have also influenced the extent to which minorities emphasize their ethnic ancestry and identities. This book argues that it is not the historical experiences that individuals have as adults, but those they had during their formative years as youth that have the greatest and most lasting impact on their ethnic consciousness throughout their lives. My interviews indicate that the internment of the prewar nisei when they were young during World War II and the discrimination and prejudice they continued to suffer immediately after the war were certainly the primary historical factors that discouraged them from maintaining their ethnic heritage and language. In contrast, the much greater ethnic tolerance and the celebration of cultural diversity today along with positive images of Japan and Japanese culture have encouraged shin-nisei and yonsei youth to retain and recover their heritage cultures.

In addition to history, the other important factors that have influenced the relative salience of ethnic heritage among Japanese Americans are assimilation and transnationalism as well as racialization and multiculturalism.

## Assimilation and Ethnic Heritage

It may strike some readers as peculiar that ethnic heritage is the central theme of this book, since most Japanese Americans have been in the United States for many generations and their assimilation to mainstream American society is quite advanced. Studies that have examined them over the generations note their progressive social and cultural incorporation into mainstream American society (Kitano 1993; Montero 1980; Spickard 1996; Takahashi 1997; Tuan 2001: chs. 3, 5). Because Japanese Americans have been in the United States longer than other Asian American groups, they have generally shown higher rates of socioeconomic mobility and cultural assimilation (Akiba 2006:164–165; Jiobu 1988; Spickard 1996:143). Japanese Americans currently have higher educational levels on average than Caucasians, and a majority of them have become successful middle-class white-collar workers, professionals, or business owners who live in white suburban communities (Akiba 2006:163, 165). The integration of Japanese Americans into mainstream society has caused many of them to become disengaged from their ethnic communities and to interact mainly with whites in their daily lives (Fugita and O'Brien 1991:11; Spickard 1996:159). Because of the dismantling of Japanese American ethnic enclaves during World War II and the subsequent scattering of Japanese Americans across the country and then into the suburbs through upward mobility, the "Japan-towns" of the past have largely disappeared,[13] and Japanese American ethnic organizations are suffering from declining membership and participation, especially among youth (see Chapter 5).

The cultural assimilation of Japanese Americans is also quite advanced. With the exception of the shin-nisei, most of them cannot speak Japanese nor have they retained any notable Japanese cultural customs or ties to their ancestral homeland (Spickard 1996:145–147, 159;

Tuan 2001:106). Since they lead daily lives that are not that different from those of white Americans, a number of them refer to themselves as "whitewashed" because of their loss of Japanese cultural heritage over the generations (Pyke and Dang 2003). As in the case of white ethnics, the only aspects of their everyday lives that remain ethnically distinct are cultural activities known as "symbolic ethnicity" (Gans 1979), such as eating Japanese food, collecting Japanese artwork, listening to Japanese music, or participating in ethnic activities and festivals in local communities (Okamura 2008:140–144; Tuan 2001: ch. 3). For Japanese Americans, the process of cultural assimilation appears to be accompanied by an apparent decline in ethnic identification over generations (Masuda, Matsumoto, and Meredith 1970; Newton et al. 1988).

However, the progressive cultural and social assimilation of Japanese Americans does not always mean that ethnic heritage no longer has any significance for them. In order to understand the continued relevance of ethnicity to their assimilated lives, this book resists the temptation to regard assimilation and ethnic heritage as irreconcilable opposites that are in constant tension. In fact, such assumptions have been implicitly embedded in the scholarly history of ethnicity. The assimilation perspective, which thrived into the 1960s and continues to have more recent proponents (Alba and Nee 1997), was initially countered by scholars who emphasized the persistence and continuation of ethnic cultures and differences, often under the banner of cultural or ethnic pluralism (Gans 1997; Kazal 1995; Omi and Winant 1986: ch. 1). Indeed, previous research about Japanese Americans has also considered how their ethnicity and communities have managed to persist and endure through the generations despite the inexorable forces of assimilation (Connor 1974; Fugita and O'Brien 1991; Hieshima and Schneider 1994; Kendis 1989; Kurashige 2002; Masuda, Matsumoto, and Meredith 1970:205–206; Matsuo 1992; O'Brien and Fugita 1991; Spickard 1996:151; Wooden, Leon, and Toshima 1988; Woodrum 1981).

The oft-cited segmented assimilation literature is also based on similar assumptions about the dichotomy between assimilation and ethnic heritage. This perspective posits three options for the children of immigrants: upward assimilation to the middle class, downward assimilation to the underclass, or (more preferably) selective acculturation, which enables them to retain their parent's culture and language to a certain extent because they are raised in cohesive ethnic communities and families that partly insulate them from the pressures of assimilation (Portes and Rumbaut 2001). Therefore, even when the second generation does not fully assimilate, they are able to retain their ethnic heritage only because they have the means to hold off the assimilation process.

Because assimilation and ethnic difference are often positioned in an oppositional manner, the increased assimilation of immigrants and their descendants is naturally assumed to lead to a progressive weakening of distinct ethnic heritage cultures and identities over the generations. Even the ethnic persistence/retention perspective regards assimilation and ethnic heritage as antithetical and assumes that ethnicity wanes over time due to the corrosive effects of assimilation. The only real difference from the assimilation perspective is that instead of claiming that ancestral cultures eventually disappear, it simply argues that the remnants of ethnicity continue to be relevant among later-generation immigrant descendants, albeit reduced to symbolic practices and identifications. This perspective also assumes that ethnic heritage is always the product of the native culture brought to the host country by the original immigrants, which is then passed down to subsequent generations in attenuated form because of eventual assimilation.

This book explicitly avoids such linear ethnic narratives and histories, where assimilation always erodes ancestral heritage and identity over the generations. Although ethnic heritage did weaken among prewar nisei and continues to do so for their even more assimilated sansei descendants, it has actually become stronger and more salient among the most recent generations of Japanese Americans, namely the shin-nisei and the fourth-generation yonsei. Japanese American history has followed a clearly *nonlinear* ethnic trajectory.

Tomás Jiménez (2010), in his path-breaking book on later-generation Mexican Americans, has suggested a more innovative way to think about assimilation and ethnicity among later generation, immigrant-descent minorities. This perspective, which can be called "ethnic replenishment theory," argues that large-scale Mexican immigration to the United States in recent decades has allowed later-generation Mexican Americans to "replenish" their ethnicity. While this is a definite improvement over the ethnic persistence/retention perspective, it is still based on an understanding of assimilation and ethnic heritage as irreconcilable. Because later-generation ethnic minorities have lost their ethnic heritage due to assimilation, they must rely on a continuing infusion of new, still-unassimilated immigrants from the ancestral homeland to sustain their ethnicity. In addition, it again assumes that the ethnicity of later-generation minorities is always inherited from immigrants. Instead of arguing that their heritage cultures have been passed down from immigrant ancestors, it simply claims that they are acquired from current immigrants. In addition, this theory generally does not apply to ethnic minorities like Japanese Americans who have not experienced large-scale immigration from Japan since 1965.

Instead of regarding assimilation and ethnic heritage in mutually exclusive ways, I suggest we explore how they can also simultaneously coexist, as well as how the former can actually produce the latter. This is not to deny that they often pull minority individuals in opposite directions, as seen in the case of prewar nisei and sansei, whose progressive Americanization seems to have occurred at the expense of their ancestral culture, language, and identities. However, the postwar shin-nisei and yonsei are examples of how assimilation is not incompatible with the continued salience of heritage cultures. The shin-nisei have become quite culturally assimilated and are fully incorporated into mainstream American society but have *simultaneously* maintained their heritage culture and language through their immigrant parents and Japanese expatriate communities, thus becoming fully bilingual and bicultural. In the case of the fourth-generation yonsei, they have actively reclaimed their ancestral culture and language because of what they consider to be their overassimilation to American society and serious concerns about their loss of ethnic heritage in a multicultural America. For later-generation ethnic minorities, the assimilative condition can actually become the catalyst for the active production and revival of ethnic heritage. Assimilation therefore becomes *constitutive* of ethnic difference.

The maintenance of Japanese heritage among the shin-nisei is indeed a product of ethnic persistence, since the original homeland culture brought to the United States by their Japanese immigrant parents has been successfully passed down to the second generation. Their ethnicity is directly inherited from the previous immigrant generation. However, the situation for the yonsei is quite different and cannot be explained by simple ethnic retention or continuity since they have actively reclaimed an ancestral culture that was mostly lost among previous generations of Japanese Americans. Therefore, we cannot assume that ethnic heritage is always the product of ancestral immigrants whose homeland culture has been transmitted to subsequent generations. Instead of simply inheriting their ethnicity from previous (or current) immigrants, yonsei Japanese Americans have actively recovered and revived it by reconnecting with Japan and remaking traditional Japanese culture in the United States. Again, ethnic histories can follow distinctly nonlinear trajectories.

### Transnationalism and Ethnic Heritage

As noted earlier, the maintenance and production of ethnic heritage is also based on transnational movement and mobility, which allow ethnic minorities to develop cross-border connections with their ancestral homeland. In contrast to the apparently corrosive effects of assimilation, transnationalism is usually regarded as enabling immigrants and their descendants to maintain homeland cultures. In an era of globalization, an increasing number of ethnic minority individuals are "returning" to their ancestral homelands to visit and even to reside there for longer periods, allowing them to explore their ethnic roots and ancestry

However, even if minority individuals do not travel to their ethnic homelands (or do so only briefly), they can still connect transnationally with their cultural heritage through what I call *non-contiguous globalization*, which refers to the flow of information and images across national boundaries such that the globalizing agent influences local societies over a geographical distance without being physically present (Tsuda 2003:356–358; Tsuda, Tapias, and Escandell 2014:127–129).[14] Through digital media such as the Internet, as well as mass media, satellite TV, and other forms of telecommunication, later-generation ethnic minorities can remain transnationally linked to their homeland cultures and even recover their lost ethnic heritage without ever traveling to their country of ancestral origin. This is especially true for immigrant-descent minorities like Japanese Americans who live a considerable geographical distance from their ethnic homeland and therefore have mainly an emotionally transnational connection to it (Takeda 2012).

The transnationalism literature in immigration studies was also initially developed in opposition to assimilation theory. Researchers interested in transnational processes have often offered their perspective as an alternative to the traditional immigrant assimilation paradigm, claiming that immigrants and their descendants do not simply assimilate to the host society and sever their transborder ties to the homeland, but that instead they continue to maintain them over time (Eckstein and Barberia 2002:799–800; Levitt and Jaworsky 2007:130; Portes, Guarnizo, and Landolt 1999:227–229; see Tsuda 2012c:633–634 for further discussion).

However, it is quite apparent that assimilation does not preclude the development of active transnational social relations with the ethnic homeland. In fact, there has been a growing number of studies that document how the assimilation of immigrants in the host country and their transborder engagement with the country of origin are not incompatible (Guarnizo, Portes, and Haller 2008; Levitt 2001; Levitt and Glick Schiller 2008; Smith 2006; Tsuda 2012c).

Nonetheless, there seems to be an inherent assumption in the literature that transnationalism, and the ethnic heritage that is partly constituted by it, gradually wanes over time among the descendants of immigrants, which makes it similar to the ethnic persistence/retention perspective. This assumption is reflected in debates about whether transnational ties to the parental homeland persist among second-generation children (Levitt and Waters 2002). Some argue that transnationalism naturally declines and becomes quite limited among assimilated members of the second generation (Kasinitz et al. 2002; Menjívar 2002; Portes and Rumbaut 2001: ch. 6; Rumbaut 2002), while others claim that it remains significant (Levitt 2002; Smith 2006).

In this manner, transnational connections to ethnic homelands are again understood to be inherited from immigrant parents or grandparents (Levitt and Waters 2002; Smith 2006) and then to progressively attenuate among members of each subsequent generation due to assimilation, likely disappearing by the third generation. Even those who suggest that transnationalism may persist into the third generation attribute it to the influence of immigrant grandparents, who may take their grandchildren to their country of origin for visits (Smith 2006:196–202). In addition to the assumption of ethnic linearity, we again have the notion that cultural heritage based on transnationalism is always dependent on the cross-border ties of immigrant ancestors.

As is the case with assimilation and ethnic heritage, such simple, linear transnational histories are challenged by an analysis of Japanese Americans across the generations. Transnational connections to the ethnic homeland of Japan did indeed attenuate among the prewar nisei and further weakened among third-generation sansei. However, the latest generations of Japanese Americans, the shin-nisei and the yonsei, have actively maintained or reactivated cross-border ties with Japan despite their assimilation, which has thus been instrumental to their ethnic heritage experiences.

Therefore, progressive assimilation does not prevent the active development of transnational relations with the ethnic homeland. Instead, assimilation and transnationalism can coexist simultaneously. In fact, in the case of the yonsei, it is precisely their overassimilation that has caused them to reach out transnationally to their ancestral homeland in an effort to reconnect with their ethnic roots and cultural heritage. Not only can assimilation and transnationalism occur together, but assimilation can actually *increase* transborder activity.

Finally, like ethnic heritage, transnational ties to the ancestral homeland among ethnic minorities are not based simply on the persistence of cross-border relations that the original immigrants developed with their country of origin. Although such *inherited transnationalism* can remain important to the second generation and its ability to maintain their parents' heritage culture (as shown by the shin-nisei), it does indeed decline as a minority group ages. However, as is the case with fourth-generation yonsei, transnational ties to the ethnic homeland can also be reactivated and recreated for various reasons long after they have been lost by previous generations. Such *forged transnationalism*[15] and its impact on ethnic heritage must also be analyzed.

## Racialization and Multiculturalism

The relative strength of ethnic heritage for immigrant-descent ethnic minorities is not based simply on the dynamics of assimilation and transnationalism. Although Japanese American ethnicity is partly the result of the assimilative patterns or the transnational opportunities they have inherited from the previous generations, each new generation has also negotiated its own ethnic positionality in response to the pressures of racialization and multiculturalism. Therefore, we must also take these additional factors into account in order to understand why ethnic ancestry is of paramount importance for certain generations of Japanese Americans while it has lost much of its significance for members of other generations. Again, the complex social dynamics that constitute the ethnicity of each generation of Japanese Americans ensure that their ethnic history does not unfold in a predictable manner, but remains inherently contingent and nonlinear.

Despite the cultural assimilation of Japanese Americans, they continue to be racialized as "Japanese" by mainstream Americans simply because of their physical appearance and last names, as shown in the opening ethnographic vignette about George Okamoto. Therefore, the experiences of later-generation racial minorities remains fundamentally different from that of white ethnics (such as those of southern and eastern European or even Jewish descent), who have disappeared into the majority white population to become ethnically unmarked "Americans." Although assimilated third- and fourth-generation Japanese Americans have come to culturally resemble white Americans, they have never been able to escape their racialized ethnic minority status and are still not regarded as true Americans.

In fact, this type of racialized ethnicity continues to pervade the daily lives of all Japanese Americans, regardless of generation and level of assimilation. Therefore, any understanding of their ethnic heritage experiences must take such processes of racialization into account. However, despite its importance, few studies of Japanese Americans have analyzed their ethnicity explicitly from the perspective of race and racialization (Okamura 2014; Yoo 2000).

"Racialization" refers to the process through which specific cultural meanings are attached to perceived phenotypical differences. Such racial categories are embedded in and reinforce hierarchical systems of power relations, constituting what Michael Omi and Howard Winant (1986:61) call racial formations. Moreover, "racialization" is usually defined in the literature as involving the ascription of racial meanings to nonracial social relations, situations, or groups (Omi and Winant 1986:64; Bonacich, Alimahomed, and Wilson 2008:343; Silverstein 2005:364). In contrast, I argue that in complex, multiethnic societies, there is indeed no previously nonracialized social group or relation, since racial identifications and understandings permeate all social interactions regardless of gender, class, kinship, or generational status. All individuals and groups are judged by phenotypic appearance and the various racial meanings associated with it (as noted above, even whites are racialized as non-ethnic, mainstream Americans).

Therefore, racial categories and meanings are not simply historically created. Instead, preexisting racial categories are constantly contested and modified. Of course, this is not to deny that they are often naturalized either by reference to biological and hereditary processes or, more recently, by culturally essentialized understandings and stereotypes. Instead, the point is that the changing and contextual nature of racial categories is not always fully acknowledged in public discourse and is often subject to the historical amnesia of biological and cultural essentialization.[16]

While Omi and Winant (1986:71–72) certainly acknowledge that racialization processes are continuously subject to contestation and change, they focus on grassroots political struggles and social movements in relation to states, whose institutions structure and enforce a racially unequal order. Likewise, Lisa Lowe (1996:21–29) directly applies this perspective to the history of Asian Americans. In this book, however, I do not focus on the history of Japanese American political struggle, such as their crucial involvement in the Asian American movement of the 1960s and 1970s or their subsequent political efforts to obtain redress for their World War II incarceration. These were one-time events, despite their long-term impact, and their history has been well-documented. Instead, I am more interested in how racialization affects the contemporary lives and everyday interactions of Japanese Americans, how they respond to and contest their racialization, and how it impacts their ethnic heritage. It is also important to remember that racialization is not simply based on panethnic categories such as Asian, black, or Hispanic. Although Japanese Americans are racialized as generalized "Asians," they are often categorized more specifically according to national origins as "Japanese." This is what makes racialization processes so relevant to their particular ancestral heritage and identity.

Because racialization is structured by and reproduces racial inequalities and hierarchies, it is often seen as synonymous with racism and racist meanings (Murji and Solomos 2005) and associated with a host of negative consequences, such as discrimination, exclusionary treatment, exploitation, and denial of citizenship rights (Bonacich 2008). Likewise, the literature on Asian Americans has emphasized how their racialization has led to social marginalization, racial stereotyping and scapegoating, experiences of prejudice and discrimination, and hate crimes (Kim 2008:14–19, 212–219; Tuan 2001:39–45, 79–86; Wu and Song 2000:xvi–xviii). This was definitely the case with the prewar nisei, who were incarcerated during World War II because they were racialized as "Japanese enemy aliens" and who continued to endure racism and discrimination after the war simply because of their ancestry. As a result, they emphasized their Americanness and cultural assimilation and distanced themselves from their ethnic heritage and identity.

While much racialization is negative and purely discriminatory, its effects are not necessarily detrimental. We must also acknowledge that racialization can be instrumental for constituting the ethnicity and identity of racial minorities, even among members of the later generations. In contrast to later-generation Italian or Irish Americans who are seen (that is, racialized) as part of majority white society and have mostly lost their ethnicity and communities, third- and fourth-generation Japanese Americans continue to maintain ethnic communities and identities, as well as a sense of ancestral heritage because they are forever racialized as ethnically different.

At the same time, Japanese Americans' understanding of their ethnicity is conditioned not only by their racialization, but also by the shift from a previous assimilationist American ideology to one espousing multiculturalism and ethnic diversity. Although the prewar nisei came of age during an assimilationist era, the shin-nisei and the yonsei, who mainly grew up in the last few decades, have been very much affected by contemporary multicultural ideologies that encourage them to maintain their ethnic heritage and cultural differences. Multiculturalism is based on the notion that in a plural society such as the United States, different ethnic cultures can coexist and should be equally recognized and respected (Alba 1999:8; Glazer 1997:14; Turner 1993). In addition to being a general ideology, multiculturalism has actually been implemented through political and educational policies based on the right of minority groups to maintain and practice their different cultures and languages.

However, multiculturalism has also come under criticism for reifying, essentializing, and homogenizing cultures as well as promoting ethnic separatism, national disunity, and fragmentation. Others have noted that it overemphasizes cultural differences at the expense of class, gender, and race, which are the real basis for ethnic inequality and marginalization (Bloemraad, Korteweg, and Yurdakul 2008:161; Glazer 1997:41–48; Joppke 2004:242–244; May and Sleeter 2010; Turner 1993:412). Nonetheless, ethnically diverse societies like the United States, which regard themselves as multicultural, continue to be positively perceived and are associated with ethnic tolerance, civil and minority rights, inclusivity, freedom, and equality. Even in public discourse, multiculturalism is seen more favorably than assimilation, which is often associated with the coercive eradication of minority cultures and differences.

However, very few scholars have examined the possibly coercive dimensions of multiculturalism particularly in relation to racialization, which in turn can have an impact on ethnic heritage. Like all ideologies, multiculturalism is embedded in systems of power that can produce ethnic essentialisms and exclusions, especially when they operate alongside racialization processes. In plural societies like the United States where multiculturalism is a pervasive ideology, the maintenance and practice of cultural differences for racial minorities ceases to be simply a voluntary and freely exercised right, but becomes somewhat obligatory and expected. I call this *racialized multiculturalism*.

Therefore, as will be discussed in Part II of this book, not only are Japanese Americans racialized as a "Japanese" ethnic minority, but in accordance with multicultural assumptions, they are also expected to be culturally different. In other words, they are often presumed to speak Japanese, know about Japan, practice traditional Japanese culture, and even think and act like Japanese from Japan. This expectation of multicultural difference is imposed even on third- and fourth-generation Japanese Americans simply because of their racial appearance, despite the fact that they are completely Americanized and generally have nothing to do with Japan or Japanese culture. Therefore, racial differences are assumed to correlate with different ethnic cultures and immigrant nationalities in a multicultural world. As a result, racialization can make multiculturalism somewhat compulsory, resulting in exclusionary ethnic practices where even later-generation Japanese Americans are seen as not real Americans, but are Orientalized as immigrant others who are forever tied to foreign cultures and ancestral homelands.

In general, Japanese Americans have responded to their multicultural racialization and ethnic exclusion in two divergent ways. Some have asserted what I call their *racial citizenship* by demanding that they be accepted as culturally assimilated Americans despite their racial differences, thereby claiming national belonging and rights. For others, racialized multiculturalism has provoked interest in either maintaining or recovering their ancestral culture. Generational differences are again quite clear in this regard. Whereas the postwar shin-nisei have maintained their parent's native language, culture, and transnational ties to Japan in a racialized, multicultural world, the third-generation sansei and some fourth-generation yonsei have contested their racialization as "Japanese" by insisting on their national inclusion as Americans. Nonetheless, the yonsei have also responded to the pressures of racialized multiculturalism by actively exploring their lost ancestral cultural heritage and forging transnational connections to their ethnic homeland. Although some Japanese Americans have been able to successfully challenge and possibly reorder hierarchical racial formations and inequalities, others have reacted in ways that inadvertently reproduce and even reinforce racialized expectations and structures. Regardless, the combination of racialization and multiculturalism ensures that ethnic heritage and identities continue to be relevant to contemporary Japanese Americans.

Multiculturalism is in apparent conflict with another dominant contemporary ideology—namely, colorblindness, which claims that racial inequality and discrimination are no longer significant in a "post-racial" American society because minorities apparently no longer suffer from racism and lack of opportunity (Omi and Winant 2015:256–260; Bonilla-Silva 2013). By denying the continued significance of race, colorblind ideologies attempt to circumscribe race consciousness among ethnic minorities and discourage them from exploring and asserting their heritage cultures, in direct contrast to multiculturalism. This is manifested in anti-immigrant policies that prohibit the use of Spanish (and other languages) in the workplace, declare English to be America's official language, and outlaw bilingual education, ethnic studies courses in high school, and other activities that apparently promote ethnic pride.

Whether multiculturalism or colorblindness is a more pervasive ideology in the United States remains open to debate. The relative strength of colorblind ideologies also very much depends on the ethnic minority group, since they are more relevant to some groups than others. Unlike other non-white racial minorities, Japanese Americans are not subject to colorblind ideologies because they tend to be socioeconomically successful and culturally assimilated and because their Japanese ethnic heritage and homeland evoke positive images and reactions. This situation contrasts with that of some poor and culturally unassimilated immigrant minorities, whose native cultures can provoke anti-immigrant backlashes under the guise of colorblind ideologies. Therefore, the social class status of racial minorities very much determines whether they benefit from an environment that valorizes ethnic difference or one that discourages and stigmatizes it.

## Methodology and Fieldwork

I conducted fieldwork and participant observation with Japanese Americans for one and a half years in San Diego and Phoenix between 2006 and 2009. Fifty-five in-depth interviews were completed, which generally lasted from two to three hours and were recorded and transcribed. Initial contacts were made with the Japanese American Historical Society of San Diego (JAHSSD), the Nikkei Student Union (NSU) at the University of California at San Diego, and the Japanese American Citizens League (JACL) in Phoenix, but through snowball sampling, I also interviewed many Japanese Americans who did not participate in these organizations. In addition, I conducted extensive participant observation by attending numerous organization meetings and community events, including those held at the Japanese American Buddhist Temple in San Diego. During my fieldwork, I was an active and participating member of JAHSSD, NSU, and JACL and also socialized with various Japanese Americans on many occasions.

My interview sample consists of roughly equal numbers of Japanese American men and women of all ages from the second to the fourth generation (the first generation was excluded). My interviewees are generally 100 percent Japanese descent with the exception of a limited number of biracial individuals (about 8 percent of my sample). In general, they are well-educated professionals, business-owners, or college students and virtually all of them currently live in middle-class suburban communities. Over 60 percent of my interviewees are married, mainly to other Japanese Americans, and most intermarriages are with whites. Interview questions covered topics such as historical consciousness, family and cultural background and upbringing, ethnic identities and communities, and relations with other Americans and ethnic groups. I also asked about their experiences in Japan (for those who had visited or lived in the country) and their connections with and knowledge of Japanese descendants in other countries. Pseudonyms are used for all individuals described in this book.

Because most of my initial contacts were through Japanese American organizations, which consist mainly of middle-aged sansei and a diminishing number of elderly prewar nisei, I soon found myself interviewing many sansei and then being introduced to other potential sansei interviewees. As a result, I started to ask interviewees to introduce me to non-sansei and also actively searched for young shin-nisei at UC San Diego and for yonsei through the university's Nikkei Student Union, where they are heavily represented. Therefore, I was able to effectively use snowball and purposive sampling to acquire more balanced generational samples, although the sansei still clearly outnumber interviewees of other generations. As noted earlier, only five out of my fifty-five interviewees were of mixed generation, which led to the issue of which generation they should be classified under. Instead of trying to determine whether a mixed-generation Japanese American resembled one generation more than another, I included them in the samples of both generations, highlighting the characteristics they shared with each generation.

When mixed-generation individuals are double-counted in this manner, my entire interview sample consists of seventeen prewar nisei, thirteen postwar shin-nisei, twenty-four sansei, and eleven yonsei. Because a number of my book chapters focus on only one of these four generations, this means that my sample sizes for these chapters are admittedly quite small, except for the sansei. However, a systematic study of purposive sampling found that "saturation" (the point at which no new information or themes are observed in the data) was reached with the first twelve interviewees (Guest, Bunce, and Johnson 2006). Although my sample of yonsei falls slightly below this threshold, I should note that all my extensive participant observations at NSU meetings and discussions were almost exclusively with yonsei students. In addition, during the interview and qualitative data coding process, I was repeatedly struck by the remarkable similarities in experiences among members of one generation as well as stark and consistent generational differences. This suggests that even if I had conducted more in-depth interviews, they would simply have further reinforced the generational patterns I had already uncovered.

All interview data and fieldwork notes were coded using ATLAS.ti, which allowed me to directly compare the relative significance of specific themes (such as cultural heritage, assimilation, transnationalism, racialization, discrimination, and ethnic identity) according to gender and generational differences as well as place of residence (as noted earlier, there were no discernable class differences among my interviewees). Generational differences clearly outweighed all other social variables, including gender, as noted earlier. I was also somewhat surprised to find that residence in San Diego (with a relatively large population of Japanese and other Asian Americans) versus Phoenix (with a small Asian American population) did not have a significant impact on ethnic experiences, although Japanese Americans in Phoenix seemed to report slightly higher levels of ethnic discrimination and more cases of racialization. In addition, the fact that a number of my interviewees had moved to these cities relatively recently from various parts of the United States made cross-urban comparisons rather difficult.

Finally, I should note that my sample includes only a limited number of Japanese Americans living in a particular region of the United States (the American Southwest). As indicated in subsequent chapters, the generalizations I make refer specifically to Southwest Japanese Americans in my sample. I make no claims that my description and analysis pertain to all Japanese Americans, especially those living in the Midwest, on the East Coast, or in Hawaii, although I would suspect that some similar generational patterns would be found among them as well. Particular care must be taken to differentiate Japanese Americans living in the mainland United States from those in Hawaii. Hawaii Japanese Americans have a longer and different immigration history, have been a larger and much more dominant part of the local population, and have lived in a state characterized by different ethnic relations than the rest of the United States (Okamura 2008, 2014). In addition, they were not incarcerated during World War II.

## Is "Native Anthropology" Really Possible?

As a Japanese American anthropologist, my research for this book has been a sort of ethnographic homecoming, a career trajectory that other anthropologists have also taken (Behar 1996; Motzafi-Haller 1997; Rosaldo 1989).[17] I should also note that this project arose not out of personal interest in my own ethnic group, but because of my previous research. I began my anthropological career as a Japan specialist and conducted fieldwork among Japanese *Brazilians* who have "return migrated" from Brazil to Japan as unskilled immigrants who work in Japanese factories (Tsuda 2003).

During this research, I became interested in a future project comparing Japanese Brazilians in Brazil with Japanese Americans in the United States as part of the "diaspora" of Japanese descendants scattered throughout the Americas. It was a natural extension of my previous research and a great opportunity to study two ethnic minorities of the same ancestral origin who have been living for many generations in countries with different race relations and histories. As a result, I expected some similarities in their contemporary ethnic minority status, but also stark differences.

Initially, I did not think that fieldwork as a "native anthropologist" studying my own ethnic group in my own country would be that interesting. For me, Japanese Brazilians had been an exotic other from a foreign, Latin American country. In contrast, not only are Japanese Americans familiar to me, but they are well-educated middle-class Americans, no longer suffer from serious discrimination, and generally do not migrate. As a result, they seemed rather ordinary, if not somewhat dull. I kept telling myself that only the comparative dimension of this project would be interesting.

However, as I began my fieldwork, I was immediately drawn to, and eventually fascinated by, the experiences of Japanese Americans, who were not at all as familiar or ordinary as I initially expected. Although I had been acquainted with Japanese Americans my entire life, they somehow remained an anthropological "other" for me. In fact, I eventually found them to be so interesting that I decided they should be analyzed in their own right. I quickly decided to first write an independent book about them, before I eventually moved on to my comparative magnum opus about the "Japanese diaspora."

In contrast to previous images of white (usually male) anthropologists studying the "natives" (usually darker peoples) in faraway lands, the apparent rise of "native anthropologists" has been a topic of considerable discussion in the last few decades. It has been repeatedly mentioned that in contrast to "non-native" anthropologists, native anthropologists' cultural and linguistic familiarity with the people we are studying provides us with superior access, rapport, and empathy and ultimately leads to more emic, sensitive, and authentic ethnographic portrayals that are less subject to Westernized, colonizing, and objectifying perspectives (Anae 2010:230–232; Hayano 1979:101–102; Kanuha 2000:441–443; Ohnuki-Tierney 1984; see also Aguilar 1981 and Narayan 1993:676–677 for summaries of such claims). Because native anthropologists are members of the groups they study, their ethnographies are also described as more politically engaged and activist-oriented, thus uncovering social inequities, as well as systems of power and domination (Abu-Lughod 1991:142–143; Anae 2010:227–228; Hayano 1979:101–102; Motzafi-Haller 1997:215–217). Nonetheless, native anthropologists may take certain observations for granted as insiders and apparently have more difficulty maintaining "objective" detachment from the peoples they study (Hayano 1979:101–102; Kanuha 2000:441–443; Ohnuki-Tierney 1984).

I suggest that we question this simple dichotomy of native versus non-native anthropologist. Even insider anthropologists will still encounter educational, social class, gender, generational, urban/rural, or cultural differences with the peoples they study because all social groups (even the most homogeneous) are fragmented by internal differences (Aguilar 1981:25; Kuwayama 2003:9; Motzafi-Haller 1997:217–219; Narayan 1993:671, 675; Nelson 1996). As a result, there are plenty of examples of native anthropologists who are seen as outsiders and have difficulty being accepted by their own communities or who conversely become embroiled in internal conflicts (Aguilar 1981:21; Hayano 1979:100; Jacobs-Huey 2002:796–797; Tsuda 2003:32–33).

Therefore, even for those of us who study our own ethnic group, the distance between the anthropologist and the "natives" remains. Just like non-native anthropologists, we must constantly negotiate our positionality in the field as we move along a scale of relative distance from those we study, in terms of what Linda Williamson Nelson (1996) refers to as "gradations of endogeny." All anthropologists are both partial outsiders and partial insiders and experience various degrees of acceptance and cultural insight.

The distinction between native and non-native anthropologists is therefore not absolute; rather, the two exist on a relative continuum, with the former simply more likely to be culturally and socially closer to their research participants. Indeed, regardless of what type of anthropologist one may be (native, non-native, semi-native), the distance and differences between researcher and researched always persist and can never be completely eliminated. Nonetheless, I argue that such cultural differences are not detrimental, but productive for fieldwork. Ultimately, difference is essential to the generation of anthropological knowledge.

## The Importance of "Othering" in Fieldwork

As mentioned at the beginning of this introductory chapter, I am a shin-nisei. My father immigrated to the United States in the 1960s as a biochemistry graduate student at the University of Chicago. I grew up partly in the Japanese expatriate business community in Chicago where I attended Japanese Saturday school from fourth grade to the end of high school primarily with children from Japan, although there were a few U.S.-born shin-nisei like myself in my classes. Our parents also forced my brother and me to speak only Japanese at home and took us to Japan a number of times. As a result, like other shin-nisei, I became bilingual, bicultural, and transnational.

As was the case with Steve Okura, the shin-nisei in one of the opening vignettes, I never identified as "Japanese American" or "nisei" when I was growing up. Neither my parents nor my Japanese classmates in Saturday school ever referred to me in such a manner. Instead, I saw myself as a "Japanese" (*nihonjin*) who just happened to be born and raised in the United States. I have felt much more connected to Japan throughout my entire life than to the experiences and history of Japanese Americans in the United States. In fact, even to this day, other Americans often mistake me for a Japanese from Japan (perhaps 1.5 generation who immigrated to the United States as a child?). This is probably because my English continues to have a Japanese inflection, and I have a very distinctive Japanese first name (in contrast to most Japanese Americans who have American first names).

Growing up in Chicago, I always regarded Japanese Americans as people who were quite different from our family. They were completely Americanized, had lost their connections to Japan, had a different history that included internment during World War II, and lived on the other side of the city. In fact, my mother had strong prejudices against Japanese Americans, to whom my parents referred only as "nisei" (of course, my brother and I were also nisei, albeit of the postwar historical generation). My mother regarded the "nisei" as descendants of low-class, uneducated, and poor rural Japanese who could not survive economically in prewar Japan and had no choice but to abandon their homeland for America.

I still remember my first encounter with a "nisei." It was when my parents took me to a Japanese food store located in the near north side of Chicago. My mother pointed to an elderly customer near us and told me, "That person is a nisei." I looked at the man. Although he looked completely Japanese, he was dressed very casually, spoke English without an accent, and appeared very Americanized to me. I was literally gazing at the ethnic other. Even without talking to him, I could sense the cultural, historical, and age differences between us.

Although I did become acquainted with a number of Japanese Americans growing up, virtually all of them were other shin-nisei with similar bilingual and transnational Japanese backgrounds like myself. Of course, I did not think of them as "shin-nisei" or even "Japanese American" back then. Like me, they were American-born "Japanese." In fact, it was probably not until graduate school that I started to actively refer to myself as "Japanese American" in the ethnically diverse environment at the University of California at Berkeley.

Given my personal background, when I first started my research on Japanese Americans, I felt like a cultural outsider. Although I was technically studying my own ethnic group, I was familiar with only the shin-nisei, a small subpopulation that was detached from the broader Japanese American community. Like Steve Okura and other shin-nisei, I had never felt like an "authentic" Japanese American. Therefore, the cultural differences I experienced with most Japanese Americans were based not necessarily on educational level, professional status, social class background, or even gender, but on generation.

My first Japanese American contact in San Diego was an elderly san-sei woman who ended up becoming one of my best informants and a good friend. After we got acquainted, the first question she asked me was: "Are you from Japan?" Great, I thought. Even when I am speaking in English, Japanese Americans think I am "Japanese" and cannot tell that I am actually a fellow Japanese American!

As I began actively attending local Japanese American community events in San Diego, I initially felt like an intruder who did not belong, although I was always openly welcomed when I met people. I had never had any contact or interest in the broader Japanese American commu-nity while growing up and was completely unfamiliar with their cultural activities, although some of them certainly resembled festivities I had seen in Japan. Almost everyone I encountered was either a prewar nisei or a sansei, and they were quite different from the shin-nisei Japanese Americans whom I had known my entire life. In fact, none of the dozens of people I met through Japanese American community organizations were shin-nisei, as far as I could tell.

Because of my strong Japanese cultural background and lingering accent, I always felt that the people I met would wonder whether I was a real Japanese American. I was struck (actually a bit distraught) when I noticed that a few elderly Japanese American women actu-ally *bowed* when I spoke with them! Since a Japanese American would never bow to another Japanese American, I assumed this indicated they thought that I was a Japanese foreigner from Japan. Bowing is of course a polite gesture, but for me, it meant "We don't think you are one of us." Apparently, the cultural and generational differences were palpable on both sides. On those occasions when Japanese Americans seemed confused about my ethnicity, I would actually say, "I'm also a Japanese American."

Of course, once I identified myself as Japanese American, no one contested my ethnic claim, especially when I told them I am actually shin-nisei. Once it became clear to them that I was born in the United States, I felt accepted as a fellow Japanese American, even if I had ini-tially appeared to them to be a Japanese from Japan. Therefore, shared nationality became a critical factor that helped overcome the differences between us.

Yet, the generational differences were still there. Ayako Takamori (2010:103–106), a shin-nisei anthropologist who conducted fieldwork among Japanese Americans living in Japan, recounts how she once introduced herself to a Japanese American gathering in Japan as a "nisei." She wanted to immediately identify herself as Japanese American in order to facilitate fieldwork. However, an elderly man abruptly grabbed the microphone and clarified that she is *shin*-nisei, not a (prewar) nisei and did not suffer through the same historical experiences.

As my fieldwork progressed, I became acquainted with many Japanese Americans and eventually became a familiar face in the local San Diego and Phoenix Japanese American communities. In fact, when I showed up at community events, a number of people would be familiar to me, and some would come up to greet me. It is evident that because I am technically Japanese American, I was able to blend into the ethnic community much more than a non-Japanese American. My ethnicity also probably made Japanese Americans more willing to meet for an interview and talk freely about their experiences. I was even asked to deliver a keynote speech at the annual meeting of the Japanese American Historical Society of San Diego about my research. There were hundreds of attentive Japanese Americans in the audience, and the talk was very well received.

Despite my progressive immersion in the field, the cultural differences between my research participants and me were never erased; nor are they with any anthropologists. It was only when I was interviewing other shin-nisei and sharing our similar experiences that I felt I was truly with my "own people." Yet, it was generational differences that made Japanese Americans so inherently fascinating to me, not ordinary and dull as I initially expected.

Indeed, I argue that difference is productive and essential for fieldwork and "good to think" for both anthropologist and research participant alike in the mutual creation of social knowledge. In contrast to those who have claimed that the insider similarities of "native anthropologists" endow them with privileged, emic insight, I actually found that it was the generational differences of most Japanese Americans that led to ethnographic and even theoretical insight. This was especially true with prewar nisei. Although we were both second-generation offspring of Japanese immigrants, I constantly felt how our cultural, ethnic,

The anthropologist in the field: *Mochitsuki* (pounding rice to make rice cakes) at the Buddhist Temple of San Diego (photo by author).

and historical consciousness were very different, causing me to realize how different historical experiences can produce considerable variation within the same immigrant generation. As a result, in Part I of this book, I emphasize the importance of properly recognizing historical generational differences within specific immigrant generations.

Difference was actually productive for my interviewees as well. During our conversations, I would often talk about my own experiences as a Japanese American, allowing my interviewees to use me as a sounding board to reflect on how their ethnic background was different. Many of these were the obvious generational differences already mentioned. Some of the elderly prewar nisei reflected on how their internment experience had affected their ethnic consciousness and Americanization compared to postwar shin-nisei like myself who are more bicultural and transnational. Older sansei interviewees spoke about how their loss of heritage culture and language was caused by greater generational distance from their immigrant grandparents and because they were not raised in a contemporary, multicultural environment. The sansei, as well as yonsei youth, sometimes remarked how great it was that I spoke Japanese fluently and had maintained my cultural background, something they were not able to do.

Therefore, "Othering" is essential for fieldwork regardless of all the existential and postmodernist angst the term now evokes among some anthropologists. Indeed, cultural difference has been the intellectual justification and cornerstone on which anthropology has been built. One of the hallmarks of our discipline has always been to bring the detailed, emic experiences of different (and yes, exotic) others to our audiences in a sympathetic, readable (and also unreadable) manner. No one wants to peruse a fieldwork-based account of an exotic tribe living in the African bush only to hear that they are "just like us."

But more importantly, cultural difference is the foundation of knowledge for both "native" and "non-native" anthropologists alike. If our fieldwork and research simply elicit information about people with whom we are already completely familiar, it is not producing new knowledge, but simply confirming what we already know. If most Japanese Americans had in fact been very similar or even identical to me, or if I had studied only the shin-nisei, I would not have learned as much that was new about them. Therefore, I acquired the greatest amount of new anthropological knowledge from Japanese Americans who were from other generations. In contrast to the standard postmodernist position that the epistemological status of the "Other" makes them ultimately unknowable, I argue that it is precisely this "Otherness" that is the subject of anthropological knowledge.

Apparently, some anthropologists have recently become wary of our discipline's constant emphasis on cultural difference. For instance, Matti Bunzl (2004) argues in our flagship journal that we need to move beyond the dichotomy of self/other in ethnographic fieldwork. As other anthropologists (such as Abu-Lughod 1991) and I have argued, this is not possible nor desirable, even for those of us who study our own ethnic group. If we are to avoid the contemporary othering of the peoples we study in fieldwork, we threaten to undermine one of the most fundamental aspects of anthropological investigation. While we need to be constantly wary about essentializing and exoticizing the cultural differences we encounter in the field, we should not hope to escape them.

## Chapter Summaries

As is the case with all ethnographies, much of this book consists of narratives told from a specific point of view based on my ethnic and generational positionality as a Japanese American shin-nisei anthropologist. As always, I have attempted to maintain the integrity of the analysis by avoiding implicitly ethnocentric (or more specifically, generational-centric) value judgments that lead to more sympathetic portrayals of certain generations of Japanese Americans over others.

Part I, "History and the Second Generation," is about Japanese American nisei in the American Southwest and emphasizes the importance of historical cohort differences among members of the second-immigrant generation. By examining the significant differences between prewar nisei and postwar shin-nisei, I show that there are actually two separate historical generations within the same second-immigrant generation. Chapter 1 focuses on the prewar nisei, whose Japanese parents emigrated from rural Japan before 1924. They grew up during a period of increasing American hostility toward their ethnic homeland and were eventually interned in concentration camps during World War II because of their Japanese ancestry. As a result of being subject to discriminatory racialization as well as to the assimilationist pressures of the immediate postwar period, many of them developed nationalist identities as loyal Americans, distanced themselves from their Japanese heritage, and demanded racial citizenship in the nation.

Chapter 2 then looks at the postwar shin-nisei, who are the children of wealthier, post-1965 Japanese immigrants who came to the United States as students, professionals, and elite business expatriates. In contrast to the prewar nisei, they have come of age in a multicultural and increasingly globalized America in which Japan's image had considerably improved because of its postwar rise in the international order as an ally of the United States. As a result, the shin-nisei have not experienced much ethnic discrimination and have had many more opportunities to become transnationally engaged with their ethnic homeland. In response to their multicultural racialization, many have become fully bilingual and bicultural and have developed transnational identifications with both America and Japan. Despite being culturally assimilated, they have simultaneously maintained their ethnic heritage and have successfully inherited both the culture and the transnationalism of their immigrant parents.

Part II, "Racialization, Citizenship, and Heritage," moves on to later-generation Japanese Americans in the American Southwest. In Chapter 3, I focus on the sansei, who have followed the assimilative trajectory of their prewar nisei parents. They were generally raised in white, middle-class suburbs, experienced further upward mobility (as well as increasing intermarriage mainly with whites), and have become well-integrated into mainstream American society. Although they have generally lost their ancestral heritage, they have also experienced the ethnic activism of the Asian American movement in the 1960s and 1970s, the gradual turn toward multiculturalism, and the emergence of Japan as a respected global economic power. Therefore, despite their assimilation, the sansei claim to have inherited aspects of the ancestral Japanese culture, and they express greater pride in their ethnic identities as Japanese Americans compared to the prewar nisei.

Before moving on to the yonsei, Chapter 4 deals specifically with the persistent racialization of Japanese Americans, which affects later-generation sansei and yonsei the most. Although their families have been in the United States for generations, they are still racialized as foreigners simply because of their Asian appearance. Because of large-scale immigration from Asia and an American national identity that is racially defined as "white," their Asian phenotype continues to have a foreigner connotation. I analyze how later-generation Japanese Americans are racially marginalized as outsiders in their daily interaction with other Americans, which is often accompanied by essentialized assumptions that they are also culturally "Japanese." In response to such racialized multiculturalism, the sansei, as well as the yonsei to a lesser degree, engage in everyday struggles for racial citizenship by demanding inclusion in the national community as Americans despite their racial differences. It is still uncertain whether such attempts to contest their racialization will cause currently monoracial notions of American identity to be reconsidered in more inclusive and multiracial ways.

Chapter 5 examines how fourth-generation yonsei youth are attempting to recover their lost ethnic heritage and reconnect with their ancestral homeland. Although some of them have responded to their continued racialization by demanding racial citizenship like the sansei, they have also become concerned about their overassimilation to American society in an era of multiculturalism where ethnic heritage and homeland have come to be positively valued. As a result, they have reclaimed their ethnic ancestry by studying Japanese and majoring in Asian Studies and have actively forged transnational homeland ties by living in Japan as college exchange students. Therefore, instead of assimilation obliterating cultural heritage, it has instigated an ethnic revival among the yonsei under conditions of racialized multiculturalism. Although this return to ethnic roots involves a more serious commitment than the superficial symbolic ethnicity observed among white ethics in the past, it indicates that ethnicity remains involuntary for racialized minorities, even after four generations.

Ethnic heritage is not simply experienced, but also performed. The first two chapters of Part III, "Ethnic Heritage, Performance, and Diasporicity," analyze how later-generation Japanese Americans have enthusiastically embraced taiko (traditional Japanese drumming) in an attempt to recover their cultural heritage and ancestry. Chapter 6 illustrates how the search for ethnic roots through taiko involves not just the persistence and reiteration of ancient cultural traditions but their active recreation in the present to reflect the contemporary social conditions under which Japanese Americans live.

Although the ethnic homeland of Japan is often positioned as the source of cultural authenticity, Chapter 7 argues that the remaking of traditional taiko by Japanese Americans also produces a type of performative authenticity that causes it to resonate with their current lives and feel more real. This is quite empowering on a personal level, allowing them to display ethnic and gender identities through performances that challenge demeaning stereotypes of Asian Americans. However, despite its subversive potential, taiko's reception by American audiences ironically reinscribes Orientalizing discourses that racially essentialize Japanese Americans as the exotic Other and is rather disempowering at the collective level.

Chapter 8, "Diasporicity and Japanese Americans," analyzes the extent to which Japanese Americans can be considered part of a larger, transnational diasporic community of Japanese descendants dispersed throughout the Americas (collectively referred to as *nikkei*, or the Japanese diaspora). Instead of engaging in intellectually fruitless debates about the definition of "diaspora" and whether peoples like the nikkei are diasporic, I argue that we should examine *diasporicity*, which refers to the relative strength of a geographically dispersed ethnic group's transnational connections and identifications with both the ancestral homeland and co-ethnics residing in other countries. Although Japanese Americans are members of the Japanese-descent nikkei diaspora, they do not manifest a high level of diasporicity in their transnational ethnic relations. However, like other diasporic groups, they have much stronger social connections to their ethnic homeland than they do to other Japanese-descent communities in the Americas.

The conclusion reassesses the various factors that cause some generations of Japanese Americans to emphasize ethnic heritage more than others and the extent to which their diverse reactions to racialization may reorder hierarchical racial formations. It ends with some thoughts about the future of the Japanese American community, including biracial individuals of half-Japanese descent whose numbers will continue to increase in the coming decades.

PART I

History and the Second Generation

1

# The Prewar Nisei

## Americanization and Nationalist Belonging

### Divergent Histories and the Second Generation

For quite some time, the leaders of the Japanese American community have been concerned about the steady decline in participation among youth in organizations such as the Japanese American Citizens League (JACL) and various Japanese American historical societies.[1] This is especially a concern for the Japanese American Historical Society of San Diego (JAHSSD). Started by a group of elderly second-generation Japanese American nisei who had been interned in concentration camps during World War II,[2] the JAHSSD has a large membership—its annual meeting draws close to two hundred members—and is more active than the JACL in San Diego.. However, the JAHSSD focuses primarily on historical events surrounding World War II and has really struggled to attract Japanese American youth, who are either fourth-generation yonsei or postwar second-generation shin-nisei. Both of these younger generations are removed from the internment experience, the exploits of the 442nd Japanese American Regimental Combat Team (which served in Europe during World War II), and the successful effort in the 1970s and 1980s to seek redress for wartime incarceration, all of which were defining moments for today's elderly second-generation nisei as well as the third-generation sansei. As a result, the members who attended JAHSSD events are almost exclusively elderly and middle aged; the only youth I observed were children whom families brought with them, and even they were few in number.

In order to address the lack of youth participation, the JAHSSD and the JACL decided to hold the annual Day of Remembrance event at the University of California at San Diego (UCSD) campus in collaboration with the university's Japanese American student organization, the Nikkei Student Union (NSU). The Day of Remembrance is the annual commemoration of the internment of Japanese Americans during World War II and is held on February 19, the date on which President Franklin D. Roosevelt signed Executive Order 9066.

Unfortunately, the event was poorly organized. It was held in the central courtyard plaza of UCSD's student center. The speakers were mainly elderly nisei from the JAHSSD who spoke at length about their experiences of being interned during World War II. They sat at a makeshift table on a stage in front of the student theater under a sign that advertised an upcoming performance of *The Vagina Monologues*. The event was constantly disrupted by the hustle and bustle of UCSD students, who were either walking through the plaza on their way to class or having lunch and conversations at nearby tables and paying no attention to what the speakers were saying. To make matters worse, music and announcements blared through the courtyard from another student organization trying to recruit new members, constantly threatening to drown out the Day of Remembrance speakers.

Although there were plenty of students in the courtyard, it was distressing to see how few Japanese American students had bothered to show up. Most of the audience members who had come specifically to attend the event were elderly nisei and older third-generation sansei mainly from the JAHSSD and the JACL. They listened intently to the speakers and reacted a number of times to what they were saying. However, only a handful of Japanese American students were present, in contrast to other Nikkei Student Union events, which draw large numbers of Japanese American (and other Asian American) students. They stood near booths located at the side of the plaza, which provided information about the internment. Most were fourth-generation yonsei whom I instantly recognized, since they were NSU board members whom I knew through my fieldwork. Partly because of the noise and distractions in the plaza, they were not paying attention to the speakers either and were mainly chatting amongst themselves. In fact, they did not even clap after each speaker finished. Given the overall lack of student attention, the general impression was of an older generation attempting to pass on their experiences and historical legacy to a younger generation, who had moved beyond the past and were too preoccupied with their daily lives to even notice.

Day of Remembrance speakers at the University of California at San Diego (photo by author).

Another speaker being ignored by students in the plaza (photo by author).

NSU board members chatting amongst themselves at the booths during a speech (photo by author).

However, most conspicuous in their absence were any shin-nisei students from the postwar second generation. Although the yonsei NSU board members were not listening to the speakers, at least they had come, perhaps out of respect for their elders. In contrast, the shin-nisei from NSU did not even show up. "I've never attended Day of Remembrance events," one of them once told me. "I didn't even know what that was until I joined NSU. I don't relate to the internment of Japanese Americans, since my family didn't go through it."

One of the most notable generational divisions within the Japanese American community is between the elderly prewar nisei, whose Japanese parents immigrated to the United States from Japan before World War II, and the younger, postwar shin-nisei generation, who are mainly a product of Japanese immigration after the 1960s. Although they are technically of the same second generation, the prewar nisei were shaped by their internment experience during World War II, a life-changing tragedy that continues to define who they are as shown by their participation in community events, their efforts at establishing memorials to commemorate it, and their periodic reunions with others who were interned in the same concentration camp.

In contrast, the shin-nisei came of age mainly after the 1980s and are far removed from the prewar discrimination and struggles of the elderly nisei. Although they are definitely aware of the internment experience and its importance, having studied about it in school or visited remnants of the internment camps, they feel little personal connection to it since it is not part of their family's history (Yamashiro 2008:258). As Takehiro Watanabe, an older shin-nisei, whose family immigrated to the United States in the early 1950s, notes,

> I grew up in a Japanese American community, and the internment was so critical in the formation of their identity. For me, that didn't make any sense because I had no connection to it. My father was in the Japanese Navy during World War II, not in the internment camps or serving in the 442nd [Japanese American regiment]. So he had different stories to tell me than the internment ones.

Similarly, in a discussion about the Japanese American internment experience during the "Culture Forums" held by the Nikkei Student

Union, Steve Okura, one of the shin-nisei board members, was rather blunt about his different historical consciousness. "All of this focus about internment in the Japanese American community kind of alienates shin-nisei like me," he stated in front of the others. "I'm also Japanese American, but I have a different history. If other Japanese Americans don't see me as Japanese American because of this, that's OK. My family wasn't in the camps. My family was in Japan during World War II. I feel much more connected to the Japanese war experience than I do to the internment."

Although the prewar nisei and shin-nisei are of the same generation in terms of immigration, they are clearly from completely different generations in terms of history. In other words, they have had different generational experiences because they are a product of different historical eras. Part I of this book examines how these two separate groups of Japanese American nisei in the American Southwest are historically constituted and how this has led to quite divergent ethnic heritage and identity outcomes.

The prewar generation of nisei are primarily the descendants of agricultural immigrants from Japan who arrived in the United States after the turn of the twentieth century. Because they grew up during a period of increasing American hostility toward their ethnic homeland and discrimination against Japanese Americans, they suffered from the negative impact of their racialization, which eventually led to their internment in concentration camps during World War II. They also had fewer opportunities to maintain transnational connections to their ethnic homeland. Those who did temporarily live in Japan had quite ambivalent experiences. As a result, many of them eventually distanced themselves from their Japanese heritage, assimilated to American society, and demanded racial citizenship by emphasizing their national identity and loyalty as Americans despite their racialized status as non-white minorities.

In contrast, the postwar second generation are children of wealthier Japanese immigrants who came to the United States as students, professionals, and elite business expatriates starting in the 1960s (Takamori 2011:28–29, 101–102). The shin-nisei came of age in a multicultural and increasingly globalized America, where Japan's image had improved considerably because of its postwar economic prosperity and the popularity of Japanese commodities and popular culture. Although they continue to be racialized as Japanese descendants, they suffer much less discrimination and have been encouraged to develop transnational connections with their ethnic homeland. Unlike the prewar nisei, they maintain strong ties to their ethnic heritage and to Japan, are bicultural, and have a transnational ethnic consciousness. Therefore, because of their different formative historical experiences, the prewar nisei inhabit an exclusively assimilationist and nationalist social space, whereas the postwar shin-nisei construct their ethnicities and identities in a much more transnational context.

## Conceptualizing Immigrant and Historical Generations

As discussed in the Introduction, there are actually two types of generation: immigrant and historical. The immigration studies literature on the second generation uses the concept of immigrant generation in two ways. First, generations can refer exclusively to genealogical birth order within an immigrant-origin family. Accordingly, the first generation are the immigrant parents and the second generation are their children. Many studies of the second generation classify generations only according to family birth order, so that all children of immigrants are members of the second generation regardless of whether they were born in the country of origin or the host country (Kasinitz et al. 2008; Levitt and Waters 2002; Rumbaut and Portes 2001; Portes and Rumbaut 2001; Smith 2006).

However, immigrant generations can also refer to distance from the country of origin based on genealogical birth order (Foner 2009:3; Kasinitz et al. 2008:400). In this sense, the second generation includes only the children of immigrants who were born in the host country and are therefore farther removed from the country of origin than their first-generation parents. The children of immigrants who were born in the country of origin but immigrated as youth and were raised in the host country are called the 1.5 generation, since they are in between the first-generation immigrant parents and the second generation in terms of distance from the origin country. Because this book adopts the latter definition of immigrant generation, "second-generation Japanese Americans" refers only to those born in the United States to Japanese immigrant parents.

In contrast, historical generations are cohorts which were shaped by similar historical events and experiences. However, according to Karl Mannheim (1952: ch. 7), it is not simply shared historical experiences that define the members of a generation, but historical events experienced *at a young age* that have a determining influence on the rest of their lives. Therefore, as Mannheim points out, older and younger people who experience the same historical processes together are not members of the same generation. In this sense, historical generations are age cohorts who were born and raised around the same time and had similar formative historical experiences in childhood or youth. Mannheim is strongly implying that subsequent historical events do not have as decisive an impact on a generation's consciousness and identity as those it experienced when it first came of age.

As this chapter will demonstrate, a historically grounded concept of generation may be just as important as an immigration-based one in explaining similarities and differences within immigrant-origin ethnic groups (Eckstein 2002). There is no doubt that there are significant differences between the first and second immigrant generations in terms of educational achievement, cultural assimilation and social integration, socioeconomic mobility, ethnic identity, and transnational engagement (Boyd and Grieco 1998; Levitt and Waters 2002; Perlman and Waldinger 1997; Rumbaut 2005; van Niekerk 2007). However, certain differences within an immigrant-origin ethnic group are the product of historical cohort differences and cannot be explained simply by an immigrant generation perspective based on family birth order or distance from the country of origin.

Even among immigrants from the same country, it is clear that those who arrived during different historical periods came from different emigration contexts and faced different host country receptions and policies (Berg 2011; Eckstein and Barberia 2002). They may also vary in terms of socioeconomic or ethnic composition. Such historical cohort differences can then have a significant impact on their second-generation descendants, thereby producing major differences within the same immigrant generation, as is the case with the Japanese Americans. However, when differences are examined within the second generation in the immigration studies literature, the research involves comparison of individuals from different ethnic groups or national origins, such as second-generation Mexican Americans and second-generation Chinese Americans (Alba and Holdaway 2013; Boyd and Grieco 1998; Portes, Fernández-Kelly, and Haller 2005; Portes and Rumbaut 2001; Rumbaut 2005). Differences among members of the second generation of the *same* national origins are almost never examined.

Of course, immigration studies about the second generation are not completely oblivious to historical generational differences. A number of researchers have noted the significant differences between the current second generation, whose immigrant parents arrived in the United States after the 1960s, and the second-generation descendants of the last great wave of immigrants in the late nineteenth and early twentieth centuries (Eckstein 2002; Levitt and Waters 2002:13–14; Perlmann and Waldinger 1997; Portes, Fernández-Kelly, and Haller 2005:1001–1003; Portes and Zhou 1993; Rumbaut 2005:1041–1043). This earlier second-generation group was primarily of European origin, worked in an industrial manufacturing economy, faced greater assimilationist pressure, and was perhaps less transnationally engaged with their ethnic homelands. In contrast, the post-1960s second generation are mainly non-white racial minorities of Latin American or Asian origin, who grew up in an era of multiculturalism and diversity, work in a service-oriented economy, and perhaps lead more transnational lives. Such differences between these two historical cohorts has led to a debate over whether the current second generation is experiencing less socioeconomic mobility than the earlier second-generation group because its members apparently face greater racial discrimination as non-white minorities in American society and more restricted labor market opportunities in a service economy (Perlmann and Waldinger 1997; Portes, Fernández-Kelly, and Haller 2005:1002–1003; Portes and Zhou 1993; Rumbaut 2005:1041–1043).

Although these studies give the impression that the prewar second generation is no longer around, a good number of individuals from this earlier historical cohort are still alive today and coexist with the postwar second generation. However, research on the contemporary second generation focuses exclusively on the descendants of post 1960s immigrants, and I am not aware of any studies of the elderly prewar second generation. In general, the second-generation literature ignores age cohort differences (that is, historical generational differences) within the second immigrant generation.[3] Most second-generation studies are about young children of immigrants and do not compare them with older members of the same second generation.[4]

In addition, the second-generation literature assumes that the pre- and postwar second generation are from entirely different national origins and therefore vary in racial composition (descendants of earlier white European immigrants versus descendants of recent non-white Latino or Asian immigrants). It is true that southern and eastern European immigration to the United States subsided after the 1920s and there has not been much postwar European immigration. Likewise, immigration from Latin America and Asia occurred mainly after the 1960s; in the prewar period, there was relatively little immigration from these regions to the United States.

However, a number of immigrant groups do have a long history of immigration than spans both the pre- and postwar period. They include the Japanese, Chinese, Filipinos, Mexicans, Russians, and eastern and southern Europeans. The second-generation descendants of these immigrant groups therefore have substantial members from both the pre- and postwar periods who constitute two different historical generations and age groups. Although the prewar nisei and postwar shin-nisei Japanese Americans are members of the same second immigrant generation, they are from different historical generations, since their formative childhood experiences occurred during separate time periods. As a result, they continue to have different ethnic experiences today. For ethnic groups like Japanese Americans, it is highly problematic to ignore such historical differences among members of the second generation who otherwise share the same immigrant family birth order or distance from the ethnic homeland.

## Japanese American Internment and Postwar Discrimination

Today's elderly Japanese American second generation was shaped by historical events pertaining to World War II, which placed them on an ethnic trajectory that led to very different assimilation and identity outcomes when compared to the postwar shin-nisei. Because the prewar nisei grew up in an era of increasing anti-Japanese hostility leading up to World War II, their racialization as Japanese descendants had significantly negative consequences, including their internment in concentration camps during the war as enemy aliens. As a result, the prewar nisei had to demonstrate their loyalty as Americans in order to avoid discrimination and emphasized cultural assimilation over the retention of their ethnic heritage or transnational ties to Japan. Because of such formative historical experiences and their struggle for racial citizenship, their sense of ethnic identity and belonging remain exclusively nationalist in orientation today.

All the elderly second-generation Japanese Americans I interviewed came of age before and during World War II, when they were subject to discrimination and persecution as Japanese descendants. The prewar nisei who are alive today were generally too young to remember discriminatory experiences before the war. However, Greg Kashimura, one of my older interviewees, told me about an incident that took place in 1938, when he was ten years old, which had a tremendous impact on him. It occurred at a racially segregated swimming pool at a local school, where he accompanied a couple of white friends. Greg innocently followed his friends to the "White Only" pool. Then, as he recounts,

> The lifeguard says, "Hey you! Go over there!" He was pointing to the other pool that said "Colored." I told him I want to be with my friends. Then, he says, "No, you aren't allowed here. Can't you read?" So I had to go by myself to the other pool with the Blacks and Mexicans and swim without my friends. I was so distressed I didn't even go into the water. I didn't even know what discrimination was at that time. It was my first time experiencing it."[5]

Undoubtedly, the most formative discriminatory experience for the prewar nisei was their internment during World War II. Although they were culturally assimilated American citizens, it is quite clear that as Japanese descendants, they were seen as a national security threat because of their racialization as a nonwhite ethnic minority (Spickard 1996:100–101; Yamashiro 2008:60–64). In contrast, German and Italian Americans were never interned en masse because they were not subject to the same level of racism, although it also true that their much larger numbers and their broad dispersal throughout the United States would have made their internment very difficult if not impossible and would have led to adverse effects on the American economy.[6] The situation with Japanese descendants was very different: they were concentrated on the West Coast, their racial visibility subjected them to discrimination and racism, as well as to economic resentment and antagonism from local residents because of their success in agriculture. Thus, once Japan became a wartime enemy of the United States, they were easily branded and targeted as "enemy aliens" because of their race.

With the exception of two individuals who were living in Japan during World War II (discussed below), all of the other prewar nisei I interviewed were interned in concentration camps. President D. Roosevelt's Executive Order 9066 designated a military "exclusion zone" on the West Coast of the United States (which included all of California, and parts of Oregon, Washington, and Arizona), and all peoples of Japanese ancestry living in this zone were evacuated and incarcerated. It is a little known fact that the border of this exclusion zone in Arizona cut through the center of the city of Phoenix. Therefore, Japanese Americans who lived on the east side of this border were not interned, whereas family and relatives living on the western side of the border (sometimes on the other side of the same road) were forced to relocate to concentration camps (in fact, a few of them moved east of the border at the last minute in order to avoid internment).

While the prewar nisei I interviewed were still children and teenagers when they were interned, they continue to have very strong recollections of their experience. The great irony of the internment experience, however, is that although it was extremely difficult for the first-generation immigrant parents, it was much less so for the nisei who were still children (Fugita and Fernandez 2004:62–65; Takezawa 1995:84). The parents often lost their homes, belongings, businesses, and jobs, and their families were uprooted, relocated, and locked up in concentration camps for years in desolate locations in California or Arizona, which had extreme temperatures and dust storms. Not only were they forced to live in miserable and crowded tar-paper barracks with no privacy and poor food, husbands lost their former authority and status as economic providers, and parents often lost their authority over their children in the camps. In addition, they faced constant anxiety about their futures. Adult nisei found their careers or university educations suddenly cut short and their future aspirations initially crushed.[7] According to Bob Nakamura, the former president of the JAHSSD:

During the internment era, if you were an adult, the pain was really great. They lost everything and it was really traumatic and they sacrificed a lot. And the pain was there for a long time and they didn't want to talk about it for decades. When we had reunions, or put on exhibits, they were looking at the exhibit and tears would come out of their eyes. But if you were a youngster like me, I didn't feel any pain. And you didn't think much about the hardship that your parents, and even older brothers and sisters, went through.

In contrast to the parents, the second-generation children were relatively shielded from the trauma and emotional suffering of the internment experience (often by the parents themselves). In fact, they enjoyed the activities for children in the camps and often spent their days playing with other Japanese American children. They were relatively free from parental control, and instead of spending much time with their parents, they often ate, played, and went to school with the other children (Matsumoto 2014:153; O'Brien and Fugita 1991:76; Takezawa 1995:94).

During the Day of Remembrance at UC San Diego, I was repeatedly struck by how none of the prewar nisei speakers had any traumatic, heart-wrenching stories to tell. Instead, they emphasized that the internment experience was "fun" and "like a hell of a long summer camp." Others spoke about how "we had a good time" and "didn't have the worries of our parents." Their stories were filled with accounts of playing with the other kids, sports and games, social groups and cliques, going to (or ditching) school, and sometimes amusing anecdotes about daily camp life. There was little anger, indignation, or resentment, and the general attitude was that they made the best of a bad situation since there was not much they could do about it.

Such themes are also reflected in my interviews with the prewar second generation. "It was actually a safe environment," Ruth Morita recounted. "All the kids were together, and we could play and study and didn't really have to listen to our parents. It was actually fun like a summer camp. We didn't find it that harsh of an environment, because we were too young to be really fully aware of what was going on. It didn't mean much to us at that time, you know. We were just like, OK, so here we are. So be it." Others emphasized the intense camaraderie among youth in the camps. "All my friends were Japanese

An internment camp memorial. Poston, Arizona
(photo by author).

Remnants of the internment camp barracks, Poston, Arizona (photo by author).

[American] for the first time in my life and I hung out with them all the time instead of my family," another nisei recalled. "I enjoyed it. We played every sport you could think of—basketball, softball, judo. I made lifelong friends that I still meet during reunions—it's a strong bond."

Although other interviewees did not necessarily enjoy their camp experience, they did not characterize it as a true hardship. According to Kiyoshi Sakamura:

> It was a relatively easy life. It wasn't a hardship for me. Some would say the living conditions were really harsh. But so what? It was not true suffering. We always had three meals a day on time, a cot, and army blankets. It was an American style concentration camp, not in the true sense of a concentration camp. We were just concentrated in one camp. It was really cold in the winter, but when you're fifteen years old, you don't really get cold because you are moving around all the time. The only real hardship was that we lost our freedom and couldn't leave the camp. But who was really thinking about the loss of our constitutional rights at that time? Later, some got special permission to leave the camp.

Another informant, John Kusumoto, recounted his internment experience as follows:

> We managed. It was just a matter of existing. We just spent a lot of time fishing and playing baseball. And by the time we were about 15, we had little jam sessions and went dancing. We would go into the laundry room/ rec. hall and somebody would have a radio or a record player and we learned how to dance with girls and things like that. . . . It would get cold, down to zero at night. And so we learned how to ice skate in the wintertime. So we did a lot of things just kind of killing time. . . . There were also four or five Boy Scout troops in the camps. I remember being able to leave the camp to take these camping trips. . . . And yeah, we also went to school. But all they did was they took one block with barracks and they just put tables in there and that was our classroom. So I recall we probably goofed off a lot at school. . . . I can't say it was an unhappy period.

However, even though the internment experience was not necessarily a traumatic hardship for the prewar second generation, it still had a major impact on their ethnic consciousness after the war. Kiyoshi expressed a sentiment probably shared by others of his historical cohort:

> The experience wasn't that harsh, but you still realize, especially as you get older, that we were locked up during World War II because we were seen as enemy aliens. It didn't happen to the Germans or Italians, only to the Japanese Americans. Despite the fact that we were American citizens born and raised here, Americans saw us as the enemy, just because of the way we look. That stays with you your entire life, even to this day.

Other prewar nisei spoke about the discrimination they continued to face as a racialized minority in American society after they were released from the internment camps. At the Day of Remembrance at UC San Diego, several speakers implied that it was harder for Japanese American kids after they left camp because when they reentered American schools, they had to endure harassment, hostility, and constant teasing. According to one of the women speakers, "Some of the kids called me names and threw rocks at me and yelled, 'Your people killed my father during the war!' They didn't seem to realize my family had nothing to do with the Japanese soldiers who fought against the Americans in the Pacific."

In my interviews, elderly nisei spoke about how anti-Japanese sentiment after the war continued to have a personal effect on them. Kiyoshi told me about how he walked into a restaurant with a friend and was denied service because he was of Japanese descent. "I'm sure this happened to other Japanese Americans at the time too," he noted. One of the most poignant examples was recounted by Bob Nakamura:

> I was on active service for the Air Force [in the early 1950s] and had come back from overseas and was stationed in a little town by Buffalo, New York. We were part of the Military Police patroling the town and we took a break to have coffee. So the guy serves us coffee, and then he asks me, "Where are you from?" I said, "I'm from California." "Where were you born?" "California." "Where were your parents born?" I didn't say anything. He then says, "Are they from China? Korea?" I said, "No. My parents are from Japan." Then he suddenly goes, "I don't serve Japs!" and pulls the coffee away. I was stunned. Here I am wearing an American

military uniform and had just been serving overseas and I get treated like this!

Because internment and anti-Japanese sentiment right after the war had such a formative impact on the nisei, they continue to be concerned about the possible negative effects of their racialization as "Japanese" to this day. I often noticed that they remain more sensitive to lingering prejudice than other Japanese Americans, although some mentioned they have not experienced discrimination recently. Nonetheless, several interviewees did refer to anti-Japanese sentiment during the 1980s, when there was trade friction between the United States and Japan, and the American car industry was being hurt by Japanese imports. "I was living in Detroit at that time and there was tremendous backlash," one of them recalled.

Sally Sakamura is another prewar nisei who has remained sensitive to racialized discrimination. "Sometimes, I still feel discriminated against because of my appearance," she told me. She then recounted two incidents. The first one occurred many years ago when she was driving and cut off a man in a car in front of her. The man came out of the car and said "Why don't you go back to where you came from?" The second incident was much more recent when she was waiting in line at a grocery store and a white woman cut in front of her. When Sally protested, the woman became really upset and said "I know your kind. I was in Hawaii and they are all the same."

Although much of the prejudice against people of Japanese descent is currently expressed in a jocular manner, it still impacts the prewar nisei in a very personal way, perhaps stirring up old memories. "Some people still use the Jap word," one of my interviewees noted. "I don't know if they do it jokingly or what, but it bothers me a lot. You don't want to hear it, even if it's in fun or jest and not directed at me specifically. It can get upsetting."

The prewar second generation are especially aware of continued prejudice among American veterans who fought the Japanese in the Pacific. Even John Kusumoto, who claimed he was no longer concerned about prejudice against Japanese Americans and did not attribute the negative treatment he occasionally receives in public to his ethnicity, continued to be bothered by the behavior of one of his acquaintances who served in the United States Navy during World War II:

He would always make these little remarks about the Japanese. It's done in a friendly fashion, but he makes jokes about two-man Japanese submarines [that attacked Pearl Harbor] or kamikazes and things like that. He seems to do it specifically to Japanese Americans. He's always kidding my Japanese American friend from Hawaii too. And for a long time, every year on December 7, we'd get this nice big fax or e-mail from him that says, "Remember Pearl Harbor!"

"A vast majority of that generation is dead," his wife added (she is also a prewar nisei who was interned during World War II). "But they have passed down these negative attitudes to their children and grandchildren."

## "We Earned the Right to Be Called Americans": Nisei Reactions to Discrimination

The prewar nisei's experience of internment and anti-Japanese discrimination during and after World War II had a formative and long-term impact on their ethnic consciousness and national identities. When faced with marginalization and discrimination, racialized minorities can respond in two ways (Tsuda 2001). They can assert their ethnic minority identity as an oppositional "counter-identity" (Tsuda 2003: ch. 3) against a discriminatory majority society, which is similar to what Alejandro Portes and Rubén Rumbaut call "reactive ethnicity" (2001: ch. 7). On the other hand, they can adopt a more accommodating, assimilation-oriented strategy in order to avoid discrimination and gain greater acceptance by majority society.

Instead of strengthening their Japanese ethnic consciousness in opposition to American society, prewar second-generation Japanese Americans clearly asserted their American national identities and claimed racial citizenship and membership in the nation-state despite their racial differences. Since they are American-born citizens who had already been subject to the assimilation process, it was natural for them to respond to severe ethnic discrimination and incarceration by demonstrating to other Americans that they are just as loyal and patriotic to their country of birth as white Americans (Hosokawa 2002; Spickard 1996:130–132). For a number of my prewar nisei informants, the effort to overcome discrimination and prejudice and gain full recognition as Americans involved deliberately distancing themselves from their Japanese ethnic heritage. The continued impact of such experiences is shown in the incident recounted above when Sally was yelled at by the driver who told her to go back to where she came from. She decided to confront him by saying: "I was born here. I'm American. Why don't you go back to where you came from?"

"They really had a history of proving that they are American," a shin-nisei who grew up in the 1990s observed when reflecting on generational differences among Japanese Americans. "These people had to prove they were patriotic. Prove that they are white. So they had to leave their Japanese heritage behind." The founding and subsequent history of the Japanese American Citizens League, is a case in point. Before and during World War II, the JACL relentlessly emphasized the American national loyalties and patriotism of Japanese American nisei. They also provided information to the FBI about first-generation issei who could become spies or saboteurs in the event of war with Japan, encouraged Japanese Americans not to resist their internment during World War II, and lobbied for the creation of a Japanese American military unit in order to demonstrate their status as loyal and trustworthy American citizens (Hosokawa 2002; Kurashige 2002: ch. 3; Spickard 1996: ch. 6).

Such a nationalist, assimilation-oriented response to discrimination was reflected in the comments of my prewar nisei interviewees. For instance, Mike Oshima was quite explicit about how the internment experience had affected his sense of ethnicity. "Internment made it quite clear to all of us that we weren't considered real Americans because of our Japanese ancestry, even if we are U.S.-born citizens. In that sense, we had no choice but to become fully Americanized, to show that we *are* Americans. It was forced on us to think that way, and so I was like, 'By golly, I'm going to be that way!'"

After they were released from the internment camps, the prewar nisei had to assert their national identities as Americans in order to counter the racial discrimination they continued to face. For instance, when Bob was called a "Jap" and denied service at the coffee shop during his service in the U.S. Air Force, he responded by demanding that his status as an American be recognized: "I confronted this guy and told him, 'I don't care what you think of me, but I want you to respect the uniform I wear. Regardless of my ancestry, I am serving this country as an American.'"

"The racial epithet 'Jap' became a rallying cry for nisei," Larry Honkawa recalled. "Because of racial discrimination, designating ourselves as Americans became necessary. Even before the internment, when the war clouds over the Pacific formed in the 1930s, some of us were already identifying ourselves as *Americans* of Japanese ancestry (AJAs for short), especially in Hawaii" (see also Tamura 1994:66–67).

One of the very important ways in which Japanese Americans earned their racial citizenship and recognition as patriotic Americans was through their service in the United States military both during and after World War II. Because they were racialized as enemy aliens after the Japanese attack on Pearl Harbor, they were initially excluded from the draft. However, the American government eventually reversed its decision and approved the formation of a segregated Japanese American combat unit because of the exemplary service of Japanese Americans in military intelligence and in the successful training of the 100th Infantry Battalion (consisting of nisei from Hawaii), as well as the efforts of discharged ROTC nisei cadets from Hawaii assisting in the war effort.

The government administered a controversial loyalty questionnaire to interned Japanese Americans asking whether they would be willing to serve in the United States armed forces wherever ordered, and whether they would swear unqualified and sole allegiance to the United States and faithfully defend the country. Despite being interned as enemy aliens and having their fundamental rights as American citizens violated, a vast majority of nisei men answered both questions in the affirmative (Takezawa 1995:99), although only a small number of them volunteered to serve in the U.S. military.[8]

As a result, the 442nd Japanese American Regimental Combat Team was formed and sent to Europe, where the nisei soldiers fought heroically in order to prove their loyalty as Americans ( Takezawa 1995:95–98; Umezawa Duus 1987; Yenne 2007). Initially, the 442nd was an all-volunteer force, consisting of Japanese Americans from Hawaii who were not interned (10,000 enthusiastically volunteered, and 2,600 were inducted) and volunteers from the mainland United States who came from the internment camps (1,253 volunteered, and 800 were inducted). Eventually, the draft was instated for Japanese Americans and a total of

21,102 were enlisted (over 12,000 of them were replacement soldiers for the 442nd). They quickly became known for fighting bravely at all costs (their motto was "Go for Broke") and saw some of the heaviest combat in both Italy and France, where they helped break German lines and also liberated several towns.

"We were always used to spearhead attacks," Jim Sakura, one of my interviewees who fought in the 442nd recalled. "It was because we always completed our mission, whatever it was. So General Clark was head of the Fifth Army and he liked the way the 442nd fought." However, another elderly nisei veteran from the 442nd whom I met at a JAHSSD meeting had a much more cynical interpretation. "All our commanders were *hakujin* (whites)," he pointed out. "If there was a dangerous mission, they'd be like, 'Send in the Japanese Americans! They fight like crazy.' We were absolutely exhausted from days and days of intense fighting. But they hardly let us rest. We were ordered to fight more."

The 442nd's most famous battle was the rescue of the Texas "Lost Battalion," which was cut off and surrounded by Germany forces in the Vosges forest in eastern France near the German border. The battle is considered one of the most ferocious in the history of the United States Army and ended in a mass suicide charge by the Japanese Americans in a final desperate attempt to rescue the 211 remaining members of the Lost Battalion. Even after the battle, they were not relieved, but were instead ordered to advance farther for eight more days. While the 442nd began the Vosges campaign with 2,943 men, 2,000 were wounded (882 of them seriously), and over 200 were killed or missing in action. The 442nd eventually became the most decorated military unit in American history for its size and length of service. It also had one of the highest casualty rates, earning 9,486 Purple Hearts (awarded to those wounded or killed in action).

The 442nd veteran whom I met at the JAHSSD and who fought in the battle to rescue the Lost Battalion said that despite his company's heavy losses in the battle, they were ordered to keep charging and that after they had rescued the Lost Battalion, only eight members of his company remained (a company consists of 180–200 men) to pursue the fleeing Germans. When I asked him whether he felt the regiment was sacrificed in order to win the battle, he did not want to speak anymore (apparently my question had hit a nerve). His wife, who was sitting next to him ex-

The 442nd Japanese American Regimental Combat Team in France in 1944 (U.S. Army file photo).

Color guards and bearers of the 442nd Japanese American Regimental Combat Team stand at attention (U.S. Army file photo).

plained: "He does not want to talk about it because it was so traumatic. It was basically a suicide charge. They were willing to sacrifice everything. That was the mentality."

There were also significant numbers of Japanese Americans (about 6,000) who served in military intelligence, and many were embedded in American military units fighting the Japanese in the Pacific. Unlike those in the 442nd, these Japanese Americans were contributing to the American war effort against their ethnic homeland of Japan and served their country under the constant threat of being mistaken as the enemy by American solders (as a result, they were assigned bodyguards to protect them). They also knew that if they were captured by Japanese troops, they would be tortured and executed. These nisei intelligence officers and linguists translated captured documents, interrogated Japanese prisoners, and intercepted Japanese radio transmissions, obtaining an unprecedented amount of intelligence that was vital for Americans to defeat Japan. The nisei also helped crack Japanese military codes used to send high-level strategic communications.

Overall, the proportion of Japanese Americans who served in World War II was the highest among any American ethnic group (out of the estimated 36,000 eligible Japanese Americans, 33,300 participated in the war) (Umezawa Duus 1987:231). Although the work of Japanese Americans in military intelligence was classified, the well-publicized exploits of the 442nd helped Japanese Americans gain greater acceptance in American society after World War II (Fugita and Fernandez 2004:93–94; Kurashige 2002:121–123; Umezawa Duus 1987:231–236; Yenne 2007:247–259).[9] Jim reflected on this as follows:

> I am proud of my service in the 442nd, although I don't talk about it much. After the war, people would come up to me and say, "Did you belong to that famous regiment during World War II?" and I'd say, "Yes, I was part of that." Then they'd say, "Oh, you boys were so wonderful!" People realized the Greatest Generation wasn't just whites. Japanese Americans sacrificed a lot for our country as well. It think it really changed perceptions of us.

Even those prewar nisei who were too young to serve in the 442nd shared similar sentiments. "Being a Japanese American is a matter of pride for me," Mike, a board member of the JAHSSD, stated during our interview.

> It's because of what our generation was able to accomplish during the war years, especially the veterans. You know what they did, the sacrifices they made, and it was a matter of great pride for all of us. What they did made it so much easier for the rest of us to assimilate to American society. We earned our Americanness. Like our veterans' memorial says, "Dedicated to all Japanese American veterans who defended their country for the right to be called Americans." Those are my words.

The continued importance of the legacy of the 442nd was demonstrated at a screening at the San Diego Asian Film Festival of *Only the Brave*, an independent film produced by a Japanese American director, which provides a fictionalized account of the 442nd, focusing on the rescue of the Lost Battalion. The movie theater was packed with a large audience of Japanese Americans and other Asian Americans, along with a number of whites (including a few veterans) and even a few African Americans. After the movie, the director appeared on stage (to a standing ovation) along with most of the cast, a few of whom had parents or grandparents who served in the 442nd. Most of the male actors were quite emotional, even if their families had no connection to the 442nd or the internment camps. A couple of them mentioned how much they owe to the nisei who were interned and served in the 442nd and how their suffering and sacrifices were critical for getting the Japanese Americans to where they are today. The few 442nd nisei veterans in the audience were asked to stand up twice, and they were roundly applauded both times.

After World War II, Japanese Americans continued to serve in the military, most notably during the Korean and Vietnam Wars. A number of my elderly nisei interviewees served in the military either during World War II, right after the war, or during the Korean War.

Because of their racialized incarceration as enemy aliens during World War II and the ethnic discrimination they endured during this period, second-generation Japanese Americans demanded racial inclusion in the nation-state by demonstrating their loyalty and patriotism as Americans. By emphasizing their racial citizenship as Americans of

The "Go for Broke" memorial in Japantown, Los Angeles, which commemorates Japanese Americans who served in World War II (photo by author).

Japanese ancestry, they were among the first Asian Americans to challenge racially exclusionary notions of national belonging whereby being American is associated with being racially white. When Bob, the former president of the JAHSSD, speaks about the internment of Japanese Americans to current high school students, he ends his talk by asking them: "What's an American supposed to look like? Tell me, what's an American supposed to look like? An American is what is in your head and your heart, not what you look like or the color of your skin. Look around you, there are other types of Americans than just white ones."

## Americanization and the Weakening of Ethnic Heritage

The prewar nisei's strong desire to demonstrate their Americanness and racial citizenship in a discriminatory environment caused many to become alienated from their Japanese ethnic heritage. As Ruth aptly put it, "[We] didn't want the cultural baggage of our parents." In addition, most second-generation Japanese Americans who grew up during the World War II period did not have many opportunities to maintain their Japanese cultural background and were influenced by the dominant assimilationist ideology of the time. Therefore, a number of my interviewees mentioned that they did not really have a chance to explore or experience their ethnic heritage, even if they were raised in Japanese American communities.

The postwar nisei generally felt that their parents did not put much pressure on them to maintain the Japanese language and culture. "I don't recall a whole lot of that in our family," John said. "There were a few displays in our home regarding Japan and things like that. But my family did not have any real reference to Japanese culture or anything. This is why I used to think we were more of an American family than a Japanese one." Most interviewees mentioned that their parents did not even insist that they attend Japanese school in the local community (see also Morimoto 1997:96). "It was more something I did because the other nisei kids were doing it," Sally noted. "My friends were going to go to Japanese school, so I went too."

Most of the prewar nisei grew up speaking some Japanese with their immigrant parents, but they did not retain their Japanese language abilities into adulthood. Although they went to a weekend Japanese school or took language classes in the Japanese American community, they did so only for one or two years in most cases. As a result, most of them reported that they could speak only a little Japanese or could hold only a very basic conversation in the language at best (see also Hosokawa 2002:157–159; Morimoto 1997:96–98; Takezawa 1995:66–67).

"I speak very poorly," Jim admitted. "I only remember a few words here and there, and some phrases." Likewise, Ruth noted that she can speak only a little Japanese and then uttered a few words in the language as if to demonstrate. "But all the reading and writing, I've forgotten." In contrast to most of his cohort, John attended Japanese school for six years. However, even he did not rate his Japanese language abilities very highly. "If I go to Japan and am with Japanese for a couple days, it slowly comes back," he said. "But if someone speaks to me in regular Japanese, I have no idea what he's saying. And I can hardly read anything now. I forgot it all."

The relatively lack of cultural heritage and language retention among prewar second-generation Japanese Americans seems to be a product of the history of Japanese immigration to the United States and of the World War II era in particular. Although most prewar Japanese immigrants initially intended to be temporary sojourners and return to Japan after amassing wealth, they ended up remaining in America permanently. By the time their nisei children were coming of age, it was quite apparent that they would probably never return to Japan. In addition, their social connections to Japan were cut off by World War II and their imprisonment in internment camps, and the devastation Japan suffered as a result of the war also made the prospects of any possible future return to the homeland unlikely and undesirable.

Even the immigrant parents who did pressure their children to retain their Japanese heritage soon lost their disciplinary power once they were interned during World War II and spent less time with their children. Japanese language schools run by the Japanese American community also probably suffered because of the dislocations of internment. War Relocation Authority officials emphasized the assimilation and Americanization of nisei students who went to school in the concentration camps (Takezawa 1995:110–111; Yoo 2000:106–108, 113).

As a result, the prewar nisei assimilated to mainstream culture and became quite Americanized. In contrast to the current emphasis on multiculturalism in the face of increasing ethnic diversity, assimilation was the dominant ideology at the time and the expected and proper way for the second generation to become incorporated into an American society that was still overwhelmingly white. Japanese Americans certainly felt such assimilationist pressures, which encouraged them to Americanize, develop stronger nationalist loyalties to the United States, and leave their Japanese heritage behind (Spickard 1996:91; Takezawa 1995:116–122; Tamura 1994; Takamori 2010:220; Tuan 2001:65–67; Yoo 2000: ch. 1).

In fact, the parents of the prewar nisei often acknowledged and even encouraged the cultural assimilation of their children to American society (Tamura 1994:61–62), instead of pressuring them to retain the Japanese language and culture. "Our parents saw it as natural that we would become Americanized as we grew up," Greg said. "They didn't object at all to this."

"There was no real conflict with our parents because I think they were encouraging and pushing us to become more American," Mike observed. "They were like, 'This is your country.'"

"Without mentioning it, I think the message was already there about assimilating," Bob recalled. "Our parents had eight kids, and their names are George, Harry, Fred, Tom, Marion, Bob, Elsie, and Mary. All American names! And they came up with these names back in the 1920s and 30s when they couldn't even speak English. It gives you the strong message they intended everyone to be American, whether they admitted it directly or not."

It is therefore quite apparent that the prewar lives of the nisei were mainly confined to a national, assimilationist orientation as Americans. In addition, they did not have many opportunities to develop transnational connections to Japan or construct transnational identities in which they identified with both the United States and Japan. Like other members of the prewar immigrant second generation, it was harder for them to develop relations with their ethnic homeland because of the greater difficulty of international travel at the time and the lack of contemporary telecommunication networks, global mass media, and the Internet (that is, lack of non-contiguous globalization).

Moreover, Japanese American nisei faced additional constraints that were a product of their historical situation and further reduced any possible transnational attachments to Japan. There is some evidence that during the interwar years (between World War I and II), the nisei did develop dual transnational identifications with both the United States and Japan partly based on the notion that they could be a cultural bridge between the two countries (Takahashi 1982:31–34; Tamura 1994: 67–69; Ueda 2002; Yoo 2000:28–32).[10] However, the prewar nisei who are alive today came of age around World War II. Not only did rising anti-Japanese sentiment and their internment as enemy aliens discourage them from affiliating transnationally with Japan, the Japanese American community also lost its transnational ties to Japan because of the war and their imprisonment in concentration camps. As a result, the leaders of the Japanese American community retreated from their earlier efforts to foster an image of the nisei as bicultural people with connections to two nations. Instead, they emphasized their exclusive nationalist loyalties to the United States in the face of mounting hostility toward peoples of Japanese descent (Kurashige 2002: ch. 2; Azuma 2005: epilogue).

After the war, Japanese American families were encouraged to settle in other parts of the United States instead of returning to California and the West Coast where most of them previously resided because of fears of continued anti-Japanese hostility (Fugita and Fernandez 2004:10,

108–109; Spickard 1996:127). Although many did return to California, a good number scattered to other parts of the United States, including to the Midwest and East Coast. This wartime displacement and postwar dispersal of Japanese Americans throughout the country disrupted their community cohesion, making it more difficult to sustain their previous cross-border linkages to their ethnic homeland while increasing their assimilation to American society.

## The Legacy of World War II: Continued Nationalist Identities

As members of the prewar historical generation, the nisei had early formative experiences that continue to inform their ethnic consciousness today. Thus, they still conceive of their ethnic identity and sense of belonging in nationalist terms, and relatively few identify with their Japanese cultural heritage. Mike spoke about how the prewar period had a formative impact on the rest of his life:

> I still feel more loyal as an American than others. It's because of the internment and all we went through in World War II. Like I go to a ball game, and I always stand up and put my hand over my heart and sing the national anthem, whereas other people are running around waving their hats and not taking it seriously. I don't take my Americanness for granted like them. It's something that I earned.

Despite the contemporary multicultural environment in the United States that values ethnic diversity and cultural heritage, the prewar nisei whom I interviewed unequivocally stated that they are fully or mostly American and do not consider themselves very Japanese. This again demonstrates the continued influence that their prewar experiences have had on them. "Everything about me is strictly American," Bob declared. "I don't speak Japanese, I've never been to Japan. Number one, I'm American. I can't say I'm Japanese. I just look Japanese with a Japanese last name, but that's about it."

Some of the prewar nisei said they eat Japanese food and celebrate Japanese-related holidays such as New Years and Obon (a festival that honors the return of ancestral spirits), but that that is the extent of their Japaneseness. "I didn't have much of a chance to experience my Japanese side," Jim noted. "I'd say I'm 85 percent American, 15 percent Japanese. I would never think of myself as similar to Japanese from Japan."

Only a few prewar nisei felt that aspects of themselves may be a product of their Japanese cultural heritage. One was John, a retired manager at a local firm, who felt he was probably "100 percent American," but not as outgoing or as friendly as others. He also thought his effective managerial skills might be attributed to his Japanese heritage, but was ultimately not sure. It was quite interesting that more *third-generation* Japanese Americans spoke about what they felt was the lingering impact of Japanese culture on their personalities (see Chapter 3).

I also noticed a common tendency among almost all the prewar nisei to deemphasize or not even mention their ethnicity or Japanese heritage to others, and simply live as "ordinary Americans." This is a product of their lingering ambivalence about their ethnic heritage from their prewar and immediate postwar experiences and the fact that they did not retain much of their parents' Japanese cultural background when they were growing up.

"I don't go around saying I'm Japanese descent," Sally noted. "I don't think people really care, and it's becoming less and less important to people, especially the younger generation. So I just don't make my ethnicity an issue."

"I don't advertise that I'm Japanese," Ruth stated. "If they ask me, I'll tell them, but otherwise, I don't volunteer anything." Later in our conversation, she elaborated: "It depends on who I'm talking with. If he's Caucasian, I say I'm an American. I make a strong point that I'm an American. I don't mention being Japanese descent. If I'm talking to another Asian, and they ask me, I say, yes, I'm Japanese descent, which I'm proud of. But I'd still tell him, I'm American. I never stress the Japanese part."

In this manner, the current identities and social interactions of the prewar nisei are still nationalist in orientation. In fact, they have not expanded their identities and interactions in transnational ways that would encompass both the United States and Japan despite postwar social transformations that would encourage them to do so. Prejudice and discrimination against Japanese Americans have largely subsided since World War II, and American attitudes toward Japan have dramatically improved because of the country's economic and political rise in the global hierarchy of nations and its continuing status as a long-time and staunch ally of the United States. Therefore, the cultural meanings attached to their racialization as Japanese descendants have become much more favorable. In addition, there has been a shift from a previous assimilationist to a multiculturalism ideology that encourages immigrant-descent minorities to remain connected to and even recover their ethnic roots.

Nonetheless, the elderly Japanese American nisei I interviewed continue to be influenced by their formative youth experiences as part of the prewar historical generation, and they have not developed transnational ties to Japan or a stronger affiliation with their ethnic heritage later in their lives. In general, they have not studied Japanese as adults, reconnected with their ancestral culture, or pursued careers related to Japan. Nor have they adopted a more transnational ethnic consciousness that goes beyond a simple nationalist identification.

Although most of the prewar nisei whom I interviewed have visited Japan in the last several decades, they went as tourists and not to explore their ethnic roots per se or to become more transnationally engaged with their ethnic homeland. "It was just like being a tourist in a foreign country," Jim explained. "I just went to see another country, how other people live. I didn't feel like I was connecting to my roots or anything. No, nothing of that sort." In general, the prewar nisei enjoyed their vacations in Japan, had a wonderful time touring different parts of the country, and were treated well by the Japanese with whom they interacted.

Most did meet briefly with their relatives in Japan, who showed them photos of their family, took them to the ancestral village or grave, and shared memories from long ago. John recounted his experiences as follows:

> The travel agent kind of arranged this reunion with my family. We got there and had dinner and two of my relatives and the family of my father's oldest brother showed up. And then, I saw this picture on the wall and I asked them, "Who are those people?" And he said, "They're your grandparents." And that really hit me. I never knew what they looked like. We really went back to our roots that day. We saw where my grandparents were buried and found out that two of my cousins or something like that were Catholic nuns.

However, because these trips to Japan were brief, one-time visits and their experiences as tourists in the country were rather superficial, the prewar nisei did not establish any long-term and sustained transnational relationship with the country. Nor did they develop a greater transnational consciousness in which their identity as Americans was simultaneously accompanied by a greater identification with Japan. Instead, they experienced their ethnic homeland as essentially a foreign country.

"My cultural background and heritage was embellished," Larry Honkawa said about his trip to Japan. "But I was fully aware that Japanese Americans are *gaijin* [foreigners] in Japan. So I came home and appreciated my American birthright and background more."

"It was great to reconnect with my relatives and see photos of my grandparents. I felt like I went back to my roots," Mike recalled. "But it didn't make me feel more Japanese or anything. I'm really a clueless foreigner in Japan. It actually reinforced in my mind that I'm an American of Japanese descent."

In addition, few postwar second-generation Japanese Americans had any social relationships with current immigrants from Japan living in the United States, which would allow them to maintain or reactivate ties to their ethnic homeland and heritage (Okamura 1998:22–23). Several had met Japanese from Japan who had connections with the Japanese American community (such as through the Buddhist temple, Christian churches, or senior centers), but they were Japanese who had been living permanently in the United States for decades and were substantially assimilated.

Other Asian American communities have large numbers of recent immigrants from Asia who not only have an important social and cultural impact on these communities, but constantly provide a cultural and social link back to the ethnic homeland. As Tomás Jiménez (2010) notes, such new immigrants are a source of "ethnic replenishment" for later-generation immigrant descendants of the same national origins. In the case of the Japanese Americans, however, there has not been a large influx of Japanese immigrants since the 1960s because Japan's increasing postwar economic prosperity reduced the economic incentive to immigrate to the United States (Okamura 2008:144).

There is little contact between the relatively small number of Japanese immigrants and the older Japanese American community for a number of reasons (Spickard 1996:151–152). In addition to the language barrier, a large historical and social class divide exists between these two communities, since the Japanese Americans are generally descendants of unskilled agricultural immigrants who arrived in the United States before the 1930s, whereas Japanese immigrants who came to the United States after the 1960s are relatively elite and highly skilled. Many of the latter group also have a temporary, sojourner mentality and live in their own separate expatriate communities, and thus have little incentive to associate with Japanese Americans.

## Transnational Prewar Nisei: The Kibei

The only prewar nisei who have lived more transnational lives are the *kibei*, who were sent back to Japan by their parents for their education before World War II and then returned to the United States after the war. Although the exact number of kibei is not known, it has been estimated at 11,000 (Daniels 1988:176), making them a small percentage of the overall Japanese American population. Two of my interviewees were actually kibei. Both had been sent to Japan during elementary school and had been stranded there during the war, an experience common among kibei (Takamori 2011:75). Because they spent their formative years in both countries, they continue to have a much more transnational outlook today than other prewar nisei.

In contrast to the relatively positive experiences that contemporary ethnic return migrants from developed countries have in their ancestral homelands (Tsuda 2009b, 2009c, 2009d:333–334), both of my kibei informants had quite difficult experiences living in Japan as youth (see also Azuma 2005:151–156; Morimoto 1997:99–103). Greg Kashimura was taken to Japan by his mother for his education because his parents expected to eventually return to Japan. His mother taught him Japanese and enrolled him in the local school. After six months, she suddenly returned to the United States without informing him. "I couldn't believe it!" Greg recalled. "I started crying. I think I cried for over a month."

Because Greg did not speak much Japanese when he first went to Japan, he was enrolled in the second grade although he was a fourth grader. "I was much taller than everyone else," he recalled. "So the other kids picked on me. They picked on me incessantly until sixth grade. Even when I could finally keep up with them in class, they treated me like some kind of retarded kid." Once World War II started, Greg recounted that he was really scared because he knew what the United States could do: "It was OK when Japan was winning. But then, the American airplanes started bombing and strafing and all that. And I had to constantly report to the local police station about my activities because they knew I was an American citizen." However, the most difficult experience was how he was treated in school. "The kids knew I was an American nisei. My nickname was *amerikajin* [American]. They threw rocks at me and all that. Thinking back on it, I'd much rather have been locked up in internment camps in the U.S. At least, no one harassed you there!"

My other kibei interviewee, Sally Sakamura, was taken to Japan by her parents, who wished to retire there (her father died soon afterward). She summed up her childhood experiences in Japan as follows: "I hated it. I didn't want to go because I knew I would have to learn Japanese and I was way behind the Japanese kids [in Japan]. . . . It's one of those bad experiences, but you're kind of glad you had it. It broadened my horizons and I learned a lot, but it was a hard time." Initially, she had difficulties keeping up in the classroom and was taunted by the other kids, who would encircle her in the courtyard and chant, "Amerikajin! Amerikajin!" However, she was eventually accepted by the Japanese students and got along with them really well.

Like Greg's experiences, her life in Japan became much more difficult once the war started. "We didn't have enough food," she recalled. In addition, she had a brother who was born in Japan and was drafted into the Japanese Army. Meanwhile, her brother in the United States was drafted into the 442nd Japanese American regiment. "I had one brother in the U.S. Army and one in the Japanese Army!" she noted. "Good thing they were fighting in different parts of the world. But I was constantly worried about both of them." Also, she could not continue her education because the girls from her school were sent to work in a Mitsubishi war factory. "We slept in a dorm and far away from home," she recounted. "We made airplane engine covers for Japanese Zero fighters. So I knew all about riveting and cutting aluminum and all that kind of stuff."

Toward the end of the war, American B-29 bombers started flying overhead and eventually bombed her factory. Sally gave a riveting account of her terrifying experiences during this period:

The air raid sirens would go off and we'd have to run into the forest with our helmets on. But towards the end [of the war], they had fighters coming down to shoot at people. And I remember this was in broad daylight and a couple of these planes came down and they saw us. They actually strafed us! I jumped into this foxhole. These bullets were hitting all around me and kicking up dirt. I thought I was going to die! It was the first time I actually believed in God. Another time, I was caught in this open riverbank when this American fighter plane came at me. I didn't know what to do. He swooped down on me, and I could actually see the pilot! He flew up and started to U-turn and come back at me again. I thought, "Oh my God. This is the end!" But then he just looked at me and went on. I guess he spared me because he realized I was a child.

Despite the difficult experiences of both kibei in Japan before and during World War II, they have continued to remain connected to their ethnic heritage as adults to a much greater extent than other prewar nisei. They are also the only ones who have a transnational orientation and consciousness because they had grown up in both the United States and Japan. Greg has forgotten some of the Japanese he had learned in Japan, but he can still understand about 75 percent of Japanese television news, sometimes speaks Japanese with his wife, who is also kibei, and remains able to read and write in Japanese to some extent. Sally remains fluent in Japanese, and when she goes to Japan, she can mix in with the Japanese and does not stand out like an American foreigner.

Greg, however, is the prewar nisei whose life has been the most transnational. He has returned to Japan a number of times and has stayed in touch with his relatives there for decades. He also has a satellite TV subscription and watches Japanese television on a regular basis, including the news and sports programs. In contrast, Sally has taken trips to Japan but did not stay in active touch with anyone there and was less transnationally engaged than Greg.

Surprisingly, in terms of his ethnic identity, Greg feels he is much more culturally Japanese than he is American. Although he blends in as an American in public, he feels quite Japanese at home. Sally, however, seems to have a more transnational ethnic consciousness based on a dual affiliation with both countries. She explained as follows:

In the U.S., I'm definitely more American than Japanese. But I've adapted in the past to both countries. When I go to Japan, I'm more Japanese. When I was there recently, it really made me think that I really appreciate the Japanese cultural background. I wanted to be like them more in many respects. But here, I'm American. So I use both sides of my ethnicity and take on the identity of the country I'm in. But there is much more refinement and formality over there [in Japan] and it's kind of restricting to me. So I feel more natural when I'm with Americans than with Japanese. I can be myself more here.

## Conclusion

This chapter has demonstrated the continued importance of particular histories on the contemporary ethnic experiences of second-generation immigrant descendants. Depending on the different historical periods when they came of age, their past experiences of racialization can vary considerably and produce significant internal differences among members of the current second generation. The prewar nisei, who grew up during a period of intense discrimination against those of Japanese descent and were interned as enemy aliens, had to fight (literally and figuratively) in order to have their national loyalties and racial citizenship as Americans recognized. Theirs was a purely negative and discriminatory racialization that discouraged them from maintaining their Japanese heritage and culture. In addition, because of the historical constraints of interment and war and the assimilationist pressures of the period, they had relatively few opportunities to develop transnational connections to their ethnic homeland. As a result, they became quite assimilated and Americanized.

However, the prewar nisei's struggle for racial citizenship and national belonging led to a gradual postwar decline in discrimination against Japanese Americans. This eventually enabled them to become upwardly mobile and socioeconomically successful and to enjoy much greater acceptance in mainstream society. As a result, they have been able to effectively challenge their racial subordination in a white-dominated society.

As members of the prewar historical generation, such formative experiences during and after World War II continue to inform the lives of the prewar nisei today. Thus, most elderly nisei I interviewed in the American Southwest still inhabit exclusively nationalist spaces of belonging and identity and have not explored their ethnic heritage despite the current multicultural climate. In contrast, postwar shin-nisei are products of a different historical period, in which their racialization as Japanese descendants has completely new meanings, causing them to develop a considerably different ethnicity than their prewar predecessors.

## 2

# The Postwar Nisei

*Biculturalism and Transnational Identities*

## A New Generation of Nisei

Although there is a considerable amount of historical research about the prewar nisei (Hosokawa 1992; Matsumoto 2014; Takahashi 1997; Tamura 1994; Yoo 2000), postwar second-generation Japanese Americans have not been extensively studied. As descendants of Japanese immigrants who arrived in the United States after the 1960s, the shin-nisei are generally still young, were raised during a different historical era than the prewar nisei, and therefore have a quite different ethnic consciousness. Although they are of the same immigrant second generation as the prewar nisei, they are members of a completely different millennial historical generation that came of age primarily after the 1980s and 1990s. They have grown up in a much more ethnically diverse and globalized environment where their multicultural racialization as "Japanese" often has positive connotations. As a result, they have retained their Japanese cultural heritage to a much greater extent, their ethnicity and identities are bicultural, and they are transnationally engaged with their ethnic homeland.

## Being Japanese American in Postwar America

Since the end of World War II, a number of obvious but significant changes have caused shin-nisei youth to remain much more strongly connected to their ethnic heritage and homeland than their prewar counterparts (Kitano 1993:202–203; Takahashi 1997:211). In contrast to the mainly white, assimilationist world in which the prewar nisei came of age, the postwar nisei are a product of a multicultural America that tolerates and even encourages the second generation to maintain their native cultures and languages and transnational commitments (Foner

2002; Levitt 2001:203). Several shin-nisei interviewees spoke of how the climate of ethnic diversity in the United States has allowed them to become bicultural instead of adopting a singular American nationalist identity. Yuki Sumimoto spoke about his past experiences in this respect as follows:

> I don't remember feeling too much pressure to assimilate and become Americanized. I was already pretty Americanized at that point, and in the U.S., there are so many different peoples of different backgrounds. So I didn't have to consciously decide to become either American or Japanese. I could kind of be both.

Another shin-nisei, Takehiro Watanabe, who is a university faculty member, remarked:

> I grew up in a really diverse community: there were blacks, Mexican people, and Japanese Americans. So I just blended into the local community and tried to fit in. There wasn't that much pressure to show that you're really American. For me, Japanese American identity was more hybrid, a mixture of cultures. It wasn't just defensively asserting your Americanness. I like the notion of fluid, flexible, transnational identities.

Meanwhile, American attitudes toward Japan have completely changed, as a formerly despised, enemy nation has become an economically prosperous and respected First World country that is the United States' oldest and closest East Asian ally (O'Brien and Fugita 1991:127; Fujitani 2011:230–231). As a number of Asian American scholars have noted, the status of ethnic minorities is shaped not only by their socioeconomic location in the United States, but also by the position of their ethnic homeland in the global order (Kim 2008:2–3; Tsuda 2009b; Wu and Song 2000). This is especially important for Japanese Americans, who have been significantly influenced by America's changing relationship with Japan (Kitano 2003:3). Along with the current positive images about the country, some Americans have considerable fascination with Japan, including its culture, history, food, global commodities, technology, and popular culture (see Chapter 5). This has encouraged postwar second-generation Japanese Americans to identify with Japan to a much greater extent than the prewar nisei. Their experiences are also very different from those of recent immigrant minorities of lower social class status, whose homelands are regarded as poor developing countries, and whose ethnic differences are met with prejudice and discrimination.

Ayako Takamori (2010:224) aptly summarizes these changes and their impact on shin-nisei ethnicity as follows:

> Shifts in Japan's place in the global economy over the last sixty years are reflected in the generational differences among Japanese Americans in their attitudes toward Japanese language. . . . Later generations of Japanese Americans, including shin-niseis, were more likely to embrace their biculturalism. Informed by the popularization and global circulation of manga, anime, Japanese toys, and other forms of Japanese pop-cultural production, younger generations of Japanese Americans are less hesitant about identifying themselves with Japan, consuming Japanese products, or expressing curiosity about or interest in Japan.

As a result, the "emotional transnationalism" of my shin-nisei interviewees, which connects them to their distant Japanese ethnic homeland, is mainly positive (compare with Takeda 2012). They generally feel that American images of Japan are quite favorable, and they noted how the country is regarded as a modern, highly advanced, and rich nation that is a pro-American ally of Japan. They also mentioned favorable perceptions of the country's technology, electronics, cars, computer games, and anime as well as the American fascination with Japanese art and historical images of samurais, ninjas, and geishas. A few of them also spoke of perceptions of Japan as an orderly and harmonious society grounded in social obligations and hierarchical respect. The postwar nisei seem to feel that any negative American reactions toward Japan are mainly a thing of the past. A number of them mentioned prejudice against Japanese in the context of Pearl Harbor and World War II, but felt it was mainly confined to elderly people and old war movies and not really relevant today. Likewise, they thought that American resentment toward Japanese economic prosperity, which arose in the 1980s was no longer an issue. "Americans used to be concerned about Japan kicking our ass economically," one of my interviewees observed. "But now, most of this is directed toward China. No one complains about Japan anymore." The only negative contemporary perceptions that the shin-nisei mentioned were Japanese tourist behavior and the patriarchal nature of the country.

Therefore, the dynamics of racialization for Japanese Americans in the United States have completely changed so that being "Japanese" no longer has the unfavorable meanings it did in the past, nor does it lead to serious discrimination or racism. As noted earlier, levels of discrimination also have a strong impact on the ethnic culture and consciousness of the second generation. In contrast to the racial hostility and incarceration that the prewar nisei suffered, the postwar nisei feel that they are no longer subject to much discrimination. Most of them cannot remember an instance when they were directly mistreated or personally discriminated against because of their ethnicity, except when they were children and were teased by other kids.

"You hear instances of discrimination against other people, like blacks, or Muslims after 9/11," Steve Okura noted. "That gets me upset. And I definitely have this awareness of institutionalized discrimination against Japanese in the past. But personally, I've never experienced anything that I consider discrimination."

Yuki, one of my shin-nisei interviewees, had been called "Jap" once by elderly World War II veterans at a state fair in California. However, his reaction to this racial epithet was quite different from that of the prewar nisei. "I didn't make much of it because I knew it was from the war long ago," he explained.

In contrast to the prewar era, most discrimination against Asian Americans today seems to be structural or relatively hidden (as in the case of the "glass ceiling") and is rarely overt or direct. In fact, studies show that second-generation Asian Americans are less likely to experience discrimination than other non-white second-generation groups (Kasinitz et al. 2008:37). Even my most socially aware shin-nisei interviewees, such as Takehiro, found it difficult to attribute possible unequal treatment directly to racial discrimination:

Professionally, I can't say there was an incident that was blatantly racist or discriminatory. It's very hard to say. If I don't get an academic job that I felt I was qualified for, is that because I wasn't white? Or because I didn't have a Ph.D. from Harvard? When I started new faculty positions, I felt the staff weren't treating me well, or they gave me a really terrible office until I made a big fuss about it. Is that because of my race, or because I was still a junior faculty member? I don't know.

"It's probably more perceived on my part than anything," Matt Honkawa, a college student, noted. "It's like when I was looking for a job on campus, or even interviewing for some internships, I feel like if I was a white guy, I'd probably have a better shot of getting the position because my interviewers tend to be white. But I just feel like it's a slight disadvantage, not a major hurdle."

When asked about American perceptions of Japanese Americans, the shin-nisei referred to positive stereotypes about Asian Americans in general. Almost all of them mentioned that they are seen as model minorities who are smart and hard-working academic overachievers and are good at math, science, and computers.[1] Some felt they are regarded as socioeconomically well-to-do and as quiet, good citizens. Others mentioned more ambivalent attitudes with respect to gendered images of Asian American women as being traditional and submissive, as well as sexually attractive, and of Asian men as wimpy computer nerds who are asexual and effeminate. Nonetheless, the shin-nisei generally feel that being Japanese American is a much more positive than a negative experience.

Finally, second-generation Japanese Americans today have had significant opportunities to maintain active transnational ties to their ethnic homeland of Japan compared to the prewar nisei. As a number of researchers have noted, today's second generation live in a much more globalized world characterized by the greater ease of international travel and the growth of global mass media and the Internet, all of which enable them to stay connected with their parents' country of origin to a much greater extent (Kasinitz, Mollenkopf, and Waters 2004:5–6, 2008:4). In addition, because of the postwar economic prosperity of Japan, the parents of the shin-nisei immigrated to the United States as generally well-to-do students, businessmen, and professional expatriates and have subsequently often traveled back and forth between the United States and Japan in the course of their careers. As highly skilled, relatively elite immigrants, they have the economic means to live transnational lives and have been able to pass on their transnationalism to their children. As Cecilia Menjívar notes (2002:537–538), children of immigrants with middle-class backgrounds are more likely to develop transnational ties to the ethnic homeland compared to those from poor backgrounds. Most shin-nisei have therefore visited Japan numerous times during their lives with their parents, and some have actually lived there by themselves in order to work, go to school, or teach English. Thus, they have grown up in a much more transnational ethnic context compared to the prewar nisei, who have either never been to Japan or visited only one or twice for brief trips mainly as tourists (the exception again are the kibei).

## Ethnic Heritage and Biculturalism

Because postwar second-generation Japanese Americans in the American Southwest grew up in a transformed ethnic landscape, they have a much stronger attachment to Japan and their cultural heritage than the prewar nisei, and most of them are fully bicultural. It is important to remember that when members of the second generation strengthen their ethnic minority identity or affiliation with their national origins, they are not always practicing a "reactive ethnicity" against majority discrimination and socioeconomic marginalization (compare with Portes and Rumbaut 2001: ch. 7). They may also do so in an affirmative manner in the context of racialized multiculturalism and the positive meanings that can be associated with their heritage and homeland.

Several of my interviewees explicitly mentioned that they felt a certain pride in their Japanese cultural background. "I wouldn't say it's a nationalistic pride, or anything," Matt remarked. "But I do take a bit of pride in being Japanese, or maybe satisfaction is a better word. I enjoy being Japanese, like the food, culture, and being able to speak the language. I don't proudly assert it, but it is part of who I am."

Likewise, Doug felt he was "sort of proud to be Japanese American." He elaborated: "Because of the community here, there is a sense of pride in who you are. The Japanese are humble and have some good qualities. And being Japanese American, even though it's been a short time, has a pretty good history. . . . I don't say 'I'm Japanese American,' just to clear up ambiguity or confusion. I'm more proud to say it."

"I really like the Japanese culture and the language," another commented. "I see my heritage in a positive way and feel pretty attached to it."

A few of my shin-nisei informants were more ambivalent about their Japanese ethnicity when they were children but eventually came to embrace it. This is the case for Takehiro, whom I consider to be an older, transitional nisei whose parents immigrated right after the war. Because he grew up in the Japanese American community during the 1950s and 1960s, he experienced both the prewar historical legacy of the Japanese Americans and the changes that were occurring at that time that were making the United States more multicultural in outlook. "When I was growing up, I hung out with mostly [Japanese American] sansei," he told me. "And back then, Japanese Americans weren't interested in studying Japanese. They had assimilated. And like them, I wasn't interested in learning Japanese. My parents tried to make me go to Japanese school, but I didn't want to and was always making trouble. So they kind of gave up."

However, Takehiro eventually became involved in the anti-Vietnam War movement and was influenced by the Asian American movement of the 1960s and 1970s. "That was very important for me," he recalled. "It really made us think about our history. People in the movement were talking about getting back to their ethnic roots. The image of Japan had improved a lot since the war, too. So I got more interested in Japanese things and history and Asian things in general. I started to take intensive Japanese language courses. Then, I went to Japan and just really worked hard at learning the language."

Like other young Japanese Americans, Matt was raised in a white middle-class suburb in the 1990s. He faced assimilationist pressures at school and distanced himself from his ethnic background as a child. "Growing up, a lot of my friends were white," he recalled. "My close friends weren't Asian. So I wanted to Americanize more." He spoke about how his mother would make Japanese lunches to take to school. "I'd be like, 'Oh man, I don't want to. . . . Make me a sandwich.' The other kids would be like, 'What's that?' I felt embarrassed a bit." Eventually, his mother began making him sandwiches because he wouldn't eat Japanese lunches at school. "My Japanese-ness wasn't like the bane of my existence or anything," he added. "But the pressure to be American was definitely there. So I didn't enjoy it and wasn't too proud of it." As a result, Matt did not want to go to Japanese school, but he did so because of parental pressure. "But it was bearable because I had a lot of friends there and they didn't all want to be there either. So we kind of just stuck together." However, as he grew older and entered college, he came to value his ethnic heritage and eventually took pride in it. "You start realizing that being Japanese is a good thing, that it's fine to be different. I also met more nisei like me, especially in college, who had similar experiences."

Doug, who is 2.5 generation, had a somewhat similar experience. He spoke about how his parents wanted to take him to Japan as a child but he did not want to go. "I would just fight it," he recalled. Also, he did not want to study Japanese. "There was this sense of me being an American, and I was like 'Why am I studying Japanese? None of my friends speak Japanese. Why do I have to speak it?'" However, as he grew older, he developed a positive perception of Japanese culture and a greater appreciation for his ethnic heritage.

It was rather remarkable that all the shin-nisei I spoke with are fully bilingual and bicultural.[2] Although biculturalism is similar to the concept of selective acculturation that is used in the second-generation segmented assimilation literature, I prefer the concept of biculturalism. Selective acculturation refers to children of immigrants who grow up in large, cohesive co-ethnic communities that allow them to partially retain their parents' home language and culture, therefore slowing down their cultural assimilation to mainstream society (Portes and Rumbaut 2001:54). Such selective acculturation is seen as preserving parental authority and providing a bulwark against discrimination and thereby promoting their socioeconomic success. However, as noted in the Introduction, selective acculturation theory implies that ethnic heritage retention is opposed to assimilation in a zero-sum game, so that the more second-generation individuals maintain their parents' language and culture, the less they will be assimilated to mainstream culture and vice versa.

In fact, very few of the second-generation Japanese Americans I spoke with mentioned that all the effort they put into studying Japanese hindered their English language acquisition or performance in American schools. The concept of biculturalism does not assume that the persistence of cultural heritage gets in the way of cultural assimilation (or vice versa), since both can happen simultaneously. In fact, although my interviewees went to Japanese Saturday school in Japanese immigrant expatriate communities for many years, this did not seem to have impeded their simultaneous cultural assimilation (almost all spoke English without an accent, for example).

Given their bicultural and bilingual backgrounds, the shin-nisei generally rated their Japanese as quite fluent. They can also read and write with some facility. Again, we see a stark contrast to the older, prewar nisei, who are generally monolingual English speakers with only basic or minimal ability in the Japanese language. Takehiro gave a typical assessment of his Japanese: "I'd say I'm pretty fluent. I can more or less speak like a Japanese and don't stand out as a foreigner in Japan. I don't really have an accent in Japanese. But I don't write very well and don't like to write in Japanese. If I read a [Japanese] book, it would take me at least twice as long as a book in English."

Most of the shin-nisei explicitly spoke about how their parents pressured them to study the Japanese language, in contrast to the rather laissez-faire attitude of the parents of the prewar nisei generation. "There was a lot of pressure in my family about the language thing," Takehiro recalled. "My parents really wanted me to study the language. They were pretty proud Japanese nationalists, especially my dad." Because a good number of the Japanese parents of the shin-nisei are professionals and businessmen who initially came to the United States as temporary sojourners and planned to return to Japan, they insisted that their children study Japanese and maintain their cultural heritage. In addition, even after they became permanent settlers, they have retained strong transnational ties with their homeland and sometimes continue to entertain the notion of eventual repatriation. One shin-nisei woman described her experiences as follows:

> My parents always said they would return to Japan. At the beginning, it was after my dad got his Ph.D. When that didn't happen, they said my dad would eventually get a job in Japan and they'd return. When that didn't happen, they said they would return after my dad retired. After a while, it became really obvious that they would never return. But that didn't stop them from insisting that we go to Japanese school and keep studying Japanese.

In general, it seems that the shin-nisei complied with their parents' wishes. Most of them attended Japanese Saturday schools, which were created for the children of Japanese businessmen and other professionals in large American cities with significant Japanese expatriate communities. Since most of these Japanese children intend to repatriate in a matter of years, these schools can be quite rigorous and attempt to keep up with the curriculum in Japan. The shin-nisei I interviewed generally attended these schools for many years (sometimes from first grade to the end of junior high school or even high school) and therefore took classes mainly with students from Japan, although there were other Japanese Americans in their classes as well. In this sense, although recent Japanese immigrants and their expatriate communities have not provided any ethnic replenishment for the prewar second-generation Japanese Americans, they have certainly done so for the shin-nisei. Without the ready availability of expatriate Japanese Saturday schools, it is unlikely they would have become so fluent in Japanese.

The shin-nisei attended Japanese Saturday school not simply because of parental pressure, but also because it was something they wanted to do. This may be related to the positive meanings and experiences attached to their Japanese heritage and ethnic homeland as well as to the current multicultural climate. A couple of them also mentioned that being bilingual may help them in their professional careers later in life. According to Yuki, "I don't think [my parents] forced the Japanese on me. I mean, they did make me go to Japanese school, but I didn't mind it too much. I just naturally did it. Actually, it was mostly for the friends. I wasn't too crazy about having to study such a difficult language every week. But in hindsight, I'm glad I did it."

"I had very strict parents, so quitting [Japanese school] was not an option," Steve said. "But I didn't really complain. Actually, I didn't want to quit myself. The thought never really crossed my mind. I had a lot of Japanese friends [from Japan] in Japanese school and enjoyed going." Steve even contemplated applying to Japanese universities.

In addition to learning the Japanese language, shin-nisei youth also felt more culturally Japanese when compared with the older prewar nisei and spoke about positive aspects of themselves that they attributed to their cultural heritage and upbringing. Yuki feels that he is group-oriented like the Japanese in Japan and has a more communal attitude compared to other Americans:

I think more about the good of the community and about forgoing individual gains for the group. I think that stems for my going to Japan and the schools there. Students there have to do everything themselves, like clean the school and serve themselves. Here, I think people tend to be more selfish and take it for granted that other people will do things for them and they don't have to give back. Sometimes that annoys me. Because of my experience in Japan, I realize the importance of conforming and doing things for the benefit of others.

Doug also spoke about the value of "sacrificing for others and the betterment of other people" as well as his ability to compromise and his respect for elders, which he attributes to his Japanese upbringing. He appreciates the respect and politeness of Japanese culture and the ability to preserve and live in harmony with the environment, which he observed during his stays in Japan.

In fact, only one shin-nisei, Steve, did not regard his Japaneseness in positive terms. He does love the Japanese language and its expressiveness, and he thinks that his Japanese respect for elders empowered him when he worked with seniors and was able to relate to and assist them better than other American youth could. However, he feels limited by other Japanese cultural characteristics he has acquired:

I grew up Japanese and get really mad at myself that I have these Japanese tendencies that are built into how I was raised. Like if I see a stranger on the street, I'll bow. I won't smile or make full eye contact when I meet someone and instead look down. I have this pretty ridiculous attachment to hierarchy. I won't disrespect someone who is above me and am too apologetic. I've realized recently that once I get a job and start worrying about promotions and stuff like that, this type of behavior may drag me down and I might create my own glass ceiling. I have to work hard to break these stereotypes.

## At Home in the Ethnic Homeland

Compared to the prewar nisei, the postwar shin-nisei have much more sustained and significant transnational engagements with their ethnic homeland of Japan. Their transnationalism has been inherited from their immigrant parents, who have taken them to Japan on many occasions. However, they have also sustained their transnational lives on their own, and some have lived in the country for extended periods for personal, educational, or professional reasons. In addition, because they are fully bilingual and bicultural, their level of interaction and engagement with the Japanese in Japan is deeper than other Japanese Americans.

In general, the shin-nisei have quite positive experiences in their ethnic homeland. They reported that their cultural adaptation to Japan is quite smooth and they feel comfortable living there. In contrast, other ethnic return migrants, who are often not fully bicultural, can have alienating experiences as cultural foreigners in their ancestral homeland (Tsuda 2003, 2009a, 2009d). For the shin nisei, Japan is not truly a foreign country, and they are able to speak and "act Japanese" to the point where they have little trouble being socially accepted. As a result, they feel very much "at home" in their ethnic homeland.

For instance, consider the experiences of Matt, who has worked in Japan as a completely bicultural shin-nisei and tries to "act as Japanese as possible" in the country:

> My experiences in Japan are quite positive. I can easily switch to a Japanese identity. Otherwise, if you stick out, you make things difficult for yourself there. I know how to be Japanese because growing up, my mom taught me Japanese manners, customs, and spoke both languages to me. I had plenty of Japanese friends growing up and related well to my teachers and peers at Japanese school, so I knew what Japanese culture was like. Interacting with Japanese in general is pretty natural for me. So in terms of living in Japan, it was very easy and comfortable for me. . . . It was sort of a reproduction of my Japanese school experiences in the U.S.

"I can be totally accepted as Japanese in Japan if I want," Steve remarked. "I used to be really sensitive about acting Japanese in Japan. It used to bother me when the Japanese saw me as different. So I felt I had to be more Japanese than other Japanese people."

Nonetheless, even though the shin-nisei are bicultural, because they are neither Japanese from Japan nor native speakers, a number of them noted that they introduce themselves as Americans in Japan partly to avoid any initial confusion and disorientation among the Japanese. Take for instance, Takehiro, who lived in Japan for years and became fluent in the language. He reported that:

> For short conversations, it's not noticeable that I'm a foreigner. So if I go into a store, I just act like a Japanese. But if I get into a longer conversation, I like to tell people I'm American. It makes things so much easier that way because otherwise, you become an idiot if you don't know something all Japanese are supposed to know or make a mistake speaking the language.

Likewise, Steve mentioned that he introduces himself in Japan as a *nikkei amerikajin* (an American of Japanese descent).

Nonetheless, my shin-nisei interviewees generally felt that Americans are well-regarded and treated in Japan. For them, their Americanness is more of an ethnic asset and a source of interest than a disadvantage because of the cultural affinity and favorable perceptions Japanese have toward the United States (see also Yamashiro 2011:1512–1513). This is quite apparent from Takehiro's comments:

> I didn't feel any prejudice being a foreigner in Japan, except the language thing. The Japanese friends I choose were really interested in America and American pop culture. I was their informant about America, and they seemed to like me for that. My Americanness was therefore more of an asset than anything else.

Although Yuki was a bit more ambivalent about how Japanese reacted to him as an American, he had similar favorable experiences in Japan:

> I think Japanese attitudes towards Japanese Americans are positive. A lot of [Japanese] people wish they could go to the U.S. There's even a sense of awe. Japanese like to come here and go to Las Vegas. They like American popular culture, American movies, and American franchises are everywhere, so they are pretty aware of Americans. So having an American background is quite positive.

Indeed, as an American, Steve even felt a sense of superiority in Japan. "In Japan, my ethnicity isn't really an issue because in the end, I'm like,

'Sorry, America is above you, Japan. You don't tell me what to do, I tell you what to do. I'm arrogant and egotistical. I feel this superiority in Japan as an American. In fact, I make a point that I'm American."

In contrast to Japanese Americans of other generations, whose exposure to Japan is often limited to short visits as tourists, which leave them with very positive impressions, a few of the shin-nisei I interviewed who have lived in Japan for extended periods tended to give more balanced and ambivalent accounts of the country. Consider the comments of Takehiro, who had lived in Japan as both a student and researcher:

> Over time, I started getting disenchanted with the romantic visions I had of Japan, because you start seeing all the warts, in addition to the cherry blossoms. I had this image of [Japanese] aesthetics that I was attracted to, so I used to love going to temples and gardens. Also museums to see the artwork. I was attracted to the exotic part of Japan. But being in Japan longer, you get this critical distance—not just how beautiful the artwork is. I was stuck by things that are Japanese characteristics that I didn't like, such as the over-excessive social hierarchy, and I distanced myself from that. That was what was the most disturbing. And also the racialized nationalism.

Likewise, a shin-nisei woman who had lived in Japan for a long time expressed frustration over the gender expectations that constrain women in Japan, especially the pressure to dress up with makeup and "look perfect." "I felt like rebelling," she recalled. "I was like, 'I'm not going to wear *any* makeup. I'm going to wear everyday sweatshirts and jeans.'"

Despite some ambivalence about their experiences, which arose from their greater immersion in Japanese society, most of the shin-nisei who have lived in Japan have strengthened their identification with the country over time. Although some of them have felt more American in Japan because of the cultural differences they encountered, they have also developed a transnational ethnic consciousness based on a dual affiliation with both America and Japan. For instance, according to Yuki:

> In Japan, I definitely feel my Americanness more because I notice more differences than similarities [with the Japanese], even though I can do a decent job of getting by. But I also have a Japanese side I can activate, and

a lot of times, I do, for courtesy's sake. I don't need to advertise that I'm from the U.S.

Although Takehiro mentioned that he has distanced himself from aspects of Japanese culture that he did not like, he was ultimately conflicted and vacillated between his Japanese and American sides. "It was a sense that I could never completely fit in there. Would never be like them. It was a combination of distance but also intimacy with the Japanese." Likewise, Matt also initially reinforced his American identity as a partial reaction to those aspects of Japan he disliked when he was younger. However, he was quite explicit about how he eventually came to adopt a more accommodating, transnational ethnic consciousness as part of a gradual maturational process:

> When I was younger, it [his trips to Japan] probably reinforced my Americanness. I could relate to the culture and it was not hard for me to fit in, but I didn't like it. I preferred American culture—it's more free and not as strict. But as I got older and more mature, I realized that's just how it is. It's not necessarily bad, just different. I went [to Japan] the past summer, and the year before, and came to reinforce my sense of relating to my Japanese side, because by that time, I had grown and can appreciate Japan. I don't act defensively anymore and say I'm American. I just totally fit in and embrace Japan. When I'm in Japan, I feel great, like I could live there for a long time. But when I get back to the U.S., I feel great being back home. I can operate fine in both cultures.

## Transnational Ethnic Consciousness

Because my shin-nisei interviewees grew up partly in the postwar Japanese expatriate community and are much more connected to Japan and Japanese culture, a good number of them do not identify much with the broader Japanese American community (see also Takahashi 1997:208–209; Yamashiro 2008:258). Only a few have belonged to Japanese American organizations. The shin-nisei are thus quite different from prewar nisei, sansei, and fourth-generation yonsei. The only exception is Takehiro, an older shin-nisei who grew up in a Japanese American community after World War II.

"I've never had any contact with the Japanese American community and know nothing about them," one of my shin-nisei interviewees remarked. "I grew up with Japanese kids from Japan [in the Japanese expatriate community]. So my life was much more oriented toward Japan and I feel much more culturally Japanese than most Japanese Americans."

Matt has had a similar experience: "When I say I'm Japanese American, I'm not identifying with Japanese American history or anything like that. I'm identifying mainly with Japan. It's not that I don't relate to Japanese Americans. I have sansei and yonsei buddies. But I feel different from them because my understanding of Japanese culture is greater." Although he was a student at UC San Diego, he never went to campus events hosted by the Nikkei Student Union (the Japanese American student organization). "They're yonsei. They don't speak any Japanese," he noted. "The purpose of the club isn't to continue Japanese culture. For me, it's just not important that I surround myself with other Japanese Americans."

"I actually never used the word 'Japanese American' when I grew up," Yuki explained. "It's not a term I really became aware of until college. I just thought of myself as Japanese. Actually, a group of us used the term 'American-born Japanese,' or ABJ."

The only shin-nisei I interviewed who was active in the Japanese American community is Steve, who was a past board member of the Nikkei Student Union and past president of Asayake Taiko (a Japanese American drumming group at UC San Diego). However, even he did not consider himself Japanese American when he was growing up. He described his reaction when he went to Japan as a child and was called *nikkeijin* (a Japanese ethnic term that refers to Japanese descendants born abroad, such as Japanese Americans): "I was like 'Hey, that's f—ked up! I'm not nikkeijin. I'm *nihonjin* [Japanese].' So that was my first major culture shock and I really felt bad back then." However, over time, he came to identify more with the Japanese American community and now calls himself *nikkeijin* in Japan. He also began to use the ethnic term "Japanese American" in college. Nonetheless, he does not always feel like a true Japanese American and sometimes struggles to be included in the community:

> Sometimes I feel like I'm not an authentic Japanese American, because
> I'm not a product of their history of internment and redress [the move-

ment to seek reparations for wartime internment]. I'm much more connected to the history of Japan. But I'm trying to understand and identify
with Japanese American experiences too. . . . When I say I'm shin-nisei,
I'm making a political statement saying, "You know what? Being Japanese American is not just about being sansei and yonsei. It's about being shin-nisei too." And to deny this distinction within the community
is absolutely unacceptable. There are minority elements in the bigger
community.

Instead of strongly identifying with the Japanese American community, the postwar shin-nisei have developed ethnic identities that
are more transnational in orientation because of their bicultural background as well as their experiences in Japan, as noted above. In contrast,
the elderly prewar nisei have an exclusively nationalist consciousness.
In the immigration literature, one of the key variables that determine
the level of transnational engagement is again immigrant generation,
with the first generation seen as being more actively connected to their
country of origin than their second-generation descendants. As a result,
there has been considerable debate about the extent to which the second
generation maintains transnational ties to the parental homeland (Levitt
2002; Levitt and Waters 2002; Kasinitz et al. 2002; Menjívar 2002; Portes
and Rumbaut 2001: ch. 6; Smith 2006).

I argue that we need to reorient the discussion of transnationalism
across generations. First, as the case of the Japanese Americans demonstrates, differences in historical generation can be just as important
as differences in immigrant generation in determining the level of
transnational activity and consciousness. The postwar shin-nisei live in
transnationalized social fields while the lives of their prewar nisei counterparts are limited to a predominantly nationalist context. Therefore,
the amount of transnational engagement between two historical cohorts
of the same immigrant generation may vary more than the difference
in transnationalism between immigrant parents and their second-
generation descendants. Although a few immigration specialists have
noted the greater amount of transnationalism among today's immigrant
second generation compared to their counterparts from the prewar era
(Foner 2002; Kasinitz, Mollenkopf, and Waters 2004:5–6, 2008:4), this
issue has not been extensively explored. Studies that examine different

levels of transnational activity among members of the same second generation compare only those from different ethnic groups or national origins, not historical cohorts (Kasinitz et al. 2002, 2008).

In addition, it is important to distinguish between the transnational *social* connections of the second generation and their ethnic *identities*. While it is quite apparent that transnational social relations with the ethnic homeland become considerably attenuated among those of the second generation compared to their parents, they are more likely to construct transnational identities based on a simultaneous, dual identification with the host and origin countries (Tsuda 2012c:462–463). There has been some confusion in the immigration literature about the nature of transnational identities. Examples of immigrants identifying with their home country across borders is often referred to as a "transnational" identity (Guarnizo and Díaz 1999:414–415; Levitt and Glick Schiller 2008:287; van Niekerk 2007; Vertovec 2004:978–980). However, immigrants' affiliations to their homelands are simply transborder (or long-distance) *nationalist* identities (since they involve identification with only one nation-state) and are not transnational unless they simultaneously identify with the host country.

In general, first-generation immigrant parents often do not identify in transnational ways since they continue to maintain a strong nationalist identification with their home countries and do not develop as much attachment to the host society. In contrast, their second-generation children come to identify with their country of birth, while at the same time, they may simultaneously develop a significant affinity to their ancestral homeland because of the influence of their parents and trips they take to their parents' country of origin. In addition, increased access to information about their ethnic homeland through the mass media and the Internet has given them new opportunities to develop a more expansive transnational ethnic consciousness.

In terms of cross-border social relations, the shin-nisei youth are not as transnationally engaged with Japan as their parents. They have traveled to Japan a number of times, a few have lived there briefly, and a number of them continue to maintain both actual and virtual connections to their ethnic homeland. However, unlike their parents, they do not travel as often to Japan and most do not have transnational business or professional connections to the country. Nor do they stay in constant touch with their relatives in Japan or vote in Japanese elections.

Nonetheless, the shin-nisei have developed prominent transnational identities based on a dual affinity with both the United States and Japan, in contrast to their parents, whom some of them described as "Japanese nationalists," "gung ho Japanese," or "patriotic toward Japan." Michiko Kawamura reflected on this generational difference as follows:

> My mother never really assimilated in America and doesn't speak much English. She's forever Japanese in her thinking. The thought of becoming an American citizen has never even crossed her mind although she's been here for decades and will never go back to Japan. In fact, it bothers her because I've recently started to call myself Japanese American. When I grew up, she kept saying I'm "pure Japanese." Of course, I have both cultures inside of me and am connected to both countries. I don't think of myself as just one or the other. I'm actually a dual national.

A number of scholars have used the concept of hybridity instead of transnational identity to understand the ethnic consciousness of the second generation (Brettell and Nibbs 2009; Hickman et al. 2005; Potter 2005). This concept of hybrid identities provides an alternative to analyses of the children of immigrants as being caught between the two competing and opposing cultures of their parents and mainstream society (see, for example, Hickman et al. 2005; Portes and Rumbaut 2001: ch. 7). Instead of choosing to emphasize one identity over the other, second-generation individuals are bringing together two separate and incompatible identities and blurring the differences between them. (Brettell and Nibbs 2009:680). This "lived hybridity" prevents them from experiencing identity fragmentation that pulls them in opposite directions.

However, there are a number of problems with the concept of hybridity (Robbins 2004:327–333). First, it assumes that there are two separate and pure cultural identities (based on the country of origin and the country of birth) that somehow become synthesized and integrated as a hybrid mixture among those of the second generation. However, each of these initial cultural identities is based on hybrid combinations of different cultures (especially in the United States) and are not self-contained, homogeneous entities. In addition, hybridity implies that the conflict between the two incompatible identities is resolved through a dynamic balance and stable equilibrium, producing a coherent self. This obscures the inherently unequal, hierarchical ordering of these identities and the continuing tension between them.

Instead of presuming some kind of smooth hybrid integration and balance between two conflicting identities (which is often difficult to achieve), the concept of transnational identity emphasizes how multiple selves simultaneously coexist within the individual and are deployed at different times in different situations. The two identities can certainly struggle for supremacy with one becoming more dominant during certain occasions or periods of time. Nonetheless, the dynamic tension between the incompatible identities often persists and is not resolved. However, this does not always fragment the subject because the different selves are not always manifested at the same time and are often compartmentalized.

Because of their biculturalism, my shin-nisei interviewees have developed a dual, transnational affiliation with both the United States and Japan and therefore have fluid, multiple identities. However, the two parts of their bicultural selves are not in some type of hybrid balance but are inherently unequal, since one side is privileged over the other (usually the American side). For instance, according to Michiko,

> I would say culturally I'm much more American than Japanese. I feel more natural in terms of the way I behave when I'm with Americans versus Japanese. With Japanese I have to be more conscious of like, "I shouldn't be saying this because this is Japan." Or "I shouldn't act this way because I'm in Japan." Whereas in the U.S., I can just act naturally and be myself. So if you were to ask, it's natural that my American side is much stronger because I was born and raised here.

Others such as Yuki have similar assessments of their transnational identities:

> I wouldn't say my American side completely overrides my Japanese side, but I think in general, I identify as American first, although there are a lot of things about me that are still based on my Japanese heritage. So I think in English more than Japanese. I grew up Japanese, so everything in my mind was Japanese in the past. But I think it slowly transitioned to American as I grew older.

In contrast, only a small number of shin-nisei feel more Japanese than American. For instance, according to Steve, "I can be Japanese or American. But if I had to choose sides, I'm inevitably more Japanese than American."

Although the shin-nisei generally feel that their American and Japanese cultural identities are incompatible, they are not that concerned about reconciling them or somehow creating a coherent, hybrid integration of their two selves. Instead, their two identities coexist simultaneously as multiple, transnational affiliations that are appropriately deployed on different occasions and countries. Michiko described her experiences in this regard:

> I'm fully bicultural, but that doesn't mean I act American and Japanese at the same time. That's not possible. My identity is a very situational thing. When I'm with white Americans here [in the United States], I consider myself fully American. I feel like I'm accepted as an American and I can act and speak like one and I have no trouble. When I go back to Japan or I hang out with Japanese from Japan here in the U.S., I feel very Japanese. I can speak like a native. I can bow. I can mix in with Japanese well enough that I don't stick out. So I can use both sides of my identity completely proficiently.

Likewise, Matt also spoke about how he "switches identities" from American to Japanese when he goes to Japan, which he found is quite easy to do. "Depending on which country I'm in, I can feel pretty Japanese or feel quite American," he remarked. "I can totally fit in and embrace Japan. When I'm in Japan, I feel great, like I could live there for a long time. But when I get back to the U.S., I feel great being back home. I can operate fine in both cultures."

For Steve, who feels he "can be Japanese or American," this type of transnational ethnic identity is more a product of being caught between two different cultures and countries:

> Ultimately, I feel more shin-nisei than either American or Japanese. I'm in a bind because I'm not Japanese, but I'm more Japanese than most Japanese Americans since I have these Japanese cultural tendencies inside me that I keep fighting. I can easily be Japanese and go to Japan and get

a job and seriously be Japanese. But then, I'm here and I want to be here and stay here and want my children to stay here. So I've got to be more American or it's going to hurt me in the U.S.

Steve seems to favor his American side, not in a restrictive, nationalist sense, but because of its more cosmopolitan, global nature compared to an insular Japanese national identity. "I get mad at myself that I have these Japanese tendencies, which don't help me," he remarked. "We live in a global community, and if you want to step out and compete with the Western world, you need to be more Western. I try to break stereotypes. In Japan, I don't have to be Japanese, even if I can. It's a global community, so I'm going to act as whatever."

Finally, a few shin-nisei conceive of themselves in even more flexible and cosmopolitan ways that go beyond simply a dual transnational identification. For instance, Takehiro, a university faculty member, is not comfortable thinking of himself simply in nationalist terms as American and says he "like[s] the notion of fluid, flexible, transnational identities." However, what he was thinking of was an even more radical, multiple subjectivity. Consider the following exchange I had with him during our interview:

TAKEHIRO: I think when I was much younger I used to be more on those terms, kind of a binary, like American, Japanese. But as we know from people who work on identity, identity is a much more complicated matter than that. So what is an American? What is a Japanese? So I like the idea of not being stuck in some kind of category.

AUTHOR: So you no longer think of yourself in those kinds of binary terms?

TAKEHIRO: No, no. As I said, I probably used to, but I don't think that way anymore at all. I think of myself as having these real complicated relationships with a lot of different communities. There was a time when I identified a lot with black culture. I liked black culture.

AUTHOR: So you see yourself as a true cosmopolitan.

TAKEHIRO: I don't know if I'm a true cosmopolitan, but I feel like I have these multiple affiliations and I'm kind of a composite at the intersection of all these different kinds of identities. And not just one identity to the exclusion of the other ones. I don't even think in terms of like "Oh, I'm one third this, and one third that . . ." or whatever.

Several other shin-nisei also have an ethnic consciousness that supercedes transnational affiliations, but not because their subjectivity cannot be contained in binary terms, but because none of the essentialized, ethnic categories available to them is adequate. In other words, they feel that they are ethnically unclassifiable. According to Steve: "My experience is so unique and it's so distinct. I'm not really Japanese American. I'm not really Japanese. I'm not white. I'm always struggling to find my identity within the different communities that affect me and that I affect."

Another good example of an individual with such experiences is Karla Jones, who is biracial (she is second-generation Japanese descent on her mother's side and fourth-generation Welsh descent on her father's side). An excerpt from our interview is again quite illustrative:

AUTHOR: So have you ever identified as an Asian American?

KARLA: No. In high school I was part of the Asian American Club but I never participated. I've never called myself Asian American.

AUTHOR: So you see yourself as kind of distinct from all these groups. Do you also not see yourself as Japanese American? Or are there times when you just act like you're a white American? Or do you just go around saying "I'm American"?

KARLA: Culturally, I am American. I recognize that. But I do have other aspects of me which I cannot attribute to being white American. When I was teaching high school, I was telling my students that I use anthropology: I'm a liminal person. I'm betwixt and between.

AUTHOR: Victor Turner.

KARLA: And that's how I describe myself. I'm betwixt and between because I'm not really accepted by either. And I don't really accept either in a way. Because I feel like I'm somewhat of both but not fully. And so I can't just be categorized as one or the other.

AUTHOR: That's interesting. So you really see yourself as between these two groups. So what about the word *happa* [half Japanese, half white]? Is that something you use a lot or does it have a lot of meaning for you? Or is it just something that Japanese Americans kind of use to refer to you?

KARLA: I notice the Asian community using it. It has more meaning to them than to the white American community. But I think it
is because it kind of means a person who is half, and a person who
isn't really either. I've only used the word occasionally, and only with
Asians.

## Conclusion: Different Histories, Different Ethnicities

The last two chapters have argued for the importance of examining historical cohort differences between members of the second immigrant
generation. The immigration literature has been rather oblivious to history and often assumes that immigrant generation is the most important
factor in explaining internal differences in assimilation, ethnicity, and
identity among immigrant-origin ethnic groups. Although it is unde-
niable that the second immigrant generation will have fundamentally
different experiences from their first-generation immigrant parents,
there can be considerable diversity among members of the second
generation depending on the historical period when they came of age,
which, in turn, can lead to considerably different ethnic outcomes.

In the case of second-generation Japanese Americans, there are significant historical generational differences between those who grew up
before and after World War II. As a result, they have developed a completely different ethnicity in terms of assimilation/biculturalism, cultural
heritage, and transnational engagement and identities. Because the racialization of the prewar nisei caused them to suffer from discrimination, racism, and internment during a period of anti-Japanese hostility,
they responded by affirming and strengthening their nationalist loyalties as culturally assimilated Americans, instead of developing transnational orientations.

In contrast, the shin-nisei are not as adamant about demanding racial citizenship and national belonging. As members of the postwar
historical generation, they are descendants of transnational Japanese
professionals and have grown up in an increasingly multicultural and
globalized America where their ethnic homeland is now regarded in
favorable terms. Therefore, although they continue to be racialized as
ethnic minorities, this racialization no longer has the negative effects
that it had for their prewar nisei predecessors. As a result, they are much

more engaged with their ethnic heritage, and their bicultural lives and identities are based on a transnational sense of belonging that simultaneously encompasses both the United States and Japan. Theirs is not a reactive ethnicity asserted against a discriminatory mainstream society, but an affirmative identification with a heritage and homeland that are now positively construed. As a result, the shin-nisei have successfully inherited the Japanese language, cultural heritage, and transnationalism of their parents. Although many of them may be just as assimilated as the prewar nisei, this has not prevented them from simultaneously retaining their ancestral culture and remaining transnationally involved.

As a result, the pre- and postwar nisei operate in completely different, historically constituted generational spaces of ethnic interaction and belonging: one national, the other transnational. As shown by the Day of Remembrance at UC San Diego, there is currently little contact between these two second-generation communities. Although this is partly because of their age differences, it is mainly because of their histories. Whereas the prewar nisei are a product of Japanese American communities before and right after World War II, the shin-nisei grew up in the postwar Japanese expatriate community as well as in white, middle-class neighborhoods. Some do not even identify strongly as Japanese American and are generally not involved in Japanese American organizations. Therefore, although the pre- and postwar nisei are members of the same immigrant second generation, they are generations apart in terms of history. Such historical cohort differences may be just as significant as immigrant generational differences among nisei, sansei, and yonsei when explaining the relative strength of ethnic heritage among various groups of Japanese Americans.

Japanese Americans are, of course, not the only ethnic group that has significant historical generational differences among those of the second immigrant generation. Plenty of other ethnic groups have a long history of immigration to the United States, such as Mexican Americans, Chinese Americans, and Filipino Americans, as well as various white ethnic groups. For all these groups, members of the same immigrant generation may come from completely different historical generations. For instance, Tomás Jiménez (2010:127–128) notes that earlier generations of Mexican Americans were raised in an era of assimilation and had parents who insisted they Americanize. As a result, they did not assert a Mexican American identity, whereas for younger Mexican Americans, who came of age after the 1960s and 1970s, Mexican ethnicity has become an important part of their lives.

However, even when immigration researchers have examined these ethnic groups, they have focused almost exclusively on the members of the postwar second generation and have ignored historical differences with their prewar counterparts and the varying types of contemporary ethnicities and identities these have produced. Even if the age gap between two groups of the same second generation is not as large as it is between the pre- and postwar nisei, it is important not to lump them together because they can still be members of different historical generations with varying ethnic experiences. For instance, the age difference between members of the Baby-Boomer Generation and Generation X is less than twenty years.

When examining the impact of different histories on the second generation, however, we must not neglect the important influence of age. After all, second-generation members from different historical periods are usually of quite different age groups. For instance, shin-nisei are more bilingual and engaged with their ethnic heritage and homeland, not only because they are members of the postwar multicultural and transnational historical generation, but also because most of those in my sample are still young. Much of the learning of cultural heritage and native languages as well as visits to the ethnic homeland occur under the auspices of parents when the second generation are still children or youth.

In addition, college is when a number of Asian American youth explore and fully discover their ethnicity (Espiritu 1994; Kibria 2002a; Thai 2002; Levitt 2002:140), partly because of the tolerant, multiethnic social environment that prevails on university campuses, the presence of large numbers of other Asian American students, and opportunities to study abroad in the ethnic homeland.[3] In fact, when the prewar nisei were young, a number of them had spoken and studied some Japanese while growing up in immigrant families and communities. However, they forgot the language as their parents passed away and they grew older. As Peggy Levitt (2002) points out, transnational (and I would also say ethnic heritage) activity does not remain constant throughout the life cycle, but ebbs and flows at different stages.

This issue of age is also relevant to the ethnic future of the second generation. Although the shin-nisei youth are currently bicultural and transnationally engaged, will they eventually become more detached from their ethnic heritage as they grow older, like the prewar nisei? It is quite evident that second-generation ties to heritage and homeland are very much dependent on transnational immigrant parents, who foster, if not insist on, the maintenance of the native language and culture and take their children with them to visit to their country of origin. Therefore, it is possible that the second-generation youth of today will become less ethnic and transnational as their first-generation parents pass away and they become busy adults preoccupied with their professional careers (see, for example, Smith 2006: ch. 8) and with their own children, who will be another generation removed from the ethnic homeland.

Although the lives of current second-generation Japanese American youth may indeed unfold in this manner as they grow older, I would argue that they will continue to remain connected to their heritage and homeland to a notable extent. Two of my older, middle-aged shin-nisei informants are still fluent in Japanese, and one continues to conduct research in Japan. The other, who no longer travels to Japan as often as in her youth and has become more detached from the country over time, mentioned a continued desire to visit or even live there in the future. We have seen that the lives of prewar nisei were shaped by their experiences during World War II, the historical period when they came of age. Despite the postwar turn toward multiculturalism and the rise of East Asia, they remain culturally nationalized and have shown little interest in recovering their ethnic heritage or developing ties to Japan. Likewise, the shin-nisei will continue to be influenced by their multicultural and transnational upbringing as they grow older. As members of different historical generations, pre- and postwar nisei have had early formative experiences that have placed them on different ethnic trajectories that will continue to determine their future identities and sense of belonging. In this sense, history is indeed destiny.

# Racialization, Citizenship, and Heritage

3

# Assimilation and Loss of Ethnic Heritage among Third-Generation Japanese Americans

## Assimilative Trajectories and Ethnicity

As noted in the Introduction, Japanese Americans are one of the oldest Asian American groups in the country. Because they are mainly a product of Japanese immigration before World War II, a majority of them today are of the third and fourth generations (sansei and yonsei). Part II of this book examines these later-generation Japanese Americans in the American Southwest and how they situate themselves ethnically as they negotiate the various pressures of assimilation, racialization, and multiculturalism.

Third-generation sansei are perhaps the largest group of Japanese Americans today. They are usually of middle-age, although some are older, and I met a few who were younger. As the descendants of the prewar nisei, their ethnicity to some extent reflects the histories and experiences of their parents. Being another generation removed from their ethnic homeland, they have followed the assimilative path of the prewar nisei. Raised in Americanized families in white, middle-class suburbs, the sansei are well integrated in mainstream American society and have experienced further upward socioeconomic mobility as well as cultural Americanization. Those whom I interviewed characterized themselves as detached from their Japanese cultural heritage and their ethnic homeland of Japan. Although Hansen (1952) famously observed increased ethnic interest and identification among third-generation white Americans, in the case of Japanese Americans, this ethnic awakening seems to have generally been delayed until the fourth generation (see Chapter 5).[1]

However, while inheriting the ethnic legacy and histories of their prewar nisei parents, the sansei have also negotiated their own ethnic positionality in response to the historical moment when they came of age.

While their further Americanization is a product of the assimilationist ideology that was prevalent when they were youth, they also experienced the ethnic activism of the Asian American movement in the 1960s and 1970s and the gradual shift from assimilationist to multicultural ideologies. In addition, they were influenced by the decline of discrimination against Japanese Americans in the post–World War II period and the emergence of Japan as a globally prominent and respected economic power. As a result, despite their assimilation, the sansei feel the impact of their Japanese cultural heritage on their ethnic consciousness to a greater extent than the prewar nisei and their identities as Japanese Americans are a source of considerable pride.

## Growing Up Sansei

In terms of social integration and mobility, the sansei seem to have continued the assimilative trajectory initiated by their prewar nisei parents (Connor 1974:163–164; Fugita and O'Brien 1991: ch. 5; Montero 1980; Spickard 1996:145–147; Takezawa 1995: ch. 4; Woodrum 1981). After their internment, a good number of the nisei dispersed throughout the United States instead of returning to their previous ethnic communities on the West Coast. In addition, many of them moved to the suburbs as they became socioeconomically mobile. As a result, my sansei interviewees tended to grow up in white suburban neighborhoods where they generally did not have much contact with Japanese Americans or other Asian American children, although a few of my interviewees did grow up in minority neighborhoods with black and Latino children. Only a small number of them came from families who were closely connected to the Japanese American community and grew up with Japanese American kids. Most did not develop relationships with Asian Americans until college. In addition, the sansei have also increasingly intermarried outside the ethnic community, furthering their socioeconomic integration into mainstream society. For instance, although virtually none of my prewar nisei interviewees had married non-Japanese Americans, close to half of the sansei I spoke with had intermarried, usually with white Americans (see also Fugita and O'Brien 1991: ch. 8). They also had higher levels of educational attainment than the prewar nisei (almost all of them had college degrees and a number had more advanced degrees) and a vast majority worked (or had worked) as white collar professionals, some attaining prominent positions.

Although the nisei made a conscious effort to culturally assimilate and demonstrate their Americanness and national loyalty because of their internment and the general discrimination they endured, they did not seem to have directly pressured their sansei children to culturally assimilate. Only a few of my sansei interviewees mentioned that their parents explicitly told them that they are Americans and should assimilate (compare with Takezawa 1995:137–-138), although a number of them did mention that their parents pushed them to excel in school and succeed socioeconomically, which they associated with their assimilation. Several attributed such pressures to the internment, which deprived their parents of educational and professional opportunities to fully succeed in American society. Others saw it as a product of Japanese culture and its emphasis on academic achievement and hard work and on not bringing shame to the family.

It is generally known that the prewar nisei did not speak about their internment in concentration camps to their children (Fugita and Fernandez 2004:112–113; Maki, Kitano, and Berthold 1999:57; Spickard 1996:130; Takezawa 1995:154–157), and this was also the case with my sansei interviewees. Not only was the experience traumatic, humiliating, and something the prewar nisei did not want to recount, they also wished to move on with their lives and did not want the experience to negatively affect their children. My sansei interviewees generally reported that their nisei parents did not talk about the internment unless they specifically asked about it. In fact, most of the sansei did not know about the internment of Japanese Americans until they learned about it in college. They then asked their parents whether they were interned, which finally caused their parents to speak about it for the first time. Cindy Kushimura recounted a typical experience:

> Growing up, [my parents] said nothing [about internment]. So I didn't know about it until college, when at San Diego State, I took an Asian American class. To learn about it, I was like, "Oh my!" So I went home and asked, "Mom, dad, is it true? Were you in camp?" And then they said, "Yeah, oh yeah, we were in camp in Hart Mountain." . . . So I was like, "Why the hell did you not tell me about this before?" And then,

they gave the pat answer that it's in the history books. They said, "It was something that just happened, there was nothing we could do about it anyways." They just put it behind them. And they just wanted to go on with their lives.

A number of the sansei were shocked and outraged when they first heard about the internment. "It made me angry," Carla Simmons recounted. "I was appalled. I was like, 'How could that happen? How could the U.S. government do such a thing?' It really opened my eyes, and made me more aware of prejudice against minorities."

Other sansei initially did not understand why their nisei parents did not resist their internment (see also Maki, Kitano, and Berthold 1999:65; Takezawa 1995:83, 160). "I thought, well, what were they? Sheep? They allowed themselves to be rounded up and just herded into these camps?" Cathy remarked, her voice tinged with the exasperation she felt at that time. "But then I calmed down and realized that I was in the mind frame of the civil rights movement. That mindset wasn't in existence in the early 1940s, and if the Japanese did protest, they may have been mowed down by machine guns without a second thought." Ron Inoue recounted a similar reaction:

> When I learned about it in college, I went through the feeling of how the hell could my parents allow themselves to be interned and not fight back? I was angry that they let the U.S. government do this to them. It was only later that I realized it took guts, what they went through and endured, having to lose their homes and businesses, and still fight for their country, and then raise kids who were patriotic.

In fact, the sansei were actively involved in the redress movement among Japanese Americans to demand reparations from the United States government in the 1970s and 1980s and encouraged the initially reluctant nisei to speak about their experiences (Maki, Kitano, and Berthold 1999:230, 232; Spickard 1996:155–156; Takezawa 149–152, 160–163).

The nisei therefore did not use the internment experience as a way to encourage their children to assimilate; nor did they tell their children to de-emphasize their ethnic heritage in order to avoid possible ethnic discrimination and disadvantage. Only one of my sansei interviewees,

George Okamoto, attributed his Americanized upbringing to the fact that his parents' generation "had to prove that they were loyal Americans, so they had to kind of push their cultural identity aside." However, even he was not sure about this connection.

Instead of viewing their assimilation as a product of parental pressure, the sansei regarded it as a natural outcome of the Americanized social environment in which they were raised. They grew up in families that spoke predominantly English, went to school and socialized primarily with white children, and did not interact much at all with other Japanese Americans. For instance, Walter Aoyama characterized himself as "having lived in an environment totally immersed with whites. I never had contact with the Japanese or Asian community." He claimed that he was basically treated like a white person while he was growing up and others never emphasized his Asian ethnicity. Likewise, Cindy said:

> I didn't have close Japanese American friends. Actually, my good friends were whites because we grew up in a predominantly white, middle-class neighborhood. So my brothers and sisters, we all wanted to assimilate and be in the various groups with them. I became a cheerleader and my brother joined the football team. We wanted to do the white middle-class thing.

"I wanted to be ethnically an All-American," Ron remarked. "In high school, I wanted to be white, blond, and tall. I didn't like being Japanese American and there was pressure from other kids too. I think I could have been more popular if I was white. And I probably would have had more girlfriends if I was white." Like Ron, a number of the sansei mentioned being teased or insulted because of their ethnicity when they were children.

Because they were raised in mainstream American suburbs and did not have much contact with other Asians, a few sansei said that they basically saw themselves as white (see also Takezawa 1995:132–133). "I had always gone to school with white kids and there were very few Japanese [American] kids," Cathy recalled. "So all my friends were white. So I never thought I was different than the rest of the population. I always considered myself fully American. Even when I looked in the mirror, I never made the connection that I had a high degree of social visibility!

In fact, the first young Japanese Americans I met like me were in college." "I didn't grow up with many Japanese [Americans]," Carla said. "And so, I always thought of myself as being white. Even though I looked Asian in the mirror, I was white. I never learned my ethnic roots as far as that goes."

## Loss of Japanese Cultural Heritage

Because their lives have come to closely resemble other Americans, there has been an increased decline in Japanese cultural heritage among my sansei interviewees, as other researchers have noted (Spickard 1996:147; Tuan 2001). Because their nisei parents did not encourage them to retain their ethnic heritage, their exposure to it was generally limited to Japanese food and occasional participation in cultural activities in the Japanese American community (see also Takezawa 1995:116, 129–131). None of the sansei mentioned that their parents made any serious efforts to pass down the Japanese language or ancestral culture to their children.[2] This is not surprising, given the prewar nisei's own attempts to distance themselves from their ethnic background. For instance, Sachiko said, "My parents made no overall effort to maintain any connection with the Japanese language or culture. The way we were brought up was completely American."

"My parents never told us to stay in touch with our heritage," George Okamoto recalled. "They allowed us to do our own thing. It appeared to be kind of a common theme with the sansei kids. They were like me, where they kind of lost touch with the culture. None of us spoke the language. . . . Some of us lamented the fact that our parents weren't more forceful about it."

"We were definitely not brought up with any Japanese culture," Cathy noted. "Essentially, we knew nothing about it, except for some cultural obligations, like funerals and koden [a tradition of giving money to the family of the deceased]. That was it. The only other Japanese connection we had was with the food."

It is interesting that the sansei are the only generation of Japanese Americans I interviewed who mentioned that other Asian Americans called them "bananas" (Takamori 2011:95), a somewhat derogatory term that is used to refer to those who have become completely assimilated and "whitewashed" and have forgotten their Asian ancestry.[3] In fact, a couple of my interviewees were not even aware of what the term meant when they first heard it.

In addition to not receiving any encouragement or support from their parents to maintain their cultural heritage, a number of the older sansei grew up in an era when America was predominantly white and assimilationist, instead of multicultural and ethnically pluralist. They did not want to be ethnically different and faced assimilationist pressures in school. Carol Hashimoto was the most explicit in discussing her experiences in this regard. "We didn't really learn Japanese and the motivation wasn't there for me," she recounted. "This was in the 1970s when it was really not accepted, bilingualism was really not accepted in the U.S." She went on to talk about how even second-generation Asian and Latino kids did not want to speak their native languages at that time. "The kids who spoke English at home were really proud that they spoke only English. I don't know why we were so proud of that, but there was definitely pressure to assimilate. We didn't want to speak with an accent. And we didn't want to be associated with people who weren't American. We tried really hard to be American."

Thus, although contemporary Asian Americans often experience an ethnic awakening during their youth (Espiritu 1994; Kibria 2002a; Louie 2004:98; Thai 2002), there does not seem to have been a sustained and widespread desire to explore ancestral roots among third-generation sansei when they came of age in the 1960s and 1970s. Not only was assimilation a more dominant ethnic ideology than it is today, Japan and Japaneseness were not as positively regarded as they are currently, even if their ancestry was no longer stigmatized compared to the World War II period.

However, the Asian American movement during the 1960s and 1970s did lead to an awakening of ethnic consciousness among the sansei and caused some Japanese American activists to question their assimilationist agenda and affirm their previously suppressed ethnic heritage as a source of pride. Nonetheless, researchers who have studied this period note that the total number of sansei who actively participated in the movement was limited and its impact seems to have been rather short-lived (Lyman 1970:96; Spickard 1996:148–149, 152, 159; Takahashi 1997:1–2, 155–156). By the late-1970s, the Asian American movement had dissipated and lost its power for various reasons (Omatsu 2000:88–90; Wei 2004:306–307). However, it is important to remember that its legacy was an important reason why the sansei were actively involved in the ethnic activism of the redress movement in the 1970s and 1980s, which led to an official apology from the United States government and reparations for Japanese American internment.

In addition, the interest in ethnic roots among sansei youth during the Asian American movement was mainly a localized attempt to reconnect with their Japanese American (or Asian American) identities, communities, and history and was not an effort to recover their ancestral heritage by learning the Japanese language and culture and creating transnational ties to Japan (Spickard 2006:148–151; Wei 2004:303–304). Others became involved in minority rights issues, identified panethnically with other Asian Americans as a means of ethnic empowerment, and created panethnic organizations (Espiritu 1992: ch. 2; Maeda 2012: ch. 4).[4] Those who were involved in Asian American activism focused mainly on the specific ethnic, educational, gender, and political issues of the time, most notably the Vietnam War and the establishment of Asian American Studies programs at various universities (Espiritu 1992:35–49; Ling 1989; Maeda 2012: chs. 2, 3; Wei 2004). Such efforts by ethnic minorities eventually helped shift the country from a dominant assimilationist ideology to a more multicultural one.

It was somewhat surprising that only a few of my sansei interviewees mentioned that they became more interested in their ethnic heritage during the ethnic activism of the 1960s and 1970s. For instance, after a childhood in which he wanted to be white, Ron started to explore his ethnic identity in college when he began to read about Japanese Americans and their history. "That's when the whole Asian American identity pride thing started," he recalled. "So I got involved with some Asian American organizations like UAAC [United Asian American Communities]." The ethnic activism of the period also had a similar impact on Daniel Kushimura, who was the president of the Japanese American Citizens League (JACL) in San Diego:

> I grew up in the inner city with blacks and Chicanos and very few whites. And that was back in the 1960s, during the civil rights movement. So I grew up with a lot of blacks who were like, "Power to the People!" And

Chicanos who were into *La Raza* and everything. So it made me more aware of who I was and my ethnic background. That I have rights just like they do. I wanted to know more about being Japanese [American] and being a minority. That's probably how I came to do JACL work.

As was the case with other sansei, Ron and Daniel's efforts to reclaim their ethnicity during this period were limited to the Japanese American or Asian American community. They did not attempt to reconnect with their Japanese ancestral heritage through transnational involvement with their ethnic homeland.

Although the ethnic revival among the sansei in the 1960s and 1970s did include an element of interest in Japan (Spickard 1996:152) and some of them did visit the country (often on language and area studies programs) in order to explore their ethnic roots and reclaim their previously stigmatized Japanese heritage (Yamashiro 2008:113–114), their numbers appear to have been limited. The sansei who moved to Japan seemed to have primarily done so in the 1970s and early 1980s, generally after the peak of the Asian American movement. Their ethnic return migration was based on various personal and professional motives and was not simply related to interest in their ancestral heritage (Takamori 2011:94–98).

In sum, my third-generation interviewees did not actively explore their Japanese cultural heritage as youth through extensive study of the Japanese language or by living in Japan. The only exception was Kate Nishimoto, who resided in Japan for one year as a college exchange student and learned Japanese. However, she came of age after the Asian American movement and her study abroad was not motivated by a desire to recover her Japanese ancestral heritage (as will be discussed below). In addition, whatever interest she may have initially had in her ethnic homeland when she was young dissipated as she became older and devoted herself to her professional career. Subsequently, she did not maintain any transnational connections to Japan and can no longer speak the language.

This does not mean that the sansei did not engage in any Japanese cultural heritage activities during their youth. For instance, they were instrumental in introducing taiko (traditional Japanese drumming) to the United States, and this has been associated with the political activism of the Asian American movement (Ahlgren 2011: introduction, ch. 1; Asai 1995:438–440; Kobayashi 2006:2–3; Konagaya 2001; Terada 2001:41). However, taiko did not become really popular in the Japanese American community until the 1990s, when it was appropriated by fourth-generation yonsei as a means to reconnect with their ancestral heritage. Although taiko has caused some Japanese Americans to become more transnationally involved in Japan, it is mainly a Japanese American musical form practiced predominantly in local communities in the United States (see Chapters 6 and 7).

Despite the brief impact of the Asian American movement, the sansei in general experienced an Americanized upbringing during an era when multiculturalism, cultural diversity, and transnational connections to ethnic homelands were not yet strongly emphasized in a world that was not fully globalized. The resulting loss of their heritage language has been especially acute among Japanese Americans who are a product of Japanese immigration before World War II (Takamori 2011:111–115). My sansei interviewees reported that they could not speak or understand much Japanese and their language ability was notably less than that of the prewar nisei (see also Takezawa 1995:129). In general, they grew up speaking only English, and their nisei parents never forced or pressured them to learn Japanese. "My dad was forced to go to Japanese school and hated it," Shannon Suyama noted. "So he didn't want to put us in the same situation."

Some of my sansei interviewees had virtually no background in the Japanese language. They had heard their parents or grandparents speaking some Japanese (for instance, their parents would speak Japanese to their grandparents or sometimes to each other). However, the parents generally did not speak any Japanese to them. These interviewees gave the following types of assessments about their abilities:

"Personally, I'd say my Japanese abilities are zero."

"I don't speak any Japanese, none at all. I picked up a few words. Very little."

"I probably speak Japanese about as well as a white person! I can say *sayonara, domo arigato, sushi, ninja*, haha . . ."

In contrast, a larger number of sansei had greater exposure to Japanese when they were growing up and had some limited Japanese language ability. A few mentioned that their nisei parents spoke some Japanese to them, although they themselves always spoke back to their parents in English, while others had substantial exposure to Japanese speakers as children. About half of the sansei I interviewed had studied some Japanese. Some had taken Japanese language classes or attended Japanese school on Saturdays (for instance at the local Buddhist temple or in Japanese American Christian churches). Others had also taken Japanese language classes in college. However, even this group had very limited facility in the language and had forgotten it as they grew older. "Well, I took courses at UCSD, so I must have known something," Shannon commented, almost shrugging. "But I would never claim to speak Japanese. I would have to work really hard just to understand a little."

"I took classes at ASU [Arizona State University] and at the Buddhist church when I was a kid, but I don't speak much Japanese now at all," Stacey Nakamoto admitted.

"My language opportunities were kind of limited. Over time, they became almost nonexistent. It was not necessary," Walter said. "If I were immersed in Japan or something, I'd gradually get some of it back."

"I knew what my grandparents were saying and what they were talking about [in Japanese]," Daniel recalled. "But now, I find that if I run into people from Japan speaking Japanese, I don't understand them."

Even Kate Nishimoto, who spent the most time studying Japanese among all my sansei interviewees (she took classes in college and was on a one-year exchange program in Japan) gave a rather low rating of her current Japanese language ability: "At the end of my year [in Japan], it was pretty functional. But I don't speak any Japanese now. I don't use it at all. If I listen very carefully, I can understand it. But it doesn't come automatically."

Because of their cultural Americanization and the lack of Japanese language abilities, the sansei have retained only symbolic aspects of their cultural heritage (Okamura 2008:140-144). Most of them continue to cook and eat Japanese food, and a number of them have collected Japanese art (and sometimes plants, like bonsai) to decorate their homes. Some continue to celebrate New Year's by cooking Japanese food and attend Obon festivals at the local Buddhist temple or make and sell Japanese food for community activities. A few practiced Japanese wedding or funeral customs. Others mentioned taking their shoes off before entering their homes, bathing at night (versus in the morning for other Americans), and making banzai toasts with sake during parties.

However, none of my sansei interviewees actually practiced any Japanese arts or music (flower arrangement, traditional dance, or instruments), watched Japanese television, or listened to Japanese traditional or popular music. For instance, Walter was hard pressed to find anything in his lifestyle that he specifically associated with his Japanese ancestry:

> Well, I like to garden, but that's not necessarily Japanese. . . . I also played lots of basketball. . . . Well, that's not particularly Japanese either, but I did play in the Japanese [American] league. . . . I don't eat any Japanese food at home, although I do go to Japanese restaurants sometimes, but so do lots of Americans. We've just had typical American dishes in this house. All American dishes. Plate, no chopsticks, although we can use them. When I get invited to other people's homes, I tell them, "When you come to my house, it's going to be all American food. Don't expect sushi or anything. It'll be like, steak. And with potatoes, not rice."

## A Revived Ethnic Identity: Americans of Japanese Ancestry

Because of their backgrounds, the sansei conceived of their ethnic identities in quite Americanized ways. Indeed, earlier studies have shown a significant decline in ethnic identification among the sansei even compared to the prewar nisei (Masuda, Matsumoto, and Meredith 1970; Newton et al. 1988). Some of those I spoke with noted that they felt no cultural differences from other Americans, except for very minor Japanese customs that they had retained. Several of my interviewees called themselves "typical American[s]." Others interviewees felt much more American than Japanese.

"I've never identified with being Japanese," Shannon remarked. "Obviously, I'm an American."

"I think 98 to 99 percent of the time, I feel just like other Americans," Dan Matsushita said. "There are just small, simple things like taking shoes off before entering houses, where I might feel slight differences."

"I'm 100 percent American," Walter declared. "I'm Japanese descent, but other than that, I'm 100 percent American."

Likewise, George felt he was "American first. An American of Japanese ancestry."

Cathy spoke about how she felt completely American growing up with mainly white children, except for the fact that she ate Japanese food and looked different. It was only later in her life that she started to associate with other Japanese Americans and become more aware of her ethnic background through greater interest in Japanese art and vacations in Japan (mainly because of the influence of her white husband, who was a scholar of Japanese American history).

In fact, some of my sansei interviewees said that they never even thought of themselves as ethnic minorities in American society. One mentioned that he may be a minority in terms of appearance, but not in terms of culture or behavior. Another said she always felt part of a larger group, both when she lived in multicultural San Francisco and in predominantly white La Jolla (in San Diego). Yet another became more conscious of her minority status only when she was labeled and grouped together with other minorities such as Hispanics and blacks.[5]

While my sansei interviewees generally acknowledged their cultural assimilation and loss of ethnic heritage and some felt no cultural differences from other Americans, it was quite remarkable how others claimed to have inherited aspects of the ancestral Japanese culture later on in their interviews (see also Masuda, Matsumoto, and Meredith 1970:205) and emphasized their ethnic identity as Americans of Japanese descent. In fact, they did so significantly more than the prewar nisei, who generally stressed their Americanness. For instance, when I interviewed a nisei husband and his sansei wife, the husband noted that "I don't have as strong a Japanese feeling as I think she does. . . . She does things and makes stuff that reflect the Japanese side of her."

The sansei were undoubtedly influenced by the turn toward more multicultural ideologies starting in the 1960s and 1970s, as demonstrated by the Asian American movement. In addition, they grew up in an increasingly tolerant ethnic environment during the postwar period, when previous discrimination against those of Japanese ancestry has largely subsided,[6] and their ethnic homeland is now highly regarded because of its rise to prominence as a respected global economic power. As a result, the sansei I spoke with have more positive imaginings of their Japanese ethnic heritage, which they attribute to aspects of themselves that they favorably perceive as distinctive.

For instance, although Georgie Nakamura characterized herself as highly Americanized, she also emphasized the impact of her Japanese cultural heritage:

> I feel like I'm an American first, but with Japanese heritage. . . . My Americanism is much stronger, and everything in my life is strictly American, except for some Japanese customs like New Years. But I also feel strongly about being more culturally Japanese [compared to other Americans]. That's just my personal feeling inside. I don't tell people this, but it's because of my heritage and the way I was brought up.

"I'm about 75 percent American," Daniel said, quantifying his ethnicity. "I grew up here in a mostly American environment. But there are also some things that I've learned from my grandparents and parents and my associations [with other Japanese Americans] and my upbringing." Others gave similar breakdowns of their ethnicity. It was interesting that the sansei who quantified their ethnicity actually placed a lower percentage on their Americanness than the prewar nisei. I was actually surprised to hear one interviewee describe her American/Japanese balance as "50/50" and another claim that she was actually more culturally Japanese than American.

In our various discussions, my sansei interviewees repeatedly acknowledged the lingering effects of Japanese culture on their ethnic consciousness and behavior and gave me a very long list of traits that they believed their parents had instilled in them as part of their "Japanese" cultural upbringing. These included: a commitment to high quality work and standards; a strong work ethic and desire to excel; a quiet, reserved, and soft-spoken demeanor; courtesy and respect for others; a cooperative and group-oriented attitude; responsibility and integrity; a desire not to disturb others; a humble and modest disposition; a desire not to shame or embarrass parents or family; a tendency not to show emotion and physical affection; a willingness to sacrifice for others; patience and endurance; and even a greater tendency to give gifts. Some of them spoke about how they embodied one or two of these characteristics while others claimed a number of these "Japanese" attributes for themselves. A few even utilized Japanese words they had heard from their parents to speak about these characteristics, such as *enryo* (restraint, deference to others) and *gaman* (perseverance, endurance without complaining) (see also King-O'Riain 2006:77; Takamori 2011:118–119). Even Donald Ishii, who is only of half Japanese descent, listed the positive aspects of Japanese culture that had supposedly been passed down to him by his parents:

> I'm pretty darn whitewashed [assimilated]. But when it comes to the work ethic and heritage, I'm Japanese. I have a Japanese work ethic. The Japanese are far, far superior to any other people in terms of work ethic culture that I've ever seen. I also have a Japanese business mind. I have a Japanese respect for people. And I have a Japanese loyalty and trustworthiness.

Although it is always possible that certain Japanese cultural dispositions have indeed persisted into the third generation (Connor 1974:164–165; Kitano 1969; Masuda, Matsumoto, and Meredith 1970:205–206), such perceptions are more likely a product of positive self-attribution based on stereotypes about Japanese culture.

I also noticed that the sansei are considerably more self-assured, as well as being less reticent about their ethnicity compared to the prewar nisei. Of course, they generally do not go around actively asserting their ethnic identities in everyday life (there are few flag-waving Japanese Americans). For a few, the term "Japanese American" is mainly a label they use to clarify their ethnicity, especially when asked, and therefore does not have much personal significance (see also Smith 2014: ch. 7). A number of them said that they do not mention or talk about their ethnic identities in their daily lives unless it specifically comes up in conversation. Most of them believe that they have not been treated negatively nor encountered much prejudice because of their Japanese ancestry.

Nonetheless, I was struck by the numerous times the sansei expressed pride in their ethnicity, especially compared to the prewar nisei (see also Masuda, Matsumoto, and Meredith 1970:205). However, this relatively strong ethnic pride tends to be based more on the accomplishments and history of Japanese Americans in the United States than on positive images of Japan or the Japanese people and culture. For instance, George is unequivocally proud of his ethnic heritage, but mainly because of the achievements of Japanese immigrants and their descendants in the United States, such as their willingness to immigrate to America despite the risks, the hardships and racial discrimination they endured, and their service in the U.S. Army. "Without that, I wouldn't be enjoying the lifestyle I have today," he noted. However, he is less proud of Japan and the Japanese, which are too distant for him to relate to and tended to provoke greater feelings of ambivalence.[7] Likewise, Doug Ishimura is also proud of the history and past struggles of Japanese Americans. "Even in a short time, we've had a really good history," he remarked. "We were pretty loyal people, not many traitors among us!" Others expressed pride in the socioeconomic achievements of Japanese Americans. "We started out pretty poor, but are all educated, successful middle-class people now," Diane Akashi claimed. "You don't hear about Japanese [American] gardeners or farmers anymore."

"Because we are Japanese [American], we were all pushed to excel, to be better than the others," Jane Sakata said. "That's why we've done well in terms of social mobility." One interviewee noted that "if a Japanese [American] person does well, you kind of admire that. And if someone does something negative, like cheating, you feel bad and take it personally. It's like, 'How could a Japanese [American] do that?'" As part of his overall ethnic self-esteem, another sansei spoke about the pride he feels about Japanese American athletes (Apollo Ono, Christie Yamaguchi), and even about Japanese baseball players (Ichiro Suzuki). In fact, only a few of the sansei whom I interviewed do not feel pride in their ethnic identity or feel ambivalent about it.

## Touristic Encounters with the Ethnic Homeland

Compared to other generations of Japanese Americans, considerably fewer of my sansei interviewees have visited (or are interested in visiting) Japan and almost none of them currently has any meaningful transnational connection to the ethnic homeland. Although virtually all my nisei and fourth-generation yonsei interviewees have been to Japan, over half of the sansei have never even visited the country. Japan is essentially a foreign country for them, and they felt relatively little connection to their ancestral homeland as a source of ethnic identification or heritage. In addition to being another generation removed from the country compared to the nisei, some also cited the high cost of traveling to Japan as a reason why they have never been there. More remarkable is that half of the sansei who have never visited Japan actually claimed they had no interest in doing so in the future. For instance, John Sakata said:

> I was born and raised here. The only connection [to Japan] I have is I'm of Japanese ancestry, and that's it. For me, to go to Japan and see the temples and shrines and other things doesn't interest me. There are too many places in the U.S. I still haven't seen.

Daniel spoke about how he is actually reluctant to visit Japan:

> Honestly, I don't really want to go there. I'd just be a foreigner who doesn't speak the language and doesn't know anything about the country. I hear if you aren't pure Japanese [that is, Japanese from Japan], you won't be accepted there. And it's really expensive. So as far as vacation is concerned, there are other places I would rather see, like Europe. So Japan is kind of way down on the list of places to go!

Another sansei wanted to visit the Philippines, where his wife is from, but had no desire to see Japan. Even one sansei who said she would like to visit Japan someday makes it a low priority. She is more interested in seeing other parts of the United States as well as Europe first.

Those sansei interviewees who have been to Japan generally traveled there as tourists. Most have taken only one brief trip to the country, and only three interviewees have been to Japan twice or multiple times (one has done so because she was a flight attendant at one time in her career). Kate is the only sansei who had actually lived in Japan for any notable period (one year to study Japanese in college). My interviewees spoke highly, if not raved, about their trips and vacations to Japan, recalling nostalgic images of cherry blossoms and festivals, shrines and gardens, art and pottery, beautiful and idyllic scenery, bullet trains, good restaurants and food, and a generally clean, orderly, and safe society. In this sense, their experiences were somewhat similar to those of the prewar nisei, whose exposure to Japan was also generally limited to enjoyable vacations. "Oh, I loved it!" Cathy exclaimed. She then recounted memories of delicious tempura bars and udon restaurants, narrow and quaint streets, and a visit to a rural village that made traditional pottery in kilns. Another remembered the fog clearing and the majestic Mt. Fuji appearing before her eyes as well as the sublime beauty of Japanese gardens and temples. Shannon gushed about the "phenomenal food, the best I've ever had," the wonderful mountain *onsen* (hot springs), and the different cherry blossom festivals in each town.

Because of their relatively short sojourns as tourists, most sansei have a rather superficial encounter with Japan. Theirs is a type of external touristic gaze and fascination that does not delve sufficiently into Japanese society to discover its negative underside (Tsuda 2009b:232). In contrast, the few sansei who had more prolonged exposure to Japanese society began to notice some of its less favorable characteristics. Although Kate really enjoyed her stay there as a student, she was bothered by the incidents of sexual harassment she witnessed in the trains as well as in a department store. Carla, who had been to Japan many times as a flight attendant, actually "hated" visiting Japan because she was immediately identified and treated as a foreigner.

Because they went to Japan as foreign tourists, most of the sansei had relatively little interaction with ordinary Japanese beyond brief encounters in restaurants, hotels, and department stores, where they were in the privileged position of customers and treatment was flawlessly polite and courteous. In fact, Cathy felt that the treatment at restaurants was *too* polite. "As a matter of fact, I thought it was too much bowing and scraping," she remarked. "I felt uncomfortable with it. And it just continued. It wasn't just 'Hello, welcome.' It was every single waiter and waitress and the cook and the sushi chef. I felt like saying, 'Just leave me alone!'"

Although the sansei do not speak Japanese (despite looking Japanese), they generally reported that the Japanese were not disconcerted nor did they react negatively as a result. Instead, they were treated in a respectful and friendly manner. According to Cathy:

> I think the Japanese handle people like us very well. Actually, much better than how Americans treat foreigners who don't speak English or people of color. They never stared at us, were always courteous and very patient with us. And it helped that we could say a few words in Japanese. I didn't feel the Japanese treated me differently.

Although some of my interviewees had heard that Japanese react negatively to people who look Japanese but cannot speak the language, they
were glad that this did not happen during their trip. "No one stared
at me, or wondered who the hell I was," Doug recalled. "Even in the
countryside, people behaved respectfully. There was not one negative
experience in Japan except for leaving!" Shannon admitted that she
would often talk and laugh loudly on the bus or subway with the other
American tourists she was with, but they were still treated extremely
well for the most part in Japan. She remembered only one instance of
people looking at and talking about them and another instance when
an elderly woman changed seats on the subway because they were too
noisy.

The Japanese could often tell that the sansei were Americans because
they spoke English, dressed in a causal manner, and acted like foreigners, although other Japanese occasionally assumed they were tourists
from Asian countries (see also Yamashiro 2011:1511–1512). They were also
sometimes part of a tour group that consisted of other Americans (or
Japanese Americans). In fact, a few times, Japanese tried to communicate with them in English or were even eager to try out their English
with Americans. As was the case with the shin-nisei, a couple of my
interviewees recounted occasions when they were treated favorably because they were Americans (see also Yamashiro 2011:1512–1513). Kate,
who lived in Japan as an exchange student, recalled that

> [the Japanese] were very friendly. And the nicest thing was that we could
> be speaking English on the train and somebody would turn around and
> ask us where we were from. And then, they were so excited to meet us
> and wanted to invite us over, just because we were from the U.S. A num-
> ber of people were just like that, so open and very friendly.

Kate actually expected Japanese to be not as friendly to foreigners who
are Japanese descendants as they would be to the white American students on the exchange program. "I thought they wouldn't care about me
because I look Japanese and not American and white," she said. "But
people were still very friendly and interested in me because I'm from
the U.S." In fact, Carla, the former flight attendant who had flown to
Japan many times in the past, was the only sansei who has had negative

experiences interacting with the Japanese. "It's because they all know that I'm not Japanese," she explained. "And then they all look at me with disdain. And when I do speak, they look at me with disdain. It's like I mean you can tell right off that I'm not Japanese. I don't like that kind of treatment."

Despite their generally positive experiences, because most sansei have been to Japan for only brief vacations, few have developed any sustained and long-term transnational connections with their ethnic homeland. Cathy is the only sansei interviewee who continues to travel to Japan each year to visit Japanese friends whom she met through her previous work in the Boy Scouts. Only a few of the sansei have met their Japanese relatives in Japan or have any contact with them. For example, while Carol's relatives were excited to see her and claimed she looked exactly like her grandmother when she was young (they even showed her old photos), she could not communicate with them[8] and did not stay in touch with them after she left Japan. Several others did want to meet their relatives, but had no idea how to find them.

Despite the positive experiences the sansei had in their ethnic home-land, it is not surprising that such short vacations as foreign tourists did not make them feel more connected to their ethnic roots and heri-tage. As is the case with the prewar nisei, their sojourns were too brief and their engagement with Japan too limited to have any significant, long-term impact on their ethnic consciousness. "It was a good experi-ence, but it was just like seeing another foreign city and country, like the other ones I've seen," Walter noted. "It was just like going to France or something."

"I didn't go there because I wanted to explore my roots," another noted. "It was a nice country, but a completely foreign country as far as I'm concerned."

It was interesting that Kate, who had lived in Japan and studied Jap-anese, was the only sansei who felt some connection to the Japanese based on possible shared cultural heritage.

There was this ease that I didn't expect to feel being in Japan. It was inter-esting because I didn't speak Japanese fluently. I could only understand a little bit but I looked like I understood enough that I fit in right away. There was something about being of Japanese ancestry. . . . A lot of people said, "Did you speak Japanese growing up?" And of course, I didn't. It must have been the way I nodded or just . . . maybe there was a Japanese-ness about me that they found familiar.

Kate also remarked that she "felt a little bit more Japanese" after living in Japan. "I think it was learning the language and culture," she elaborated. "I don't know if I felt more tied to my ancestry. It was more that I was pleased I could finally communicate with my grandma [in the United States] a bit more. I also realized some of the things my parents had been doing were based on their Japanese upbringing and not just standard parenting practice. There was a cultural reason for it."

## Conclusion: Culturally American, but Racially Foreign

By most standard indices, third-generation Japanese Americans are assimilated and socioeconomically incorporated into mainstream American society, even when compared to their prewar nisei parents. They are better educated and have higher socioeconomic status, and a good number of them have intermarried with white Americans. Mean-while, they are more disconnected from their ethnic heritage, since most grew up in Americanized settings primarily with whites and never felt a strong minority ethnic identity or cultural differences. As a result, the sansei have generally not retained the Japanese language or significant cultural traditions and almost none of them have meaningful transna-tional connections to their ethnic homeland.

In some ways, this is an outcome of the assimilative trajectory ad-opted by their prewar nisei parents, who had stressed their American identities and cultures and had scattered from former ethnic commu-nities to mainstream, white suburbs. Not only are the sansei another generation removed from their ethnic homeland; they generally grew up in a period when the United States was overwhelmingly white and the cultural assimilation of immigrants and ethnic minorities was both expected and normative.

However, the ethnic experiences of the sansei are also an active re-sponse to the ethnic and geopolitical environment in which they were raised. They were influenced by the ethnic activism and pride of the Asian American movement, the gradual emergence of multicultural ideologies after the 1960s and 1970s, the global rise of Japan as a respected, advanced industrialized nation, and a significant reduction in discrimination against Japanese Americans. Therefore, they tend to acknowledge the impact of a positively regarded Japanese cultural heritage to a greater extent than the prewar nisei, even if it is only at the level of ethnic consciousness. They also tend to express considerable pride in being Japanese Americans.

Nonetheless, the sansei continue to feel quite culturally assimilated and Americanized and show considerably less interest in their ethnic roots or ancestral ties to Japan than other generations of Japanese Americans. Because less than half of my interviewees have visited Japan, and did so primarily as tourists, their ethnic homeland remains a completely foreign country. Although they had quite positive experiences in the country, Japan it is not a source of ethnic roots or identity for them. Their pride in their ethnic identities is therefore mainly a product of the history and accomplishments of Japanese Americans in the United States.

However, despite their almost complete Americanization and cultural assimilation, third-generation Japanese Americans remain racial minorities and are still not regarded as real Americans. Instead, they continue to be racialized as foreign by mainstream Americans, who tend to view all Asians as immigrants and often do not recognize significant generational differences within this population. Since such processes of racialization are important for understanding how third- and fourth-generation Japanese Americans ethnically position themselves in American society, it will be the focus of the next chapter before I move on to the fourth-generation yonsei in Chapter 5.

4

# The Struggle for Racial Citizenship among
# Later-Generation Japanese Americans

## Forever Foreigners

As indicated in the previous chapter, Japanese American sansei are culturally and socioeconomically well integrated in mainstream American
society.[1] The assimilative legacy of the third-generation sansei has in
turn influenced the upbringing of their fourth-generation yonsei children, who are similarly raised in white suburban environments and lead
very Americanized lives. Therefore, as a number of researchers have
claimed, the cultural assimilation of later-generation Japanese Americans is quite advanced, and the influence of their Japanese heritage has
become quite minimal and symbolic (Akiba 2006:163, 165; Spickard
1996:145–147, 159; Tuan 2001:106, ch. 3). As a result, their daily lives are
not that different from those of white Americans.

Nonetheless, third- and fourth-generation Japanese Americans continue to be racialized as perpetual foreigners simply because of their
Asian appearance, an experience quite common among all Asian American groups (Kim 2008:4–5, ch.8; Lowe 1996:5–6; Min 2006a:93; Park
2005:6–8; Tuan 2001). Unlike white ethnics of southern and eastern European descent, who have disappeared into the majority "white" population and have become ethnically unmarked Americans (Jacobson 1999;
Roediger 2005), upward socioeconomic mobility and cultural assimilation among later-generation Japanese Americans have not guaranteed
them full acceptance as Americans for two reasons. Because of an U.S.
national ideology that equates Americanness with being "white" (Dyson
1999:219–220; Zhou and Gatewood 2000:21), racial minorities are more
likely to be seen as foreign, or not really American. In addition, most
Asian American communities are a product of large-scale Asian immigration to the United States after 1965 and are still primarily of the first
and second generations, with immigrants outnumbering the American-

born generations. Because almost 70 percent of Asian descendants in the United States are foreign-born (Min 2006b:42–43), those with an Asian racial phenotype are often assumed to be immigrant foreigners (Tuan 2001:38–39). In this sense, racial meanings are determined not only by nationalist discourses but by immigration patterns as well.

Although the Japanese American community is older than most other Asian American ones, and less than a quarter of Japanese descendants in the United States are first-generation immigrants from Japan (Akiba 2006:159–60), the "Asian as immigrant" image is indiscriminately applied to them because of the tendency of mainstream Americans to view Asian Americans as a homogeneous ethnic group instead of recognizing internal differences within this panethnic community (Kibria 2002a:70–75; Kim 2008:210; Tuan 2001:21–22). The status of Asian Americans as non-white racial minorities is therefore fundamentally different from that of African Americans. Although African Americans continue to experience socioeconomic marginalization and serious discrimination and are positioned lower on the racial hierarchy than Asian Americans, they are not regarded as foreign because they have been in the United States for a much longer period of time.

It may not be that surprising that second-generation Asian Americans are often treated as racialized outsiders. However, the fact that Japanese American sansei and yonsei are still subject to such exclusionary practices despite being in the United States for generations indicates that in many ways, their racial appearance continues to be a much more socially visible marker than their cultural assimilation as Americans. In fact, other later-generation racial minorities seem to have similar experiences. For instance, later-generation Mexican Americans (especially those who do not look white) are often mistaken as immigrant foreigners because of continued large-scale immigration from Mexico (Jiménez 2010: ch. 5; Rosaldo 1999:256). Asian minorities in other countries are also marked as foreign, including Japanese descendants in Latin America (Tsuda 2003:58–65).

This chapter will examine the various ways in which later-generation Japanese Americans in the American Southwest are racialized as perpetual foreigners in their daily interactions with other Americans and how this leads to essentialized assumptions that they are also culturally foreign. Although this is not as pernicious as the purely discriminatory racialization that the prewar nisei suffered in the World War II period, it is still a form of racialized exclusion and is especially important for understanding the ethnic experiences of both third- and fourth-generation Japanese Americans. Most of them contest their racialization in various ways in an attempt to change such hegemonic ethnic perceptions. The denial of their Americanness by virtue of their race ultimately brings their status as Americans citizens into doubt, making their daily lives a struggle for racial inclusion and belonging, or what I have called racial citizenship.

Such responses are most prevalent among the sansei, who are no longer connected to their Japanese cultural heritage and are therefore most bothered by the fact that they are still racialized as foreign despite being culturally American. Although fourth-generation yonsei have similar concerns and experiences, their continued racialization as "Japanese" has also provoked an ethnic reawakening based on a desire to recover their ancestral heritage, as will be discussed in depth in the next chapter. While the racial marginalization of Asian Americans is often mentioned in the literature, there are relatively few in-depth, ethnographic analyses of how it is manifested in their daily lives or considerations of its implications for racial citizenship and ethnic heritage, especially for later-generation Asian Americans.[2]

## Racial Citizenship and Rights

The continued racial marginalization of later-generation Japanese Americans as immigrant foreigners indicates that despite their socioeconomic and cultural incorporation into American society, they are still not considered real and full citizens. Citizenship is the conferral of basic rights on individuals and groups based on membership in social and national communities. Although it is often associated with liberal universalism and equality, citizenship entails an inherent tension between inclusion and exclusion (Bloemraad, Korteweg, and Yurdakul 2008; Joppke 1999:660), since definitions of who is a legitimate member of the nation (and deserving of rights) involves the marginalization and exclusion of those who do not belong to the national community.

Although American-born ethnic minorities have secured legal citizenship (and civil rights) in the United States through the country's *jus soli* nationality laws (wherein citizenship is granted by place of birth), this does not always guarantee them full social membership in the national community and access to equal social rights, or what can be called *social citizenship* (Kim 2008:14; Park 2005:2, 4). Since social citizenship is based on the socioeconomic and cultural criteria necessary for national belonging and membership, those who do not meet such criteria can be excluded. For instance, the socioeconomically dispossessed are not always granted full social rights in contrast to those who have attained upward economic mobility and better integration in mainstream society. Likewise, ethnic minorities are often socially excluded and marginalized from the national community because of their cultural and racial differences, leading to the denial of some basic social rights. Therefore, both social class and ethnic inequalities can become barriers to social citizenship. Although the classic work on social citizenship by T. H. Marshall (1950) focused on its social class aspects by examining the eventual expansion of social welfare rights to the British working class,[3] he did not consider the cultural and racial dimensions of social citizenship (Bauböck 2001; Bloemraad, Korteweg, and Yurdakul 2008:157).

For ethnic minorities of immigrant origin, social citizenship and belonging in the national community often require the adoption of what is considered the majority or dominant national culture (Castles and Davidson 2000:124). Such cultural membership in the nation can be acquired through cultural assimilation or it can be externally imposed, for instance through what Aihwa Ong (1996) calls "cultural citizenship," the production of cultural beliefs and practices necessary for national belonging through the normative disciplinary forces of state and civil institutions that produce consenting subjects.[4]

However, some form of assimilation is not the only pathway to cultural inclusion in the nation-state. Marginalized ethnic minorities can also claim cultural citizenship by demanding recognition as legitimate members of the national community who deserve basic social rights despite their cultural differences from mainstream society (Flores 1997:262; Rosaldo 1994, 1999). This involves building minority cultural communities and claiming public spaces of empowerment and protest. The possibilities of such cultural citizenship for ethnic minorities have become greater in countries like the United States, which have adopted a multicultural ideology that allows cultural minorities to be accepted as social citizens without full cultural assimilation.

In contrast to social class and culture, race has not been seriously considered as another aspect of social citizenship that can determine who is included and excluded from the national community. National belonging is defined not only by socioeconomic integration and cultural characteristics but also by race. Although some societies have multiracial conceptions of nationhood,[5] others have monoracial notions of national membership. In those cases, those who do not fit the dominant racial category are often not considered part of the nation and can be racially marginalized and deprived of fundamental social rights. However, unlike the social class and cultural dimensions of citizenship, which allow ethnic minorities to strive for greater national inclusion through socioeconomic mobility and cultural assimilation, the racial dimension of citizenship is harder to negotiate, since visible racial characteristics cannot be easily changed and represent the more primordial aspect of ethnicity.

Therefore, ethnic minorities who are marginalized on the basis of race must claim racial citizenship by demanding inclusion in the national community and equal access to social rights despite their racial differences. In this sense, racial citizenship involves a type of claims-making like cultural citizenship and can involve collective mobilization and activism. However, it is also a part of the daily struggle among minorities for racial belonging and social justice. If such struggles are successful, they can cause dominant notions of citizenship to be reconsidered in more inclusive and multiracial ways, leading to the conferral of equal social rights to racial minorities as full members of the nation.

Although Rosaldo includes race in his definition of cultural citizenship (1994:57), others define the concept mainly in cultural terms (Flores 1997; Kymlicka 1995; Stevenson 2003). I argue that it is useful to maintain the distinction between cultural and racial citizenship since not all ethnic minorities are defined (and excluded from the national community) by *both* cultural and racial differences. This is especially true for culturally Americanized later-generation ethnic minorities (like Japanese Americans and non-white Hispanic Americans) for whom only racial and not cultural difference prevents them from being accepted as real Americans. In other words, their struggle is for racial citizenship, and not cultural citizenship per se.

Because Japanese Americans have been in the United States for longer than other Asian American groups, they have generally shown higher rates of socioeconomic success and cultural assimilation (Akiba 2006:164–165; Jiobu 1988; Spickard 1996:143). As a result, later-generation sansei and yonsei have certainly met the socioeconomic and cultural criteria for social citizenship and national belonging. However, because American national identity continues to be monoracially defined as "white,"[6] they lack the racial attributes necessary to be fully recognized as Americans and are often seen as foreigners simply because of their physical appearance. As one of my Japanese American interviewees succinctly put it: "We have never been really accepted as American because we're not white. If you're not white, you're a foreigner." In this sense, racial barriers to social citizenship, because of their apparently primordial nature, are more difficult to overcome than the socioeconomic and cultural barriers to national membership.

## Japanese Americans as Racialized Foreigners

Despite their Americanization, most of my sansei and yonsei Japanese American interviewees continued to be racialized as noncitizen outsiders instead of as real Americans, especially by those who are not acquainted with them personally. A number of them said explicitly that Americans make no distinctions between Japanese Americans and Japanese from Japan. "I've never heard my associates [at work] differentiating between them," Walter Aoyama, a sansei, claimed. "A Japanese is a Japanese, regardless of whether you are from here or from Japan." According to Cathy, an elderly sansei, "They just can't tell the difference, definitely. We speak English without an accent, but our faces are still Japanese, so they see us that way. It's because lots of people are not aware there is a substantial Japanese American community. So they assume Japanese-looking people are all from Japan."

Likewise, a sansei employee at the Japanese American National Museum (JANM) in Los Angeles noted: "We have people who come in here and ask, 'Where are the samurai swords?' It's like they see 'Japanese American' [on the sign at the museum entrance] but only the 'Japanese' part registers in their heads." According to a former yonsei employee of JANM, when she presents her resume to prospective employers, they often assume she worked at some Japanese art museum. "They don't notice the 'American' part of the name and just focus on the 'Japanese' part," she remarked. "I have to constantly explain to them that it was a museum about Japanese descendants born and raised in the U.S."

Undoubtedly, the racialization of Japanese Americans as non-American foreigners is most often manifested by the ubiquitous question "Where are you from?" which is asked by strangers or others who encounter them for the first time. When the expected answer is not forthcoming, the follow-up question is often: "Where are you *really* [or originally] from?" (Kitano 1993:5; Tuan 2001:141–142). Other variants are: "Where were you born?," "What is your nationality?," "Are you American?," "How long have you lived in the U.S.?," and "When did you come over [to the United States]?"

Although such questions are seemingly innocuous and inoffensive, they indicate that peoples of Asian descent in the United States are considered to be non-American outsiders (Chan and Hune 1995:205; Kibria 2002a:81–83), and therefore lack racial citizenship and belonging. Such questions continue to be directed not only at second-generation Japanese Americans, but those of the third and fourth generations solely on the basis of their physical appearance. In fact, Sherry Okamoto, a yonsei, initially even had trouble understanding the meaning behind such questions:

> When I was asked where I was from at some cocktail party, I couldn't understand what people were getting at. So I thought maybe they wanted to know where I was raised, so I'd say "Los Angeles." Then, when they asked "No, where are you originally from?" I thought maybe I was being asked where I was born, so I'd say "Seattle." Recently, it finally began to dawn on me that maybe they thought I was from some Asian country because of the way I look. When I realized this, it really bothered me! I was like, my family has been here in the United States longer than many whites. Why do I continue to be seen as some kind of foreigner?

In this manner, later-generation Japanese Americans have come to realize that such questions are often based on mistaken assumptions that they are foreign nationals and not American citizens.

Even when Japanese Americans are not directly mistaken for foreigners, mainstream Americans sometimes remain curious about their immigrant origins or ethnicity. In this regard, my informants were also asked, "What are you?" or "Are you Chinese?" "Are you Japanese?" although some of them were asked about their ethnic origins in more polite ways. Others were asked "Where were your parents born [or where are they from]?"

In addition to these types of persistent questions, my interviewees gave other types of examples of how they were racialized by strangers as non-American foreigners simply because of the way they look. Dan Matsushita, a sansei who used to be part of the United States volleyball team, recounted such an incident that occurred in Indianapolis:

> We were on tour and playing the Chinese national team. We were leaving the hotel and getting on the bus to play our match. When I walked up to the bus with my American teammates, the bus driver said, "The Chinese bus is over there." It was really surprising because I was wearing the American team jersey like the rest of my teammates! The only difference was that I was Asian and was shorter than everyone else.

Thus, even when Japanese Americans display overt symbols of their Americanness, their foreign racial appearance can often have a greater impact on how they are ethnically perceived.

Likewise, Shannon Suyama, a third-generation sansei, who recently married a Caucasian man from New Zealand, told me that people always assume that her husband is the American, despite his accent, and that she is the immigrant, despite her lack of an accent. This was especially apparent when they both went down to the local U.S. Citizenship and Immigration Services office to fill out his immigration papers:

> So we go up to the window, [my husband] hands the form over to the man behind the glass, and he looks at it and says, "Oh, she left something blank. You need to talk to her." He was speaking to my husband and saying, "What is her current address in the U.S.?" or something like that. And it became very apparent to me that he thought *I* was the immigrant filling out the form and my husband was helping me! He just made that assumption.

Japanese Americans are also sometimes referred to as "you/your people." When I was at a local bar with a sansei man (after an interview), to our surprise, we were both carded when we ordered drinks. After the bartender looked at our IDs and realized we were both in our late thirties, he said "Well, it's because you people eat all that healthy Asian food!" A yonsei interviewee, Carrie Kawamura, remembered being asked at a party by an elderly lady about "your people." "I told her I was part of a sorority in college and she wondered why a college sorority would accept 'your people,'" she said. "It was pretty insulting."

Although some scholars give the impression that majority whites are responsible for the racialization of Asian Americans (Kibria 2002a:92–96; Kim 2008: ch. 8; Louie 2004:103–108; Tuan 2001), it must be remembered that ethnic minorities also engage in such practices, often as frequently as whites. As a shin-nisei, I have been asked the "Where are you from?" question or regarded as a Japanese foreigner by Hispanics, blacks, and Native Americans, as well as by Arabs and Indians in the United States. "I guess Native Americans have the right to ask anyone where they are from, even whites," one of my yonsei interviewees noted. "It's like, 'I've been here for 10,000 years, where are you from?'"

In fact, I have noticed that Asian immigrants tend to be the ones who are most interested in the foreign origins of Asian Americans. "Whites may not care too much what kind of Asian you are," a sansei woman remarked. "But Asian people, they care. They want to know, are you Chinese? Japanese?"

"When whites ask about your ethnic background, they are pretty subtle about it," another interviewee observed. "They ask questions like 'Where are you from?' 'What is your national origin?' But when Asians want to know, they are much more blunt, like, 'You Chinese? No? You Korean? No? You Japanese?'"

The racial marginalization of sansei and yonsei as perpetual foreigners often leads to the perception that they are culturally foreign as well. As a result, Japanese Americans are often essentialized by racial appearance as people who lack the cultural attributes necessary to belong to the national community. As usual, language is the primary cultural marker of national belonging and citizenship. Sometimes, Japanese Americans are simply assumed to lack facility in English because of their race. Although she is fourth generation, Sherry claimed that some people speak

English to her more slowly and in a patronizing manner when she first meets them, or even ask, "Did you understand that? Did that make sense?" She also said that one professor in college asked her whether she would understand course materials better if they were explained to her in Japanese.

Therefore, although later-generation Japanese Americans are culturally assimilated, they continue to be marked as culturally foreign by their racial appearance. Their unaccented English does not always guarantee that they will be regarded as real Americans. As is the case with other Asian Americans, a significant number of my informants have been told, "You speak English so well" or asked, "Where did you learn to speak English so well?" In other words, it seems that some mainstream Americans still have difficulty accepting that someone with an Asian face can speak English like a native. Instead of concluding that such individuals must be Americans, the assumption sometimes seems to be that they are foreign nationals who learned to speak English surprisingly well.

There are other cases when sansei and yonsei Japanese Americans are racialized as culturally foreign despite their Americanization. I have witnessed or been told about numerous occasions when people try speaking Japanese with Japanese Americans. Several interviewees also reported instances when people wondered whether they celebrate American holidays. One sansei man was asked by a woman at a Christmas party, "Do they play Christmas carols in your country?" In this case, her husband interjected by saying "Honey, I think this *is* his country!" Likewise, another Japanese American recounted an experience at a grocery store during Thanksgiving:

> So I go up to the counter with a can of cranberry sauce and the clerk says, "Oh, I didn't know you people celebrated Thanksgiving!" Although I didn't bother to correct her, I was like, what do you mean, "You people"? First of all, I'm American, and second of all, do you think Japanese Americans eat sushi for Thanksgiving? We eat turkey, just like other Americans!

Although such treatment as racialized outsiders is generally limited to first-time encounters with strangers, for some Japanese Americans, it is quite persistent. Indeed, only a relative few sansei and yonsei said that they are *not* racialized as foreigners or that this happened only a few times in the past, such as when they visited other parts of the United States where there are few Asian Americans. Two of my informants believe that their American first names prevent them from being seen as foreigners. A few others noted that their cultural assimilation marks them as American, despite their foreign appearance. "I sound and behave too American to be seen as Japanese," a sansei remarked. "I think when I open my mouth, people can tell I'm American. Or at least that I'm no FOB [fresh off the boat]."

In general, however, it is quite apparent that most later-generation Japanese Americans cannot escape their persistent racialization and cultural essentialization as noncitizen foreigners in spite of their cultural assimilation and socioeconomic integration in mainstream American society. Such treatment makes them acutely aware that although they have been in the United States for many generations, they are still not seen as real Americans, but are forever essentialized as a foreign Japanese ethnic minority simply because they lack the racial features needed to be considered part of the American nation. Of course, later-generation white Americans are never mistaken as foreigners—which shows the power of race to define who is included in the national community as a social citizen and who is excluded. Indeed, race seems to matter more than cultural assimilation in the definition of who is American and who is not.

## Claiming Racial Citizenship: Japanese American Reactions to Racialization

When later-generation Japanese Americans find their status as Americans questioned because of their racial differences, they are forced to engage in everyday struggles to claim their racial belonging and citizenship by demonstrating that despite their apparently foreign appearance, they are American citizens by birthright and culture. However, the effectiveness of such Japanese American attempts to challenge their racialization varies, and their ability to eventually expand dominant notions of American racial membership to include non-white ethnic minorities remains uncertain.

A majority of my Japanese American interviewees are not that bothered by their racialization as foreigners and the constant questions they are asked about their supposed immigrant origins. They tend to explain such questions as a result of ignorance, confusion, simple curiosity, or inevitable because of the way they look and do not take them personally or become offended and angry. However, a minority said they are bothered and really dislike such treatment, although most do not respond aggressively. In general, I found that second-generation Japanese Americans are less bothered by the mistaken assumption that they are foreigners since they are only one generation removed from Japan. "I don't really care. It doesn't bother me," one of them said, expressing a sentiment shared by others of his generation. This was especially true for the shin-nisei, who are more closely tied to their ethnic homeland and cultural heritage and are therefore less troubled when they are regarded as foreigners.

In contrast, third- and fourth-generation Japanese Americans generally react more negatively to their foreignization, perhaps because of the absurdity of having to defend their Americanness even when their family has been in the United States for generations. Carol Hashimoto, a sansei, described her reaction as follows:

> I got really tired of people coming up to me all the time and looking at me, and then asking "What are you?" I HATED that! And I knew exactly what they were asking. So when I got to college, I started to ask people, "What do you mean what am I? What are you asking?" And they said, "What's your nationality?" And so I gave them a hard time about that because it just bothered me that people didn't see me as American after three generations!

"When people come up to me and ask, 'What are you?' I just say, 'I'm human!' and walk away," another sansei woman claimed.

Other later-generation Japanese Americans who understand perfectly well that the "Where are you from?" question is about their assumed foreign origins somewhat defiantly refuse to give the answer that people are seeking and simply state their city of residence or birth. "I know what they are asking, but I don't give them what they want," George Okamoto explained. "When they ask, 'Where are you from?,' I say 'San Diego.' Then they say, 'No, where are you really from?,' and I say, 'I'm really from San Diego.' The conversation more or less ends there!" By refusing to reveal their ethnic background, Japanese Americans are able to exercise their agency in a subtle way and actively subvert the implicit racial marginalization involved in such questions. Such evasive responses shift the power dynamic in their favor by preventing the interrogator from automatically excluding them as the racialized other and allows them to insist on their racial citizenship as Americans.

As noted above, however, it is not just majority whites who ask such questions. So do people of color. During my visit to the San Diego Zoo with Cathy, an elderly sansei friend, we encountered a family with three children while we were watching an exhibit at the aviary. The mother suddenly asked us, "Where are you from?" "San Diego!" Cathy quickly responded in an almost defiant tone. The woman was not taken aback and instead said, "We're from Puerto Rico."

Although Cathy's type of response is quite typical among Asian Americans in general (Kibria 2002a:81–83; Tuan 2001:141–142), its implicit demand that their American citizenship be recognized may not always have the intended effect or actually change dominant perceptions of them as immigrant foreigners. For instance, even if Japanese Americans state that they are from an American city, they can still be perceived as Asian immigrants who have been living in that city for a while. Consider the following conversation I overheard at the San Diego airport between two white women:

> WOMAN 1: So you ask these people where they are from and they
> say something like "San Francisco" and I'm like, that's not what I'm
> asking you, I want to know your country of origin. But they don't an-
> swer because maybe they are sick of answering this question. I don't
> know why they are like that.
> WOMAN 2: Yeah, I know, it's strange. I don't know why they don't want
> to say where they're from. Asian countries are respected these days,
> so they shouldn't be embarrassed about it or anything.

Apparently, it had not occurred to these women that the apparent refusal of Asian Americans to "properly" answer the "Where are you from?" question is an attempt to assert their Americanness, not a wish to hide their Asian origins. Instead of realizing that "these people" are real Americans because they are from the United States, the women conflated Asian Americans with Asian foreign nationals.

When the "Where are you from?" question is followed up with questions such as "Where are you really [or originally] from?," sansei and yonsei often engage in what Mia Tuan (2001:141-142) calls an "ethnic game" and continue to refuse to reveal their ethnic origins so that they cannot be racially categorized as foreign. A good example was given by Barbara Kitamura, a yonsei:

> I was at this BBQ where I was the only Asian person, and someone comes up to me and asks, "Where are you from?" I said "San Diego." Then she asks, "No, where are you originally from?" I said "I was born in Chicago." But then she asks, "Where are your parents from?" I said, "They were born in California." "And what about your grandparents?" "They were born in Hawaii."

Again, Barbara's refusal to give the desired answer allows her to actively avoid the racialized exclusion implicit in such questions, thereby claiming her status as a native of the United States despite her apparently foreign phenotype.

When questioned about their supposed immigrant origins, some of my interviewees simply state that they are Japanese Americans born in the United States. Others used the term "Americans of Japanese descent/ancestry." However, a few informants cited examples where they continued to be treated as Japanese even after they clarified their status as Japanese Americans. "Most Caucasians don't want to hear the 'Japanese *American*' part," one sansei woman observed. "They just want to hear the 'Japanese' part." For instance, I was having lunch with a Japanese American family when a delivery man appeared at the door with a new coffee table. After moving the table to the living room and asking the husband to sign paperwork, the delivery man asked, 'Are you Japanese?' The husband said 'I'm a third-generation Japanese American.' As the delivery man left, he said, 'OK, sayonara.'" A more extreme example was given by another interviewee:

> So I go to this local Subway, the owner sees my name [on his credit card] and he starts with the whole "Oh, are you Japanese? *Konnichiwa! Genki desu ka*?" Then he starts saying he was in Japan, he really liked it, he has a good friend from Japan. I made it clear to this guy that I'm not from

Japan, I'm Japanese *American*, I was born here. But it doesn't seem to register in his head that I have nothing to do with the Japanese, and he keeps up the *"domo arigato, sayonara"* thing every time I go there and sometimes talks about Japan. He's a nice guy, but it makes me feel uncomfortable, so I just stopped going there.

In the face of such treatment, instead of calling themselves "Japanese American," some of my interviewees find it more effective to claim racial citizenship by simply insisting that they are "Americans." For example, according to Carol, "I always say 'I'm American.' I never put 'Japanese' in front of it. When people ask me, 'Are you Chinese or Japanese?' I say 'I'm American.' I am really adamant about that. And when someone asks, 'What are you?' I say, 'I'm American.'"

Other later-generation Japanese Americans claim racial belonging and citizenship by demonstrating that they are culturally Americanized even though they look Asian. As Nazli Kibria notes (2002:84-87), Asian Americans attempt to neutralize or deflect assumptions of their foreignness by deploying cultural symbols of their Americanness such as language, dress, and demeanor. For instance, Doug Ishimura, a sansei living in Los Angeles, makes an effort to display his Americanness to counter the foreigner treatment he sometimes receives:

When someone says, "Wow! You speak English so well!" it is quite jarring. I'm like "What?!?" and it sort of freaks me out. So I think the way for me to approach people is to come off as more American than anything else. So, for instance, when I meet someone, I'll go "Hey! What's up!" That way, they won't say, "Oh, are you from Japan?" because I'm more like them than not like them. So sometimes, I try to be more American than necessary.

Nonetheless, as noted earlier, the perception of Japanese Americans as "Japanese" sometimes continues to persist even after they clarify to others that they are Americans born in the United States. Therefore, they face continued pressure to be recognized as culturally American even after initial greetings and introductions. According to Carol:

When people ask me where I'm from, I always clear it up by saying I was born here and am a third-generation Japanese American. But I think they still can't get away from the "she's Japanese" notion. So in such cases, I try to speak a lot more [to show she doesn't have a foreign accent] and I just try to show that I'm very American. I make sure I don't mention things like Japan, sushi, or even my Toyota!

Some sansei and yonsei contest their racial marginalization as non-American citizens more forcefully. When they are mistaken as Japanese immigrant foreigners or assumed to be culturally Japanese, not only do they correct the error, but they use the occasion to "educate" those who are apparently ignorant or misinformed. One yonsei described his reaction when someone approaches him and speaks Japanese: "I say, 'Well, if you want to practice your Japanese with someone, that is fine. But I am a fourth-generation American and don't speak the language. My parents did not speak Japanese either. Neither did my grandparents.'" A few even strike back against their racial essentialization as foreigners, even at the risk of being a bit rude. For instance, Bob Nakamura spoke about his sansei daughter:

My daughter, Wendy, teaches public speaking at a local community college and her students are always amazed they have this Asian teacher and say, "God, Wendy, you speak English so well!" She responds by saying, "My family has been in the U.S. for three generations. That's why I speak it better than you!"

According to, Daniel Kushimura, another sansei:

The stuff you deal with every day when people say, "Where are you from?" I never took that very well when I was younger. I was more militant about it. I would get angry and say, "What do you mean?" And I'd lecture them about Japanese Americans, how we've been here since the late nineteenth century. Or I'd say, "So what's your name?" And then they'll tell me and I'd say, "Oh, is that Germanic?" And they'd say, "What?" and I'd say, "Well, since you were checking my ethnic background, I'm checking yours."

Like other Japanese Americans, Daniel asserts his agency by turning this type of racialized questioning against interrogators in order to demonstrate that he is just as American as they are.

Among my Japanese American interviewees in general, the prewar nisei are more vocal than shin-nisei about demanding racial inclusion because of the racism and discrimination they endured during the World War II period. Bob, a former president of the Japanese American Historical Society of San Diego and a prewar nisei, is most effective in this regard, using invitations to speak at local San Diego high schools about his internment experiences during World War II as an opportunity to challenge students' racialized assumptions:

> There are still some of them that look at me like I'm not American. I spoke to a class a year ago, and afterwards, a couple of the students came up and said, "Mr. Nakamura, when you first came in, we thought you were Japanese. But you're more American than anyone I've seen!" I got my message across, I think! So when I speak at these high schools, I ask them: "What's an American supposed to look like? Tell me, what's an American supposed to look like? An American is what is in your head and your heart, not what you look like or the color of your skin. Look around you, there are other types of Americans than just white ones." And they finally get it.[7]

In contrast, a minority of my interviewees respond to their racialization as "Japanese" in ambiguous ways or choose not to actively contest their foreignization and demand racial citizenship as Americans. Some of these are young shin-nisei, who feel more connected to Japan and their cultural heritage and are not as bothered by or even that conscious about being conflated with Japanese nationals. One shin-nisei who speaks Japanese fluently told me that when someone speaks to her in Japanese, she responds in Japanese. "If the person wants to practice some Japanese with me, I'm willing to oblige," she said. Other interviewees (nisei as well as some sansei and yonsei) mentioned that they respond to questions about their immigrant origins or ethnicity by saying they are "Japanese." "I know they just want to know my ethnic background, so I just say 'Japanese,'" a shin-nisei explained. "I guess I'm taking it for granted that I'm American, and they just want to know whether I'm Chinese, Korean, or Japanese descent."[8] However, such responses may exacerbate the tendency to confuse Japanese Americans (including those of the later generations) with Japanese from Japan.

A few of my interviewees do not insist on their Americanness even when they are clearly mistaken as Japanese foreigners because they figure that doing so is not worth the trouble, especially in public. Therefore, they forgo their right to claim racial citizenship. Sherry, who is fourth generation, described her reaction when a store clerk sees her name on her credit card and assumes she is from Japan:

> I mean, I don't even know how to react because the likelihood I'll ever see them again is very low. And there are people behind me in line, so I can't sit there and say, "No, I'm not Japanese" and go through the whole explanation. If I'm in a situation where it's easy to have a conversation about this, I may. But I also feel that sometimes people don't want to hear me make a big fuss about this.

I have also observed Japanese Americans engaging in "ethnic play" by poking fun, if not ridiculing, essentialized images of them as Japanese. However, they may do so at the possible risk of actually reinforcing such stereotypes. For example, while I was having lunch at a Mexican restaurant with other Japanese Americans after we worked at the local historical archives, Bob had the following amusing interaction with the waiter:

BOB: What kind of beer do you have?
MEXICAN WAITER: We have Corona, Tecate, Pacífico . . .
BEN: What about Asahi, Kirin, Sapporo?
WAITER: Sorry, we don't have Japanese beers here. You will have to go to Samurai Sushi for that.
BEN (LAUGHS): OK, *yo tengo un Corona muy grande* [I'll have a large Corona]. Oh, and I'll also need a fork, knife, and some chopsticks.
WAITER: In Mexico, we use our fingers (gesturing with his index and middle finger as if they were chopsticks).
BEN: What? No chopsticks? How do you expect me to eat Mexican food without chopsticks?

It is interesting that a person who demands that he be accepted as American despite his racial differences can also behave in a manner that undermines such efforts, even if it is in jest. However, Bob said he would not joke about his ethnicity in this manner in front of Caucasians.

It is also important to note that the racialization of Japanese Americans as foreign is mostly limited to initial encounters with strangers and is usually cleared up by correcting such mistaken assumptions. Although their racial essentialization as "Japanese" may persist in later interactions, most Japanese Americans feel that those who have become close acquaintances and friends accept them as Americans and do not treat them otherwise. According to Carol:

> When I meet someone or join a group or something and people initially think I'm an Asian foreigner, it gets cleared up quickly when I tell them I'm American and my family has been here for three generations. I think once people get to know me after a half hour or hour, it's fine and I feel accepted.

Likewise, Bob acknowledged, "Once people get to know us, they accept us as American. It's mainly the people that don't know me who look at me like I'm a foreigner."

Thus, as more mainstream Americans interact with and befriend culturally Americanized, later-generation Japanese Americans and Asian Americans, they will gradually be accepted into the national community as full social citizens and Americans. However, since only a relatively small number of mainstream Americans have friends and close acquaintances who are later-generation Asian Americans, the perception that all Asians are immigrants will continue to persist. As a result, Japanese Americans must continue to struggle in their daily lives to be recognized as Americans despite their racial differences.

## Conclusion: From Racialized Foreigners to Americans

It is quite apparent that ethnic minorities can be denied full social citizenship and national belonging on the basis of not only cultural difference, but racial difference as well. Because Japanese American sansei and yonsei have been in the United States for generations and are well integrated in mainstream society, they wish to be seen and treated like other Americans instead of being forever tied to their Asian immigrant origins. However, large-scale immigration from various Asian countries continues to give their racial phenotype a foreigner connotation, especially in a country where national membership as real Americans is often limited to those who look white. As a result, even later-generation Japanese Americans are racialized as perpetual foreigners simply on the basis of their Asian appearance and excluded from the national community despite their full cultural Americanization. Indeed, their racial visibility seems to have a greater impact on dominant ethnic perceptions of them than their cultural assimilation as Americans, making their ethnicity quite primordial. Upon meeting people for the first time, sansei and yonsei are often asked a barrage of questions about their presumed immigrant origins. In addition, their racial marginalization and treatment as non-American outsiders are often accompanied by essentialized assumptions that they are also culturally foreign.

Therefore, in contrast to later-generation white Americans, Japanese Americans must continue to endure the burden of race on a daily basis and must demand racial inclusion as Americans despite their status as non-white minorities. Such demands range from refusing to answer questions about their foreign origins, clarifying their status as later-generation Americans, attempting to correct ethnic misconceptions, culturally demonstrating their Americanization, and educating other Americans about Japanese Americans. However, such struggles for racial citizenship and national belonging among sansei and yonsei are uneven. Some contest their racial marginalization more effectively, while others do so in more ambiguous ways with uncertain outcomes or even decide to forgo such efforts altogether. In fact, the power of race to exclude later-generation racial minorities as noncitizens is so strong that even when the sansei and yonsei challenge their racialization, they sometimes cannot fully shake the dominant perception that they are still essentially "Japanese" and perpetually foreign.

What is at stake in such struggles for racial citizenship is not simply the right to be recognized as American. Because later-generation Japanese Americans are racially perceived as not truly belonging to the American nation, such denial of full social citizenship also indicates that they may be deprived of certain fundamental social rights as well, such as freedom from racial and ethnic discrimination (Castles and Davidson 2000:105–106, 110). A good number of the sansei and yonsei endured harassment and ridicule when they were children as well as some prejudice in the early postwar years (in the case of elderly sansei). Although most of them generally feel they have not been subject to direct prejudice or institutionalized racial discrimination in recent years, they continue to encounter instances of informal discriminatory behavior in their daily lives (see also Tuan 2001:79–80). This includes racial slurs and stereotypes, derogatory remarks (such as those related Pearl Harbor or World War II), negative reactions and comments by war veterans, resentment for their economic success, and poor service at restaurants and stores, especially when they are the only Asian customers. Others report how they have been associated with negative images of Japan and Japanese ethnic stereotypes or have been told in anger to go back to where they came from.

In addition, I was struck by how a significant number of my interviewees strongly suspect (or are even sure) that they have been subject to more formal discrimination when applying for jobs or promotions at work and feel that they face a glass ceiling, which prevents them from advancing to top management and administrative positions. They note how such positions are dominated by whites, and give examples of managers and supervisors who were seemingly reluctant or unwilling to hire or promote them to such top-level jobs because they are not white. Such discrimination solely on the basis of race indicates that racial citizenship involves the demand not only for national belonging but also for equal social rights as Americans. Japanese Americans have been involved in the struggle for racial citizenship since the 1930s, when discrimination against them was much worse that it is today (Hosokawa 2002; Takahashi 1982:40). An effort that began with the prewar nisei now continues with the sansei and yonsei.

The United States has come to terms with its multicultural diversity as an integral part of its national identity, enabling culturally different ethnic minorities to claim membership in the nation and access to equal rights to a certain extent (that is, cultural citizenship). However, the country has yet to become a fully *multiracial* nation that accepts racially different, non-white minorities of immigrant origin as true Americans. Because American national identity continues to be defined monoracially as white, even when ethnic minorities become culturally assimilated over the generations, they can still be excluded as not American on the basis of racial difference. Although later-generation Japanese Americans speak fluent and unaccented English and behave in Americanized ways, this has not been sufficient for them to be considered real American citizens and guaranteed full social rights. Because of its social visibility, race remains the primary way that identities are initially judged and often overrides cultural markers of citizenship in determining who belongs to the American nation.

Will Asian Americans achieve racial citizenship by eventually becoming "white" (or at least, honorary whites)? It is clear that the racial category of white is more a marker of social privilege and status than a purely biological phenotype (Zhou 2004:30). Although southern and eastern European immigrants during the nineteenth century were initially seen as racially distinct and inferior,[9] their descendants were eventually incorporated into the majority white population through cultural assimilation and socioeconomic mobility (Jacobson 1999; Roediger 2005), which in turn was possible because of their phenotypic similarity to the dominant Anglo American population (Waters 1990:2). In contrast, Asian Americans will continue to be racialized as non-white and foreign because of their greater perceived differences in physical appearance from white Americans.[10] As a result, their cultural Americanization and upward mobility will not lead to their eventual acceptance as "white" and fully American (Kim 2007; Zhou 2004:35).

Therefore, in order for racial minorities like Asian Americans who are destined to be non-white to successfully become legitimate members of the nation, currently monoracial and restrictive notions of Americanness must be replaced by more inclusive and multiracial conceptions of national belonging. Will Japanese Americans and other later-generation Asian Americans be able to effectively contest and challenge discriminatory and white-dominated racial formations that forever exclude them as the racial other?

Since large-scale immigration from Asia will not decrease for the foreseeable future, the Asian phenotype will continue to be perceived as foreign. However, the population of later-generation Asian Americans will also continue to grow and eventually outnumber Asian immigrants in the United States, as happened for Japanese Americans decades ago. As Americans increasingly interact with a growing number of U.S.-born, later-generation Asian Americans, they will become more accustomed to encountering people who look Asian but are fully Americanized, especially if Asian Americans continue to demand racial citizenship as true Americans. As a result, those with an Asian appearance may no longer be automatically associated with immigrant foreigners in the future and become more recognized as part of a multiracial American nation. Asian Americans may therefore eventually come to somewhat resemble African Americans, who are racial minorities but regarded as Americans because of their long history in the United States.

In states such as California, where the population of Asian Americans is quite high, there are already indications that their racial marginalization is somewhat abating. Some of my Japanese American informants in San Diego noted that they are mistaken less often as foreigners in California and that such treatment is more frequent in other parts of the United States. For instance, Cindy Kushimura, a sansei in San Diego, remarked:

> Japanese Americans have been very much accepted as part of the society here. People out here have met a lot of Asian Americans, so they kind of have that category for us. It's only out East or in the Midwest where people aren't used to us and don't understand who we are.

In fact, almost all of the relatively small number of Japanese Americans in my sample who claimed they are not regarded as foreigners live in San Diego or southern California. In general, my interviewees in Phoenix tended to report more instances of racialized exclusion. In addition, several Japanese Americans noted that such treatment used to be more prevalent in the past. In contrast, younger Americans are becoming more aware of the growing population of Asian descendants in the United States who have become Americanized and therefore no longer automatically associate them with foreign immigrants. These may be the first steps toward undermining current hierarchical racial formations and forcing America to become a more multiracial nation where race is less of an obstacle to national inclusion for later-generation Asian Americans, or at least where culture, instead of race, is used to judge who belongs to the nation as a social citizen.

5

# Ethnic Revival among Fourth-Generation
# Japanese Americans

## Assimilation and Ethnic Revival

Fourth-generation Japanese American youth have become increasingly interested in reconnecting with their Japanese ethnic heritage and homeland in recent years (Asakawa 2004; Takahashi 1997:210–212; Takamori 2011:26).[1] The yonsei are studying Japanese, majoring in Asian studies, and visiting Japan as college exchange students while others listen to Japanese popular music, watch Japanese TV, or participate in Japanese taiko drum ensembles in the local ethnic community.

It may not be surprising that second-generation Asian American youth would seek to retain their ethnic roots (Espiritu 1994; Kibria 2002b; Louie 2004; Min and Kim 2000) since they remain connected to a certain extent to their cultural heritage and countries of ethnic origin through their immigrant parents. Their ethnicity is a product of persistence and continuity from the previous first generation. In contrast, fourth-generation Japanese Americans have become completely Americanized and culturally assimilated. They had little exposure to the Japanese language and heritage culture while growing up in mainstream white suburbs and have lost their ties to the ancestral homeland of Japan. Why have they suddenly become so interested in recovering their Japanese ethnic roots and living in Japan, generations after their full cultural assimilation and social integration into mainstream American society?

The ethnic history of Japanese Americans who are descendants of prewar Japanese immigrants seems to be a story of progressive incorporation into mainstream American society over the generations (Kitano 1993; Montero 1980; Spickard 1996; Takahashi 1997; Tuan 2001: chs. 3, 5; Woodrum 1981). As noted in Chapter 1, after the prewar nisei were interned in concentration camps during World War II, many of them distanced themselves from Japan and their Japanese heritage and attempted to culturally assimilate and become socially accepted as Americans. The assimilation process continued among third-generation sansei as they experienced upward socioeconomic mobility, scattered into white suburban neighborhoods, and increasingly intermarried with mainstream Americans.

However, there are very few accounts of the ethnic experiences of fourth-generation Japanese Americans since there has been a serious dearth of studies about the yonsei. Although they are certainly not reversing the progressive assimilation of the earlier generations, they are definitely experiencing an "ethnic revival" and actively attempting to reconnect with their ancestral roots and distinctive cultural heritage. The yonsei in my research sample are recovering and recreating an ethnicity that was apparently lost among the previous generations of Japanese Americans.

Research in the 1960s and 1970s associated assimilation with the eventual eradication of minority cultural differences through the adoption of majority Anglo norms (Gordon 1964). Even Alba and Nee's reformulation of the concept of assimilation as a two-way attenuation of cultural and social differences between groups (usually minority and majority) assumes that the distinct ethnic heritage of immigrant-descent minorities weakens and disappears over time through a process of hybrid cultural mixing (1997:834, 841, 863). However, cultural and socioeconomic assimilation does not preclude the continuation and active production of ethnic difference, even for later-generation ethnic minorities. In fact, as this chapter illustrates, assimilation may instigate the search for a distinctive ancestral heritage and identity, especially among racial minorities, and is not always incompatible with ethnic difference.

Therefore, the history of immigrant-descent minorities should not be understood in a simple, linear fashion where assimilation progressively erodes ethnicity over the generations. Nor is the continued salience of ethnicity simply the result of its "persistence" through the generations because of the ability of ethnic minorities to hold off assimilative pressures, as emphasized by previous research on Japanese Americans (Connor 1974; Fugita and O'Brien 1991; Hieshima and Schneider 1994; Kendis 1989; Kurashige 2002; Masuda, Matsumoto, and Meredith 1970:205–206; Matsuo 1992; O'Brien and Fugita 1991; Spickard 1996:151; Wooden, Leon, and Toshima 1988; Woodrum 1981). Instead of relying on such common-sense assumptions about assimilation or ethnic persistence, we must analyze how each generation responds to a particular and changing set of historical and social circumstances.

## Racialized Ethnicity, Multiculturalism, and the Search for Cultural Heritage

Fourth-generation Japanese Americans have reconnected with their ethnic heritage for a number of reasons. In some ways, this ethnic revival is a product of the current historical moment. The rise of multiculturalism in recent decades and the celebration of ethnic diversity have certainly encouraged Japanese American youth to affirm their ethnic heritage as a source of distinctiveness and pride instead of losing themselves in the ordinary homogeneity of mainstream America (Takahashi 1997:210–211; Kibria 2002a:97; Louie 2004:6–7). The increasing prominence of Asian and Asian American Studies and study abroad programs on college campuses have also provided opportunities for yonsei youth to explore their ancestry and reconnect with their ethnic homeland in a globalized world where international experience is valued.

At the same time, the rise in Japan's international stature and economic power since the 1960s has considerably enhanced its image in the United States, which has led to increased American interest in Japanese popular and traditional culture. In contrast to the prejudice and discrimination that caused the prewar nisei to assimilate and distance themselves from their ancestry in the World War II period, the racialization of Japanese Americans no longer has such negative ethnic consequences. Because Japanese Americans are now socioeconomically successful, Americanized, and well-regarded, they are not subject to colorblind ideologies that stigmatize the ethnic differences of poor, less-educated, and unassimilated immigrant minorities and discourage them from maintaining their native cultures. In addition, because a vast majority of the yonsei are college-educated and middle class, they have educational opportunities and the economic means to actively engage in ethnic heritage activities and travel to Japan to explore their ancestral roots.

Nonetheless, multiculturalism and positive imaginings of Japan by themselves would not cause an ethnic awakening among culturally assimilated fourth-generation Japanese American youth unless they continued to be racially defined by American society as an ethnically different, culturally "Japanese" minority. Because of their status as racialized minorities, their ethnic revival is fundamentally different from the resurgence of ethnic identity observed among third-generation white ethnics decades ago (Hansen 1952; Jacobson 2006; Novak 1971). As Mary Waters notes (1990), later-generation white Americans continue to identify by ethnic origins, but their ethnicity is optional and symbolic. Because of generations of social mobility, cultural assimilation, and intermarriage, they can choose which parts of their mixed ancestry to emphasize, or simply forgo ethnic identification altogether and become ethnically unmarked "Americans" or "whites." In addition to its voluntary nature, ethnicity for whites has also become symbolic and consists of relatively superficial cultural activities such as eating ethnic food and participating in local festivals and has therefore ceased to have a significant impact on their daily lives. It no longer serves as the basis for social and community solidarity (Alba 1990), nor does it lead to any negative consequences, such as discrimination and lack of socioeconomic opportunity (Waters 1990:91–92).

In many ways, later-generation Japanese Americans resemble white ethnics because they have enjoyed similar rates of upward socioeconomic mobility (Akiba 2006:163, 165), live in middle-class suburbs, and have become culturally assimilated over the generations (Spickard 1996:145–147, 159; Tuan 2001: chs. 3, 5). This has even led to mistaken mainstream perceptions of Japanese Americans (and Asian Americans in general) as "honorary whites" or minorities that are "becoming white" (Okamura 2014:209–211; Zhou 2004). However, although later-generation Japanese Americans may now resemble whites socioeconomically, their ethnicity has not become completely voluntary and optional. As discussed in Chapter 4, despite their full cultural and social integration in mainstream American society, they continue to be racialized as "Japanese" because of their physical appearance.

Although multiculturalism is often equated with tolerance, inclusivity, and minority rights (unlike assimilation), it is embedded in systems of power like all ideologies and can have a somewhat coercive element, especially when it operates alongside racialization processes. In a multicultural society, racialized, non-white minorities like Japanese Americans are encouraged, if not expected, to retain and display their ethnic distinctiveness (Kibria 2002a:97; Louie 2004:6–7; Takahashi 1997:210–211), intensifying the significance of race as a marker of cultural difference. As Mia Tuan notes (2001:46), "Asian ethnics may feel compelled to identify ethnically even if it holds little meaning for them because others expect them to."

Because of the pressures of such racialized multiculturalism, ethnic revivals among non-white minorities are not simply voluntary personal choices, but indicate that ethnicity remains involuntary and primordial for such groups, even after they have been in the United States for generations. In contrast to ethnically unmarked, white Americans who do not face multicultural expectations to retain their ethnic heritage, Japanese Americans are assumed to be culturally different by virtue of their race and do not have the option of being non-ethnic, mainstream Americans. In effect, then, ethnicity continues to be somewhat obligatory for racially visible minorities even long after they have become culturally assimilated.

The multicultural racialization of fourth-generation Japanese Americans as "Japanese" conflicts with their complete Americanization and makes them acutely aware of their loss of Japanese cultural heritage. As a result, the yonsei have become concerned about their overassimilation to American society and have developed a strong desire to explore their ethnic background and reconnect with their ancestral origins. In this sense, their ethnic heritage is not a product of cultural persistence and continuity over the generations. Instead, it is precisely the cultural discontinuity created by assimilation and the loss of ancestral heritage that have caused the yonsei to nostalgically yearn for and revive their ethnicity.

Because the recovery of ethnicity among Japanese American youth is motivated by a racialized minority identity, it is deeper than the somewhat superficial appropriation of cultural symbols and casual participation in ethnic activities that characterize white ethnics (Gans 1979). Japanese American youth are making a more serious effort to directly reengage with their cultural heritage by studying Japanese, majoring in Asian or Asian American studies, learning Japanese cultural traditions, and living in Japan as students. Their search for cultural heritage does not simply occur in local ethnic communities, but has a more significant, transnational dimension.

The racialization of later-generation ethnic minorities as culturally foreign can thus instigate two divergent responses. On the one hand, they can assert their racial citizenship by emphasizing their cultural assimilation and national belonging (as shown by the sansei discussed in Chapter 4) or they can respond by reviving their ethnic heritage, as shown by the yonsei. Indeed, the yonsei have responded to their racialization in both ways: although they are bothered by the continued perception that they are "Japanese" and demand racial citizenship as Americans, they have also become concerned about the loss of their cultural heritage and wish to reclaim a distinctive ethnicity that will make them different from ordinary Americans.

Such divergent responses to racialization among fourth-generation Japanese Americans are not necessarily contradictory nor tinged with hypocrisy since they occur in different social contexts. In ordinary, everyday life (especially among whites), the yonsei are completely Americanized and want to be recognized as real Americans since their families have been in the United States for many generations. In contrast, they attempt to recover their lost Japanese ethnic heritage in their private lives, with their families, and in ethnic communities, as well as through academic pursuits and living abroad in Japan. For example, Sherry explained the bifurcated nature of her life as follows:

> I'm mostly American. I think if anything, the Japanese American side in me probably only comes out when I'm with other Japanese Americans or family. It's probably because other people that I interact with can't relate to that part of me. So with these people, by being more American, it kind of levels the playing field so that we have a basis to relate to each other.

For Japanese American yonsei, then, the desire to reconnect with ethnic roots does not conflict with their Americanized lives nor does it make them less culturally assimilated.

## The Racialization of Later Generation Japanese Americans as "Japanese"

### Ethnic Differentiation by National Origins

Chapter 4 examined in considerable detail how later-generation Japanese Americans are often racialized as foreigners and are denied racial citizenship as Americans. Such processes of exclusion also externally constitute racial minorities in specific ways and produce specific types of ethnic identities. A number of scholars have noted that Asian Americans are homogeneously racialized as Asians because of their physical appearance, which leads to panethnic Asian American identities and affiliations (Chan and Hune 1995:207; Kibria 2002a:70–75, 191; Pyke and Dang 2003:168; Tuan 2001:46; Zhou and Lee 2004:21).

However, the experiences of my Japanese American interviewees indicate that their racialization is much more specific and ethnically differentiated than scholars have understood. Most mainstream Americans are not simply content with knowing that a given person is Asian (which is quite apparent because of his or her phenotype), but wish to know whether the person is "Chinese," "Korean," or "Japanese." In this manner, racialization processes are not simply limited to the panethnic meanings attached to general racial categories, but are accompanied by additional information that provides further ethnic specificity to racial appearance. It is the tendency of Japanese Americans to be racialized by national origins that eventually leads to their desire to recover their particular ethnic heritage. If they were simply regarded as generalized Asians, they would not feel as much ethnic pressure to be specifically "Japanese."

Since race itself does not specify national origins, mainstream Americans use various inquiries and social markers to differentiate among different groups of Asian descendants. As discussed in Chapter 4, the main way that Japanese Americans are racially categorized as "Japanese" is through queries such as "Where are you from?" "Are you Chinese/Japanese/Korean?" and various related questions. My interviewees generally felt that such questions were based on the assumption that they are from Japan simply because of the way they look. One of them described her reaction as follows:

I think when people ask, "Are you Japanese? Are you Chinese? Are you Korean?" I don't think they are asking what type of American you are. It's not, "Are you Japanese American? Are you Chinese American?" The American part is pretty neglected, I think. The strong sense I get is that they are asking whether you are this specific ethnicity or nationality. Did you come from that country?

In other cases, Japanese Americans are simply identified as "Japanese" by their last names, obviating the need to ask about their ethnic background. This was especially true in stores, restaurants, and other businesses or agencies when their names are revealed on their credit cards or documents. Some of my interviewees remarked that Americans in general are familiar enough with Japanese names that they can recognize them or at least differentiate them from Chinese and Korean names. A typical example was given by a yonsei, Sherry Okamoto: "For instance, sometimes I go to a store to buy something and the cashier looks at my name on my credit card and says something like, 'Oh, Okamoto. You're from Japan! You guys have all that cool anime! So, what do you think about Ichiro Suzuki?'" Another interviewee recounted a similar experience at work:

> I'm sitting at my desk at work, and one of the workers from the mailroom comes by to deliver a package. I've talked to this person before and I've never told him I'm Japanese American or anything, but one day, he suddenly starts using the Japanese he knows with me, like *ohayo gozaimasu, sayonara*. I don't know how he was able to tell I'm Japanese descent. He must have seen my name on the package.

There are even a few isolated cases when Japanese Americans are identified as "Japanese" solely on the basis of racial appearance, without any other information such as a name. One time when I was at a grocery store with a Japanese American friend, he was greeted by the cashier in Japanese (he had not showed his credit card). I asked him afterward how the cashier was able to ethnically identify him. "I don't know," he admitted. "I've never seen the woman before. But some people say I look very Japanese, so that must have been the reason." A yonsei interviewee recounted a similar instance:

I was at some national park and I was walking along the road with my brother to the next overlook. This car pulls over and the driver asks us whether our car had broken down. We told him we just parked at the last overlook and are walking to the next. Then he says, *sumimasen* ["excuse me" in Japanese] and drives off. I have no idea how he was able to tell we were Japanese.

As such cases illustrate, although later-generation Japanese Americans speak unaccented English, behave in Americanized ways, and have been in the United States for generations, they continue to be racialized as "Japanese" simply because of their physical appearance, which shows the power of race to define social identities.

Therefore, although there is a tendency among mainstream Americans to view Asian Americans as a homogeneous ethnic group instead of recognizing internal differences within this panethnic community (Kibria 2002a:70–75; Kim 2008:210; Tuan 2001:21–22), relatively few of my interviewees felt they were simply seen as undifferentiated Asians. In fact, the ethnic specificity that some Americans demand was even a bit surprising to one of my sansei interviewees:

If I'm having conversations with white people, I do find myself occasionally saying that I'm Asian American instead of Japanese American. I think I have this sense that sometimes Japanese American is too specific for people to understand. But then I'm surprised that there are a lot of people who ask, "Are you Japanese? Are you Korean?" And I'm like, why is it significant for you that I'm Japanese instead of Korean? What difference is that going to make?

### The Cultural Essentialization of Japanese Americans

Once Japanese Americans are categorized according to their ethnic origins, they are also essentialized as *culturally* "Japanese" to a certain extent as well. Because of the tendency to conflate race and culture, peoples of Japanese phenotype/descent are seen as inherently connected to their Japanese cultural heritage, even if they were born in the United States and are fully Americanized. "Japan is as foreign of a country to me as Zimbabwe," one sansei woman remarked. "But people continue to think I'm not truly Americanized yet and that somehow, I can't leave my culture behind, that I have some innate connection to Japan."

Thus, Japanese Americans are often expected to be familiar with the Japanese language and culture (Tuan 2001:78-79) or have a natural affinity with Japan.[2] As noted above, my interviewees reported numerous instances of strangers using Japanese words when interacting with them (*konnichiwa*, *domo arigato*, *sayonara*, and so on). This is especially true of Americans who have studied Japanese (or lived in Japan) and are eager to try out their Japanese. Others simply assume Japanese Americans know a lot about Japan and ask them about the country or its culture or talk about their prior experiences in Japan.

Moreover, it is not only majority whites who culturally essentialize Japanese Americans. Japanese immigrants from Japan are among those who most often assume that those who are of Japanese descent are culturally Japanese as well. On numerous occasions when I have gone to Japanese restaurants or stores with Japanese Americans, waiters or staff have spoken Japanese to us. Kate Nishimoto, a sansei who studied Japanese in Japan, has had similar experiences: "Whenever I go to Fujiya [a local Japanese food store], which is regularly, they always speak to me in Japanese. I could answer in Japanese, but I never feel comfortable doing that because I don't use the language. So I usually answer in English."

Another striking incident occurred in San Diego, when I went to a sushi restaurant with my friend, Cathy, and one of her acquaintances, Ruth, who is an issei who came to the United States when she was a baby and does not speak any Japanese. She is, however, very involved in the Japanese American community and considers herself to be Japanese American. As usual, the Japanese waitress spoke to us in Japanese and continued to do so even when Cathy and Ruth did not respond. Once we were seated at the sushi bar, we entered into a conversation with the Japanese sushi chef, who was a very friendly man, and knew Cathy quite well, since she was a frequent customer. He began speaking to Ruth in Japanese, and when she told him she could not speak Japanese, he gave her a hard time for having forgotten the language. "So do you only eat hamburgers now? No Japanese food?" he teased her. I was surprised he continued to speak to her mainly in Japanese (despite the fact that he is proficient in English, having lived in the United States since 1972), making Ruth feel inadequate and uncomfortable. He also spoke some Japanese to Cathy (although he used more English with her), despite the fact that she does not understand the language.

The cultural essentialization of Japanese Americans as "Japanese" is, thus, not limited only to first-time encounters, but sometimes persists even among those who were acquaintances and friends. Some of my interviewees cited examples of acquaintances who know they are Japanese Americans born in the United States but continue to use Japanese words with them or ask them whether they can speak or read Japanese. Others ask them about Japan, Japanese popular culture or celebrities, or Japanese food. Doug Ishimura expressed his frustration with this type of treatment:

> I had these acquaintances in college who were these Japan-o-philes and asked me about Japanese food and samurais and ninjas. Or they were taking Japanese language classes and wanted to try out their Japanese with me or asked about Japanese phrases and grammar. I always had to clarify that I'm sansei and I have no association with Japan.

Several of my interviewees who grew up in white suburban neighborhoods with few Asian American families recounted instances in elementary school when a student from Japan was seated next to them in the classroom. "The teacher knew I wasn't from Japan," one of them recalled. "But I think she thought maybe I'd be able to communicate with the Japanese girl. It was the strangest thing! Of course, I wasn't able to translate. I don't speak a word of Japanese!"

In addition to the general expectation that later-generation Japanese Americans are familiar with Japan and the Japanese language, a few of my interviewees cited cases of being culturally stereotyped specifically as "Japanese" by acquaintances and friends. For instance, Kate, a university faculty member, noted how her students sometimes write in their teaching evaluations that she has high standards "because she is Japanese." Such essentialized perceptions can even persist in more intimate relationships. Some of my female interviewees have been ethnically stereotyped as "Japanese women" in past romantic relationships. For instance, consider the experiences of Carrie Kawamura, a fourth-generation yonsei:

I dated a Caucasian man who, after a while, suddenly tells me I don't act very Japanese. I was taken aback that he still saw me that way after all the time we had spent together and I realized that the main reason he was dating me was because he expected me to be like a Japanese woman. I sometimes feel like telling people, "No, I don't bow. I don't speak Japanese. I'm not quiet and restrained. I don't put my hand over my mouth when I laugh." I think that's one reason I ended up dating [and marrying] another Japanese American, because I didn't have to deal with such issues.

It is quite apparent that even later-generation Japanese Americans cannot escape the racialized perception that they are ethnically "Japanese" and forever associated with Japan despite their assimilation and socioeconomic integration in mainstream American society. Of course, few later-generation white Americans are asked questions about their ethnic origins or culturally essentialized because of their ancestry. "It is pretty bothersome because I know with white Americans, they don't have to feel the pressure of being racially stereotyped even before you get to interact with someone," Sherry lamented.

## Racialization and the Resurgence of Ethnicity
### Racialized Multiculturalism and Ethnic Heritage

The perpetual racialization of Asian Americans as a foreign ethnic group has been associated with various negative consequences, such as social marginalization, racial stereotyping and scapegoating, experiences of prejudice and discrimination, and hate crimes (Kim 2008:14–19, 212–219; Tuan 2001:39–45, 79-86; Wu and Song 2000:xvi–xviii). However, it has also contributed to the persistence of their ethnicity and identities over the generations and can provoke a renewed interest in ethnic roots and cultural heritage among even later-generation Asian Americans. Racialization therefore is not always associated with racism and its negative consequences.

Although fourth-generation Japanese Americans have come to re-semble white ethnics in a number of ways, they do not have the option of being ethnically unmarked, mainstream Americans because they continue to feel the racialized pressure to be ethnic in accordance with multicultural expectations. Such racialized multiculturalism creates considerable tension between their socially imposed "Japanese" identities and their full Americanization. Sherry eloquently referred to this as "a conflict between my race and my American self. Sometimes I feel kind of inadequate because I look Japanese but am totally Americanized."

However, in the context of today's multicultural pressures, when cultural diversity is not only cherished but also expected and somewhat obligatory among racialized minorities, my fourth-generation yonsei interviewees have decided to embrace their ethnic identity instead of distancing themselves from their heritage and ancestry (see also Asakawa 2004:xii). Sally Nakamoto elaborated as follows:

> I think just the way we look, we will always be seen as Japanese. If you're third-generation German American or something, you blend in. But if you're third-generation Asian American, or even fourth or fifth generation, you're still going to look Asian and never fully blend in. And so I think you can either deny your heritage or you can kind of embrace it and deal with it and be proud of who you are. It's a little subculture and your own group.

Other yonsei youth expressed similar multicultural sentiments valorizing ancestral roots and heritage in light of their status as racialized ethnics. According to Sherry,

> I feel that the face of America is changing. Eventually, there is going to be a mix of cultures and races. And that's not necessarily a bad thing. It's just where America is headed. So I think my only hope is that people who are Japanese American still remember their roots, their heritage and not to forget where they came from. Really embracing that part of themselves as opposed to ignoring it or pretending it doesn't exist.

Because fourth-generation Japanese Americans continue to face the racialized expectation that they are ethnically "Japanese" and recognize the value placed on cultural difference and diversity in a multicultural society, many of them seem concerned about their overassimilation to American society and their loss of ancestral heritage. The continued multicultural racialization of later-generation minorities can therefore intensify feelings of ethnic loss caused by assimilation. Although a few prewar nisei and sansei expressed regret over their loss of the Japanese language and culture, such sentiments were stronger among my yonsei interviewees, most of whom live in ethnically diverse, multicultural college environments where being ethnic is not only valued as "cool," but also somewhat compulsory.

This was quite evident in the "culture forums" of the Nikkei Student Union at the University of California at San Diego, which allowed yonsei youth to discuss their experiences. I was struck by how much of the discussion revolved around the loss of ethnic heritage and community among later-generation Japanese Americans and the tone of regret that characterized these conversations. Students mentioned numerous times how assimilated and "whitewashed" Japanese Americans are and how they have lost and forgotten their Japanese ethnic roots (leading to murmurs of agreement from the group). One participant spoke about how he has become so accustomed to American culture that he did not even know about Obon because he never went to Japantown, does not know anything about Japanese culture, and never went to school with other Japanese American kids. "I feel like my culture has been stripped away from me," he lamented. Another yonsei remarked: "We aren't even a Japanese American ethnic club because we don't even speak the language and half of our members aren't even Japanese [descent]. I mean, the stuff we do is what any American college kids would do. It's not Japanese."

In addition, there was considerable discussion about how Japanese Americans no longer participate in the ethnic community, visit Japantown (Little Tokyo) in Los Angeles, or even identify as Japanese American. Some do not even know the ethnic community exists. The yonsei at these meetings also pointed out how Japanese American organizations are shrinking because of lack of membership, how the Japanese American community has become scattered and lost its cohesion because of assimilation and suburbanization, how the Japantowns of the past have disappeared, and how the Japanese American population is declining through intermarriage with whites. "There are so few of us now compared to other Asians," a female student noted. "We are a dying race."[3]

Therefore, in contrast to the importance placed on cultural assimilation and upward socioeconomic mobility among prewar nisei and sansei, a good number of yonsei youth seemed to feel that the assimilation process has gone too far and caused Japanese Americans to sacrifice their ethnic heritage and roots. According to one yonsei, "My parents were told by their grandparents, 'You have to act American to move up in this society.' So they told them, 'It's OK not to learn Japanese. It's OK to be American.' Even though my parents haven't said it, I kind of feel a sense of regret that they haven't really kept up the Japanese and the traditions." Such concerns were also reflected in the culture forum discussions in which the students mentioned how Japanese Americans have stressed academic achievement and socioeconomic advancement to such an extent that they have moved away from the Japanese American community in order to become successful in mainstream American society through assimilation. "Lots of Japanese Americans gave up and discarded their Japaneseness and became strictly American because they were so concerned about money," one of the leaders of the group remarked. "They felt they no longer need the community and can make it on their own."

Such concerns about overassimilation and regret over the loss of cultural heritage have led to a strong nostalgic desire among my fourth-generation Japanese American interviewees to explore and recover their ethnic ancestry. In this sense, instead of eliminating ethnic distinctiveness, assimilation can encourage the active production of cultural difference among racialized minorities. "If anything, the interest in the Japanese American community is getting stronger among yonsei," Sandy Hashimoto, a college student observed. "We've become so assimilated that it's kind of like, 'Where are my roots? What's happened to my heritage?' A couple of my peers are going into Asian American Studies and getting in touch with their roots. So I certainly don't see it dying out. At least, we want to maintain what we have and not lose it further." Sherry expressed this sentiment most directly:

> We've become so whitewashed in the U.S. My Asian American friends call me at home and my dad picks up the phone and they say, "Wow, your dad sounds like he's white!" I feel like I've lost my culture. But people keep seeing me as Japanese because of the way I look. It used to bother me, and I ended up wanting to explore the Japanese heritage that I lost. So I decided to major in Asian studies, learn Japanese, and study in Japan. It's kind of a way to find out where I originally came from, to reconnect to my roots.

## Cultural Pressures from Other Asian Americans

Fourth-generation Japanese American youth's concern with their loss of cultural heritage also arises from having second-generation Asian American friends, who are much more closely connected to their ethnic roots through their immigrant parents. This makes some yonsei feel somewhat culturally inadequate as Japanese descendants who have lost their ethnic heritage. Although the racialized multicultural expectation that later-generation Japanese Americans have retained their ethnic differences often comes from mainstream American society (Kibria 2002a:92–96; Louie 2004:103–108; Tuan 2001), it is important to remember that such pressures can also originate from other Asian Americans (Lowe 1996:63–64). In fact, such intra-ethnic racialization may be more immediate and direct than racialization by majority white Americans.

My yonsei interviewees cited a number of instances when second-generation Asian Americans were surprised that they do not speak Japanese or maintain Japanese customs. Tom Sumimoto described a typical interaction he has on this issue:

> So these [second-generation] kids come up to me and it's like "Oh, can you speak Japanese?"
> "No."
> "How come?"
> "My parents don't speak the language, so I don't know how to speak it."
> "What do you mean they don't speak Japanese? So do you eat sushi at home?"
> "No."
> "You mean you don't eat Japanese food every day?"
> "No. I don't eat Japanese food every day."

A yonsei woman gave a similar example:

> I remember when I first met Chinese and Vietnamese American friends in high school and brought them home. They saw that my parents and I, we speak only English to each other. But when they go home, they speak their native language. So they were looking at us like, "You guys don't

speak Japanese here?" And we were like, "Actually, we don't know how to speak Japanese!"

Some of my yonsei interviewees actually attributed their interest in reconnecting with their ethnic roots directly to the racialized multicultural pressures they face from second-generation Asian Americans. Although the relatively smaller numbers of Japanese immigrants since World War II have not served as a source of "ethnic replenishment" for fourth-generation Japanese Americans, the dramatic increase in Asian migration in the past several decades has encouraged and pressured them to reconnect with their ethnic heritage. Thus, it is important to consider not only the phenomenon of ethnic replenishment, but also that of *panethnic* replenishment. In this context, moreover, Asian Americans are not directly replenishing the Japanese cultural heritage of the yonsei; rather, they are pressuring them to reconnect with it through racialized multiculturalism.

For instance, Tom claimed that the presence of other Asian Americans motivated him to study Japanese when he was younger. "It was just something I wanted to do because my friends went to Chinese school. So I felt I should go to Japanese school," he recounted. "They were second generation and I'm fourth. But I just felt like since they can speak Chinese, I should be able to speak Japanese." He went further and attributed his general ethnic awakening to other Asian Americans:

> I think having these other Asians around can be good for Japanese Americans because it makes us more aware of our culture as Asians, and not simply as Americans. And I think it really pressures us to be Asian too. When you have friends and they are all Chinese and they have their own cultural customs and activities and speak Chinese, it makes you ask yourself, what do I have? I feel like I need my own culture.

For Sherry, the racialized pressure from other Asian Americans to reconnect with her ethnic heritage was more direct:

> In high school, most of my classmates were first- and second-generation Taiwanese American. So obviously our experiences were very different and I felt a lot of pressure to become more Asian. They would say, "How

come you can't speak Japanese? That's so weird. If you're Japanese, you should speak Japanese. You're whitewashed." And I was experiencing a lot of anger and frustration because I was so Americanized. So when I came to college, because of this pressure, I felt that "Oh, maybe I'm supposed to act Asian to satisfy other people's expectations." Because most of my Asian American friends were so tied to their cultures, I felt this need to be Japanese, as opposed to being more American. So I started listening to Japanese popular music and watching Japanese TV shows, things like that. And I think one of the motivations for me to minor in Japanese studies is that I want to reclaim my heritage in a sense. In college, I've learned not to be ashamed of being Japanese American and become more proud of who I am.

## Positive Meanings of Japaneseness

In addition, the generally favorable images currently prevalent in American society about Japan and Japanese culture have become an added incentive for my yonsei interviewees to identify with their Japanese ancestry. This is mainly the result of Japan's rise in global stature since the 1960s and the general respect the country receives internationally because of its economic power and prosperity. Some Americans also take considerable interest in Japanese popular culture (especially anime, manga, karaoke), food (especially sushi and chicken teriyaki), martial arts, technology, and various cultural traditions. As Gil Asakawa notes (2004:68), the current "Japan-fad [has] opened the way for Americans to feel hip and cutting-edge by mimicking and co-opting [Japanese] styles and artistic expressions that are sometimes hundreds of years old."

The most notable example of this "Japan-fad" that I encountered in my fieldwork is the Phoenix Matsuri Festival, the largest and most popular ethnic festival in the city, which lasts for two days. Because there are relatively few Japanese immigrants and Japanese Americans living in Phoenix, it was quite remarkable that most of the main Japanese cultural activities and demonstrations were run partly or entirely by non-Japanese descent Americans (mainly Caucasians) who are apparently fascinated by Japanese culture. This included a major Japanese taiko drumming performance, a kimono fashion show, traditional Japanese dance and a parade, and various demonstrations of Japanese martial

A kimono fashion show at the Phoenix Matsuri Festival (photo by author).

The Japanese Swordsmanship Society of Phoenix (photo by author).

The Phoenix Taiko Kai (photo by author).

arts, including karate and samurai swordsmanship. The only part of the ethnic festival that was run mainly by Japanese and Japanese Americans were the various food vendors and booths.

In effect, the currently positive meanings of Japan have changed the dynamics of racialization for Japanese American youth. Because racialization for the yonsei is no longer associated with racism and overt discrimination as it was in the past, it has encouraged them to embrace their ethnic heritage. The yonsei I spoke with were certainly quite aware of some of the positive meanings currently associated with Japan and things Japanese. "Japanese culture is kind of cool," one of them observed. "Everyone nowadays is really into J-pop [Japanese popular culture and music]." Others mentioned Japan's "very trendy culture" and how it is "technologically advanced" and "comes up with the latest gadgets." Others used words like "refined," "exotic," "sophisticated," and "chic" to describe Japanese traditional culture. As Gil Asakawa (2004:67) in his source book for Japanese Americans observes, it has become hip and desirable to be Japanese.[4]

Sandy was the most explicit in linking her racialized ethnic consciousness to the positive meanings of Japanese culture to explain her motivation for exploring her ancestral heritage:

> I've always been interested in the Japanese language and culture. So I kind of wanted to learn more and studying Japanese seemed to be the key to understanding more about it and to get in touch with where I'm from, where I came from. But the more I take classes, the more I get kind of entranced by the exoticness of Japanese culture, the way it's portrayed. It's cool, kind of interesting. It just draws me in because it is seen in a positive light.

Such favorable images associated with the ethnic heritage of Japanese Americans contrast with the experiences of socioeconomically marginalized racial minorities whose ethnicity and ancestral homelands are stigmatized in the United States. This can be the case with African Americans as well as Mexican Americans, who have experienced anti-immigrant backlashes because their homeland is seen as a poor, developing country that sends large numbers of illegal immigrants to the United States who are Hispanicizing and threatening American culture because of their supposed refusal to assimilate. As a result, even U.S.-born Mexican Americans can be subject to colorblind ideologies that discourage them from maintaining their ethnic heritage, which is a source of prejudice and discrimination from majority Americans.

It is also interesting how few of my yonsei interviewees mentioned that they are interested in reconnecting with their Japanese ethnic heritage because they feel it will increase future professional and career opportunities in an increasingly globalized world. Only when directly asked did they acknowledge such instrumental motives, which are secondary to their yearning for their lost ethnicity (compare with Kibria 2002b).

Consequently, the revitalization of ethnicity among later-generation Japanese Americans is not merely a product of external, racialized coercion. Instead, it is partly a response to the currently favorable meanings attached to Japan and Japanese culture in an era of multiculturalism when ethnic heritage and homeland have come to be positively valued. Nonetheless, such ethnic revivals are fundamentally based on culturally essentialized assumptions about ethnicity, which are imposed on the yonsei because of their multicultural racialization as "Japanese" by both mainstream Americans and other Asian Americans. Insofar as this causes the yonsei considerable ethnic unease and a sense of inadequacy about their loss of cultural heritage that later-generation white Americans never face, we see once again the somewhat involuntary nature of ethnicity among non-white minorities.

## Assimilation versus Heritage: The NSU Culture Show

The importance of ethnic heritage and ancestry for fourth-generation Japanese American youth was clearly illustrated by the "Culture Show" held by the Nikkei Student Union at UC San Diego. Organized and produced by NSU board members, who are predominantly yonsei, the Culture Show took place in the huge, main ballroom of UCSD's student center, which was packed with hundreds of students who had lined up outside the building well before the event. The Culture Show was an impressive, major production that consisted of an engaging series of music and dance performances, videos, and skits, and was even accompanied by a slick, Hollywood-type poster and a promotional video

The UCSD taiko ensemble performing at the Culture Show (photo by author).

"trailer." The audience was raucous throughout the event, clapping, cheering, and laughing at everything presented, making for an electric atmosphere.

The Culture Show consisted of a number of Japanese American cultural heritage activities, including music videos of Japanese rap artists and other popular music stars, a long performance by UCSD's taiko ensemble, and traditional Japanese dance accompanied by *enka* music (popular songs that resemble traditional Japanese music). However, the showcase of the night was a play entitled "Trouble in J-Town," which focuses mainly on a group of Japanese American undergraduate students who take a UCSD Ethnic Studies class about Asian Americans and work on a project about the Japanese American community. The play reflects the ethnic concerns of the NSU yonsei board members who wrote the script. In general, the main female students are more serious about the class project and wish to explore their ethnic heritage and visit Japantown, whereas the male students simply goof-off and joke and are more concerned about chasing the girls. Nonetheless, in order to conduct research for the project, the student characters first attend a meeting at the NSU, where Japanese Americans discuss how they are so assimilated and "whitewashed" and have forgotten their cultural heritage. I was struck by how this scene reiterated the actual conversations that NSU students had at their culture forums described above.

The student characters go to Japantown in Los Angeles for their class project and encounter a group of youth who are protesting how J-Town is being taken over by corporations, which are putting small Japanese American stores out of business. The protestors are collecting signatures for a petition against Starbucks, which plans to move into Japantown. The students also visit one of the original J-Town businesses, a *mochi* (rice cake) store, and meet the elderly Japanese American couple who are the owners (supposedly played by the real owners). The owners tell the students that youth are no longer interested in Japantown and its ethnic businesses and that their livelihood is threatened. The students realize that with the encroachment of big corporations into J-Town, subsequent generations of Japanese Americans will not be able to experience their cultural heritage through such ethnic businesses. They conclude that J-Town is important for Japanese American culture and history and therefore sign the petition distributed by the protestors.

However, one of the students refuses to sign the petition, confounding his friends. This student is Greg, who eventually becomes the main protagonist. It is later revealed to the audience that Greg does not sign the petition because he plans to start working for Starbucks in J-Town, partly to support his family. One of the poignant scenes in the play is a dinner conversation Greg has with his parents, who continue to be closely connected to the Japanese American community. They tell him that Japanese American businesses like the *mochi* store in J-Town go back to their childhood, when such businesses supported local ethnic communities and families. They emphasize how it is important for the younger generation to give back to the community and not forget about their ethnic roots. During the conversation, it becomes clear that Greg feels that his family has not become socioeconomically successful because they remain tied to the Japanese American community. He feels a need to distance himself from the community in order to pursue job opportunities in mainstream society and get ahead, but he is sacrificing his ethnic heritage and culture in the process. The play also indicates that he distanced himself from his Japanese ancestry as a kid in order to avoid teasing in school.

In this manner, the play reveals the main tension between assimilation and ancestral heritage, which drives the latter half of the narrative. The story and dialogues strongly imply that Japanese American youth are losing touch with their ethnic heritage because of their assimilation

The actor-students visit the *mochi* shop in "Trouble in J-Town" (photo by author).

The actor-students present their class project (photo by author).

and obsession to succeed in American society. In the final project presentation for the Ethnic Studies class, the students speak about how Japantowns are disappearing because of the internment and subsequent scattering of Japanese Americans, urban renewal, and the assimilation of the younger generations. They point out that there are only three Japantowns remaining (Los Angeles, San Francisco, and San Jose) and that the former Japantown in San Diego has been gone for a long time. They recount how J-Towns used to be the core of the Japanese American community and its familial, religious, and social activities, and mention the protests they encountered in the LA Japantown. They ask themselves why they need a Starbucks in J-Town, since they can go to local shops for coffee.

Greg is conspicuously absent from the class presentation (apparently he takes the course only to fulfill a general education requirement) and in the last scene of the play, he is found working at the Starbucks in J-Town during its grand opening. At this point, he is deeply conflicted about his new job and has not told his friends, hoping they will never see him working there. However, the elderly *mochi* business owners suddenly show up (apparently they drink coffee like everyone else!) and recognize him, leading to an awkward encounter that leaves Greg feeling guilty. However, the elderly couple are not angry or resentful, but are instead surprisingly sympathetic to his plight, apparently indicating the nature of the choices that Japanese American youth must make.

Ultimately, "Trouble in J-Town" does not resolve the fundamental conflict it portrays between assimilation and ethnic heritage. The play does not explicitly indicate which path Japanese American youth must take, or whether they can strike a balance between the two apparently opposing forces. However, it certainly stresses the importance of maintaining cultural traditions and staying in touch with heritage. Greg, who abandons his heritage and ethnic community in favor of assimilative upward mobility, is portrayed as a conflicted, unhappy, and overworked individual. In contrast, the other students, who have discovered the value of their ethnic heritage and give an effective class presentation, seem to be more at peace with themselves. Nonetheless, the dominant narrative of the play is structured according to a binary opposition and tension between assimilation and cultural heritage. However, as argued in this chapter, assimilation and ethnic heritage are not antithetical, and most yonsei youth in my interview sample seem to be successfully navigating both simultaneously.

## Reconnecting with Heritage and Homeland

### Japan as the Source of Ethnic Heritage

Despite the implications of "Trouble in J-Town," efforts by my yonsei interviewees to explore their ethnic roots involve directly reconnecting with the culture of the ethnic homeland of Japan and less with the

Greg encounters the *mochi* store owners at the new J-Town Starbucks (photo by author).

Japanese American ethnic community in the United States. Since many of the activities of local Japanese American organizations are not directly relevant to Japanese culture, they seem not to interest young Japanese Americans in search of their ethnic heritage. Both the nationwide Japanese American Citizens League (JACL) and local organizations like the Japanese American Historical Society of San Diego (JAHSSD) are struggling to attract Japanese American youth. Tellingly, only one sixth of my yonsei interviewees are currently actively engaged in the Japanese American community. The rest may have participated with their parents and families when they were children, but they have become detached from the community during and after going to college and most of them are not members of any Japanese American organization.[5]

Although the Nikkei Student Union at UC San Diego was quite popular and had a good number of yonsei, half of the membership consisted of other non-Japanese descent Asian Americans who were attracted to its "fun" social activities in contrast to the more civic and activist orientation of the other Asian American student organizations. When Japanese American members were asked at one meeting why they joined the NSU, most mentioned that they got involved through their friends and were drawn to its social activities, such as parties, ski trips, sports clubs, as well as its plays and skit performances. It seems that the organization serves mainly as a way for college students who are brought together on the basis of ethnicity to socialize and have fun; few see it as a means to explore their ethnic heritage. As one member (quoted earlier) aptly put it, NSU is not really an ethnic club because it does not engage in Japanese cultural activities, except for its annual sushi fest. Otherwise, its activities are "stuff that any American college kids would do."

Likewise, the main Japanese American Citizens League activities that attract yonsei youth are its sports leagues (basketball, volleyball, bowling, and so on), but these are standard American athletic activities that are not ethnic per se. The civil rights component of the JACL and its other activities do not interest my yonsei interviewees. Moreover, there was virtually no collaboration between the NSU and the San Diego chapter of JACL or the JAHSSD, except for the Day of Remembrance. In fact, during the NSU culture forum meetings, the organization's leaders noted that their members are not interested in the local Japanese American community and do not go to its events. The youth at these meetings also said that they hardly ever visit Japantown in Los Angeles because it is not in a good neighborhood and does not have anything that really interests them.

Although participation in ethnic organizations is generally declining among Japanese American youth, community activities based on traditional Japanese culture still attract significant numbers of youth. This includes the annual *mochitsuki* (pounding Japanese rice to make rice cakes) and Obon festivals (which honor deceased ancestral spirits and involve Japanese dance, music, and food) at the Buddhist Temple of San Diego. Both are well-attended by youth who accompany their parents as well as by some younger Japanese American couples and families. In addition, a number of yonsei are increasingly becoming involved in traditional Japanese taiko drumming. As will be extensively discussed in Chapters 6 and 7, the number of taiko ensembles has increased exponentially in the Japanese American community, offering an effective way for yonsei youth to experience their ethnic heritage and ancestry in an authentic manner.

Obon at the Buddhist Temple of San Diego (photo by author).

In contrast to such Japanese cultural heritage activities, events in the ethnic community that focus specifically on the Japanese American experience or history draw very few youth. Most notable is the annual Day of Remembrance commemorating the internment of Japanese Americans during World War II, described in Chapter 1. The annual meetings of the Japanese American Historical Society of San Diego are well attended by hundreds of Japanese Americans, but they are overwhelmingly middle-aged and elderly, with almost no participation by youth (even as part of families).

Instead of simply increasing their engagement with the local Japanese American community, my yonsei interviewees reconnected with their ethnic roots by going directly to the original source of their cultural heritage, Japan (see also Okamura 2008:140–142). Implicit in such efforts is the notion that authentic Japanese culture comes from the ethnic homeland, not Japanese American organizations in the United States. This contrasts with the sansei's earlier efforts, during the Asian American movement of the 1960s and 1970s, to reconnect with their ethnic roots, which were localized in the Japanese and Asian American communities and were not transnational in scope. One of the senior leaders of the San Diego JACL also observed this trend among the yonsei. "I've noticed that Japanese American youth are looking to connect to Japanese culture and find out more about their Japanese side," he noted. "They're trying to learn more about their roots. So the younger generations, they are interested in the Japanese language and in Japan. It's not an interest in Japanese Americans or the Japanese American experience. It's the Japanese culture. But that's not something the JACL can really provide them."

It is remarkable that a good majority of my yonsei interviewees seriously studied the Japanese language in high school and/or college. Most had taken (or planned to take) a number of years of college Japanese classes, and a few had participated in summer immersion programs in Japan. In addition, almost all of them had lived (or planned to live) in Japan through student programs. Because all of my fourth-generation Japanese American interviewees are well educated and from middle-class backgrounds, they have ample educational and economic resources to explore their ethnic heritage in college and in Japan, in contrast to racial minorities who are less wealthy and educated. Because of their local and transnational cultural heritage activities, my yonsei interviewees have acquired some proficiency in Japanese over the years and generally speak the language much better than the sansei, who have had no (or limited) Japanese language training or experience. "If it's not complicated Japanese, I can understand what is said," said Sandy, giving a typical yonsei assessment. "And I can get my ideas across in the language."

In addition, a majority of my interviewees are majoring or minoring in Ethnic Studies (with a focus on Asian Americans), Asian Studies/History, Japanese Studies, or the Japanese language (or had done so in the past). In fact, among this group of students, a significantly greater number is specializing in Asian/Japanese Studies instead of Ethnic/Asian American Studies, a fact that again indicates that their interest in directly reconnecting with their Japanese ethnic roots is greater than their interest in their Japanese American/Asian American background per se. "Asian American Studies never interested me as much as directly studying Japanese culture," a yonsei Asian Studies major remarked. "Maybe because Asian Americans were already familiar to me."

Most of the yonsei youth I interviewed also engage in Japanese rec-reational activities, including watching Japanese anime (animation) and other TV shows, playing Japanese video games, listening to Japanese popular music, and consuming other types of Japanese popular culture. Others have taken traditional Japanese art, music, or dancing lessons. One of my interviewees has even done some "voice acting" training for anime and Japanese video game characters. As Tom observed, "Japanese American youth listen to Japanese music and are much more attuned to Japanese popular culture than anything Japanese American or Asian American."

## Forged Transnationalism: Living in the Ethnic Homeland

It is also notable that in addition to turning to their ethnic homeland as the source of their cultural roots and heritage, almost all of the yonsei in my sample have also lived in Japan as college students on foreign exchange or study abroad programs, generally from one semester to a year, or planned to do so soon. One third have been to Japan two or three times (once as a student and other times as a tourist or on other types of programs). One older yonsei man is actually living in Japan with his spouse, who is employed at a Japanese university.

Although transnational connections to ethnic homelands are often understood to be inherited from immigrant parents or grandparents (Levitt and Waters 2002b; Smith 2006), they are not simply a product of continuity or persistence across the generations. While it is true that im-migrant descendants often depend on their parents to develop transna-tional ties, they may also do so independently without any support from previous generations. As the Japanese American case demonstrates, racialized multiculturalism can cause later-generation minorities to re-cover and reactivate transnational linkages to ancestral homelands that were lost among the second and third generations. Therefore, theirs is a type of "forged transnationality" (Schein 1998)—the creation of new transnational connections instead of the continuation of preexisting, cross-border linkages.

All of the yonsei I interviewed reported quite positive and fun experi-ences in their country of ethnic ancestry. Those who lived in Japan as study abroad students associated mainly with Japanese students, who are educated and cosmopolitan, often speak (or want to practice) English, and are quite eager to meet and talk to American students. They also experienced the fun that accompanies student life in Japan, where academic pressures are low and social and club opportunities are abundant. For example, Barbara Kitamura, a yonsei from Hawaii, recounted her experiences quite fondly:

> It was overall a very positive experience. There were few expectations for students. You didn't even have to go to class. The Japanese [university] students didn't study. They just wanted to go out and play. They had an international section at the university, so I joined the student clubs there. Being a student in Japan was so much fun. I mean, you just go out all the time and drink and everything was to have fun. But I know it would be very different had I gone to Japan to work.

Tom particularly enjoyed his time with Japanese students:

> I had lots of interaction with Japanese. In fact, that was the best part. It was only at school, but there was a group of [Japanese] students that we'd always meet for lunch. We became really good friends with them. They were learning to speak English, so they were interested in us. They would speak some English to us and we'd try out our Japanese, but most of the time it was English, because their English was good. They'd also come to our dorms and we'd party. They loved it, because it was different for them. They were interested in foreigners.

Because the Japanese Americans and the Japanese in this case share the same social status as students, this facilitated interaction across cultural and linguistic barriers, as Tom noted:

> I didn't feel that much difference from the Japanese students. Yes, there are cultural differences, but both of us were students. They basically wanted to do the same things I wanted to do. It was no big deal. I did feel the cultural gap—they knew about Japanese cultural things much better—but in everyday interaction, I didn't feel much difference.

My yonsei interviewees also reported that the Japanese they encountered outside their host universities were also quite courteous and polite, even toward foreigners who do not speak Japanese that well. "It was much better than when I went to Spain," Carrie Kawamura observed. "In Japan, everyone treated us well. I felt I blended in better because everyone looked like me and I didn't stick out as much as a foreigner. It was much better than the rumors I heard about the Japanese."

Although Japanese Americans are treated as foreigners in Japan, such ethnic exclusion does not bother them as much, partly because they are fourth generation and have not been strongly attached to their ethnic homeland from the beginning. Sandy, a fourth-generation Japanese American who lived in Japan as a student, exemplifies this attitude:

> I had no consciousness of being culturally Japanese before going to Japan. I see myself as a foreigner in Japan. Of course, I do feel some kind of affinity to Japan, but I'm still a foreigner. So it was no shock to me that I was seen as American in Japan. Even among my non-Japanese [American] Asian friends [in the United States], I felt very American. They'd call my dad at home and say he sounds white. So it's pretty obvious that the Japanese are going to treat me as a foreigner.

By contrast, ethnic return migrants who expect an ethnic homecoming in their parents' homeland can be quite bothered when they are regarded by the host population as culturally alien foreigners (King and Christou 2010; Tsuda 2003, 2009a).

Although the Japanese may sometimes be initially confused or surprised when meeting Japanese-looking people who cannot speak the language and may regard them as handicapped, strange, or uneducated (Tsuda 2003: ch. 5; Yamashiro 2011:1511), once it becomes apparent that the Japanese-looking people are American, the Japanese are reportedly quite nice and courteous (Asakawa 2004:111). "Whenever I spoke to Japanese at stores or wherever, I prefaced everything by saying I'm a student from America and my Japanese is not very good," Sandy explained. "That seemed to facilitate things. [The Japanese] seemed fine with that and I can't remember an instance when people distanced themselves from me because of it." Carrie also mentioned that interaction with Japanese in cities went smoothly once they understood she is American, although in outlying areas, they did not really have a conception of a Japanese American and were more confused.

A number of my interviewees claimed that the Japanese could tell they were Americans by the English they spoke, their demeanor and dress, and the people they were with (which sometimes included white American or biracial exchange students) and that therefore, there was not much ethnic confusion. Only one of my yonsei interviewees mentioned that she received the aloof, silent treatment when it was discovered she was American in Japan. "Then, they would basically be like, OK, just go away. Pay your hundred yen and just go away," she recounted.

Other interviewees mentioned how the positive perceptions that Japanese have of Americans benefited them in Japan (see also Yamashiro 2008:1512–1513). Carrie recalled such a case during her second visit to Japan after college:

> One time, we were stuck in a remote area at night without a train ticket with two other Caucasians and this Japanese man picked us up with his car and drove us back home. He had lived in the U.S., spoke some English, and was really kind and nice. He probably saw my Caucasian friends and assumed we were American and therefore decided to be really nice.

Because of their overall positive experiences in Japan, a good number of yonsei I interviewed have tended to identify with their ethnic homeland to an increasing degree and to feel more connected to their ancestral roots. Although about half of my interviewees mentioned that they felt quite American in Japan, this was simply a recognition of their cultural differences with the Japanese and was not based on a sense of social alienation in their ethnic homeland (see also Yamashiro 2011:1512–1513). "Living in Japan, I realized how American I am," said Carrie, expressing a common sentiment. "I didn't speak the language very well, I didn't know Japanese customs, and in terms of the way I act and think, you feel different. For instance, I realized I'm not quiet and courteous like the Japanese, but I'm actually pretty loud like an American."

On the other hand, for an equal number of my interviewees, their sojourn in Japan made them feel more connected to their Japanese ethnic roots and strengthened their sense of affiliation to their ethnic homeland (see also Asakawa 2004:116–117). "I feel somewhat of a stronger affinity with Japan now," Sandy noted. "It's because I know more about Japanese culture and how it works. Now, I want to learn more, so that Japan becomes more natural for me, so when I go back, I can fit in more." For Tom, his greater affinity with his ethnic homeland is even a matter of ethnic pride:

> Being in Japan definitely solidifies that I'm a yonsei and not from Japan. But on the other hand, going to Japan and seeing everything there makes me proud that I'm Japanese [descent], that this is where I'm from. People respect Japan. I'm now prouder to be of Japanese ancestry. I felt this is where I should be, because people looked like me, even if they don't dress like me and people there were really nice.

## Ethnic Heritage and Identity

The ethnic revival among my fourth-generation Japanese American interviewees is therefore not simply a type of symbolic ethnicity that involves food, dress, music, and casual participation in ethnic festivals. Although my yonsei interviewees certainly engage in their share of symbolic ethnicity, their commitment to their ethnic roots is deeper and motivates them to study the ancestral language, learn about Japan and its history in college, and eventually live in their ethnic homeland. It is quite interesting that when they were children, they tended to engage in symbolic ethnicity in their families and local communities (many mentioned eating traditional Japanese food for New Years and participating in Japanese American festivals). However, as they grow older, they make a more serious and transnational attempt to recover their ethnic heritage by directly reconnecting with the language and culture of their ethnic homeland.

The importance and enduring nature of ethnic heritage is also shown by its impact on the identities of my fourth-generation Japanese American interviewees. In contrast to both the prewar nisei, whose American consciousness eclipses their sense of Japanese ancestry, and the sansei, who feel completely Americanized despite acknowledging the lingering effects of their cultural heritage, the yonsei tend to stress the "balance" between their American and Japanese selves. Not surprisingly, the yonsei I spoke with regard themselves as fully Americanized and assimilated in cultural orientation. However, when discussing their ethnic identities, they had the following types of remarks:

"I think there's a balance. Because American-wise, I'm definitely like I can do what I want. But at the same time, I've gotten back in touch with my Japanese roots."

"There is an interesting balance that I think I have. Growing up in America, in a very American-type family, I consider myself American through and through. I can't really pass as Japanese. But I also kind of feel I've inherited Japanese culture, although it's not really mine anymore."

"I think after high school, I've become more content with learning how to balance my two sides. I'm no longer ashamed of being Japanese American. I'm not ashamed to be more Americanized [compared to other Asian Americans]. But I'm also not ashamed to be Japanese in a predominantly white society."

It was also interesting that almost all of my yonsei interviewees emphasize aspects of themselves that they attribute to their Japanese cultural heritage, such as a nonconfrontational attitude, quieter nature, politeness, greater self-restraint, and respect for others. In contrast, a smaller proportion of sansei made such claims. Again, it is very debatable whether such self-perceived characteristics are really a product of an original Japanese culture passed down over the generations or stereotypes about Japanese culture that yonsei have conveniently appropriated for the purposes of creating a positive ethnic self-image. For instance, Sandy, who is more self-reflexive than others about this issue, remarked, "There is this politeness about me, at least on the surface, that seems to be from my Japanese heritage. But it's probably because I've studied Japanese culture in depth, so I find affinities that I like. If I studied other cultures in depth, I'd also find things where I'd say, 'Oh that sounds like me too.'" Nonetheless, such attitudes illustrate both the extent to which the ethnic consciousness of my yonsei interviewees remains grounded in Japanese cultural heritage and ancestry and the degree to which they do not conceive of themselves in strictly Americanized terms.

The pride my yonsei interviewees expressed in their ethnic identities as Japanese Americans was also notable—and again, quite different from the prewar nisei, who generally downplay their ethnicity, and the sansei, whose ethnic pride is based mainly on the history and socioeconomic accomplishments of Japanese Americans. In contrast, the ethnic self-esteem of the yonsei is a product of *both* Japanese American history and the Japanese people and culture. Although they do not actively assert their ethnic identities in front of others, most have had experiences that are similar to Tom's. "I'm definitely proud to say I'm Japanese American," he stated. "It's partly our history. I'm proud of that, because it shows a lot about Japanese Americans. But living in Japan also made me proud of my Japanese origins and cultural heritage. People respect Japan." Likewise, Sandy shared her sentiments with me as follows:

["Japanese American"] is a term that I associate with pride. Because Japanese from Japan are seen as a very progressive, modern people in the postwar period. So it's like I have a positive thing to associate with my identity when I say, "Yeah, I'm Japanese American." A lot of it is also because I identify with the community and other Japanese Americans, a group affinity. If I actually use the term "Japanese American" to identify myself, the meaning usually includes all the history. The internment, the 442nd.

## Conclusion

The case of fourth-generation Japanese Americans indicates that ethnic histories do not follow linear trajectories wherein an initially strong ethnic minority identity gradually wanes over the generations because of unrelenting assimilative pressures. While obviously influenced by the ethnicity of their parents and ancestors, each generation negotiates its own ethnic positionality in majority society in response to the complex dynamics of racialization, assimilation, and multiculturalism, which constantly change over time. Although the second generation has inherited their ethnic heritage from their immigrant parents, the fourth generation has actively revived and recreated this heritage in response to the particular historical moment in which they live in American society. Therefore, the continued salience of ethnicity is not simply the result of the retention and persistence of the cultural differences of immigrant ancestors over time. It is also the product of active recovery among later-generation racial minorities in response to the discontinuity caused by the loss of heritage culture among previous generations. In the process, the yonsei have also reactivated and forged new transnational ties to their ethnic homeland of Japan, which is regarded as the original and authentic source of their ancestral culture.

Although later-generation Japanese Americans have come to resemble white Americans because of their upward socioeconomic mobility and cultural assimilation, they have been unable to escape their status as ethnic minorities because of their racial visibility. Not only is their ethnicity rather involuntary, it is also quite specific, since they are racially essentialized as "Japanese" and not simply as panethnic "Asians." Such racialized pressures have intensified recently with the current politics of multiculturalism whereby even later-generation Japanese Americans are expected to retain their connections to a Japanese cultural heritage and homeland that is now positively valued. Therefore, the dynamics of racialization have been reconfigured so that they no longer represent racism and blatant discrimination as they did for the prewar nisei. Instead, the advent of racialized multiculturalism has caused my yonsei interviewees to lament their overassimilation to American society and produced feelings of ethnic loss. As a result, they have nostalgically yearned for and actively reclaimed their ethnic roots and homeland.

Although the ethnic revival among the yonsei is not a defensive, reactive ethnicity constructed in response to ethnic marginalization and discrimination per se, it is also not an entirely voluntary search for ethnic ancestry. Without their continued racialization as a "Japanese" ethnic minority, it is unlikely that my interviewees would embrace the current multicultural moment and attempt to reconnect with their cultural heritage in the fourth generation. In contrast to the completely optional nature of multiculturalism for white ethnics, the racialized multiculturalism of non-white minorities like Japanese Americans is more obligatory and can compel even those of the later-generations to recover their ethnic heritage, increasing the power of race as a marker of cultural difference. Indeed, it seems that race matters much more than immigrant generation in determining the ethnic experiences of later-generation Japanese Americans.

However, because of its racialized nature, the resurgence of ethnicity among the Japanese American youth I studied is more than the superficial and residual symbolic ethnicity observed among whites and is not limited to casual participation in local Japanese American communities. In response to the multicultural pressure to be ethnic (including pressure from second-generation Asian Americans), most of the yonsei have made a much more serious commitment to their ancestral roots by turning directly to their ethnic homeland as the ultimate source of cultural heritage.

In this manner, later-generation racialized ethnics seem to have a stronger desire to maintain their ancestral background and identity than white ethnics. In addition to dedicating themselves to serious study of their ethnic ancestry and language, most yonsei in my sample have lived in Japan as students. Therefore, unlike the localized nature of the sansei's ethnic revival in the 1960s and 1970s, they have made serious transnational efforts to recover their cultural heritage. When they do get involved in the local ethnic community, it is not Japanese American issues per se, but imported Japanese cultural traditions that galvanize these youth because these traditions are what reconnect them to their ancestral roots.

Although the yonsei's return to ethnic roots is an active response to their racialization, it is rather apolitical and mainly a cultural movement, in contrast to the previous ethnic revival of sansei youth, which was linked to the political and ethnic activism of the period (compare with Takahashi 1997:212). Nor has the yonsei ethnic revival led to panethnic solidarity and political mobilization with other Asian American groups. In fact, the Nikkei Student Union at UC San Diego has been criticized by other Asian American student organizations on campus for showing no interest in political and ethnic activism and for simply engaging in "fun" cultural activities.

Nonetheless, a cultural awakening seems to have occurred among young Japanese Americans after three generations of progressive assimilation and gradual erosion of ethnic identification. This indicates that assimilation is not incompatible with the continued salience and manifestation of ethnic differences in the context of racialized multiculturalism. In fact, for racial minorities like the Japanese Americans, overassimilation can lead to a search for ethnic roots in an effort to better realign their culture with their race. Instead of being opposed to ethnic heritage (as portrayed in the NSU's "Trouble in J-Town"), cultural assimilation can actually lead to the active production of ancestral homeland cultures.

In addition, in reclaiming their ethnic heritage, fourth-generation Japanese Americans do not wish to reverse their cultural Americanization or even counterbalance it with a greater attachment to their ethnicity (Matsuo 1992:508; Pyke and Dang 2003:157). Instead of making them less assimilated, their Japanese heritage activities simply coexist with their Americanization in different contexts, thus giving their lives added ethnic significance in a society characterized by racialized multiculturalism. There is no inherent contradiction in their attempts to recover their ethnic heritage while claiming racial citizenship as culturally assimilated Americans.

Nonetheless, the revival of ethnicity among fourth-generation Japanese American youth is based on a tacit realization that they still cannot be completely accepted by majority American society despite generations of cultural assimilation because they are forever essentialized by racial appearance as foreign ethnics. In this context, not only does their search for ethnic heritage lack activist potential; it may also end up reproducing, instead of challenging, dominant racial formations that equate Americanness with being white and relegate Asian Americans to the margins as culturally foreign. By actively recovering (and displaying) their Japanese cultural heritage, they may be reinforcing the dominant racialized assumption that those of Asian descent are irrevocably tied to their ancestral cultures (even after four generations) and therefore are not real Americans. In fact, cultural heritage activities such as Japanese American taiko may even exacerbate the American tendency to conflate Japanese Americans with Japanese immigrants from Japan (see Chapter 7). In this sense, the revival of ethnicity among the yonsei may be empowering on a personal level, but disempowering on a collective level, as well as undermining their struggles for racial citizenship as Americans.

Nevertheless, the search for heritage and homeland among the yonsei indicates that ethnicity continues to matter for Japanese Americans, at least for another generation. Although racialized multiculturalism has prevented them from being recognized as real Americans, it has also enabled their ethnicity and communities to endure for a remarkably long time. It is quite notable that a significant population of fourth-generation Japanese Americans who are still of completely Japanese descent even exists. In contrast, because the ethnicity of white Americans is not racialized, they are mostly of mixed ancestry and significant ethnic participation and community attachments have long disappeared among them (Alba 1990, Waters 1990). One certainly does not find fourth-generation Italian American or Irish American youth organizing on the basis of ethnicity, lamenting the loss of their ethnic roots, or seriously attempting to recover their ancestral heritage. Ironically, because of their multicultural racialization, Japanese Americans have remained more ethnically resilient than white Americans.

# PART III

# Ethnic Heritage, Performance, and Diasporicity

# 6

# Japanese American Taiko and the Remaking of Tradition

## Encountering Taiko

The search for ethnic roots among later-generation Japanese Americans does not simply involve reaching out to the Japanese ethnic homeland but also occurs through the appropriation of homeland cultures in their local communities. As Min Zhou and Jennifer Lee note (2004:17), globalization has allowed Asian American youth to stay in touch with the cultures of their ancestral countries and created new opportunities for active cultural production and expression. Cultural heritage is not only experienced as part of ethnic consciousness or practiced in the privacy of individual families and lives. It is also actively performed in local communities and displayed to the public.

By far the most notable performative cultural activity that has become very popular among youth in Japanese American communities is taiko, traditional Japanese drumming that dates back to ancient Japanese history. The first two chapters of Part III examine how Japanese American taiko, as a performance of ethnic heritage, involves a complex dynamic of tradition, embodiment, and performative authenticity.

Growing up as a shin-nisei who was completely detached from the Japanese American community and who did not identify either as nisei or Japanese American, I used to think of taiko drumming as an ancient tradition that was rooted in Japan and had nothing to do with the United States or Japanese Americans. My first personal encounter with Japanese taiko was during a family trip to Japan when I was in junior high school. Our relatives took us to an Obon festival in the local community at night. It was a magical experience to see a circle of Japanese dancers dressed in colorful *yukata* moving gracefully with hand-held folding fans, illuminated by beautiful lanterns hanging overhead. It was an archetypical scene of Japanese cultural tradition. Behind them on a wooden scaffold (*yagura*) decked out with ceremonial paraphernalia was a male taiko drummer dressed in festival garb and a headband, playing alone. Although the taiko player was a visual spectacle, he was not really putting on a musical performance per se but simply drumming out a simple beat in the background for the dancers.

Many years later, I had my second encounter with Japanese taiko when I was Associate Director of the Center for Comparative Immigration Studies at the University of California at San Diego. One day, Stacie Walker, one of our predoctoral fellows, came to my office and asked:

"Hey, do you want to go see a taiko performance?"

"Taiko?" I was really surprised to hear Stacie, an African American, even utter the word. "You know about taiko?"

"Yeah, I *love* taiko. Kodo is performing at UCLA's Royce Hall next weekend. They are that really famous taiko group from Japan. Do you want to go?"

I was a bit bewildered. So not only do some Americans know about taiko, they go to concert halls to listen to taiko performances? For me, taiko was associated with traditional Japanese festivals and ceremonial rituals, and I had never heard of taiko performed in concert halls, and especially not in the United States. However, Stacie seemed to assume that as a Japanese American, I would know everything about taiko and naturally be interested.

"Yeah, I'd love to go!" I tried to convey a sense of enthusiasm and disguise my ignorance about and lack of interest in taiko. I had little understanding of what a taiko performance was or what to expect. I also did not tell Stacie that I would never have been willing to drive two hours to Los Angeles to attend a taiko performance had she not been so interested.

We eventually recruited another predoctoral fellow, who happened to be from India, and the three of us drove to UCLA. Royce Hall is a huge and impressive concert hall, and I was surprised to see that the entire place was completely packed. As expected, a good portion of the audience was Asian, but there were plenty of whites and people from other ethnic groups as well. (In fact, our group itself ended up being quite multiethnic, since it consisted of a Japanese American, an African American, and an Indian).

The performance was utterly enthralling and like nothing I had seen before. Kodo is a large taiko ensemble (called *kumi-daiko*) and plays a wide array of drums in different size groups. In contrast to the traditional practice of having the drumming performed by men, the ensemble includes a few women drummers. The instruments ranged from small *shime-daikos* to huge *odaikos*, and each piece was played with a different group of drums, often arrayed in various positions around the stage. As a result, their beats combined to produce various complex rhythms and drumming effects. The percussive variety of the ensemble was impressive, ranging from the loudest beats on massive drums to the barely audible tapping on smaller drums, sometimes within the span of a few minutes.

Despite the free-flowing power that the Kodo ensemble projected, the drumming always remained structured and disciplined and appeared very traditional and true to classic Japanese artistry. The performers were dressed in traditional garb and perfectly synchronized as they drummed in unison, and their motions were always beautifully choreographed and coordinated. At times, they moved gracefully from drum to drum like dancers while releasing brief shouts or yells (*kiai*). This intensified the physical energy of the performance, making it very powerful and exciting. The general effect was a dramatic and sublime combination of collective force, artistic beauty, rhythmic precision, and spirituality. The most memorable part was when a massive *odaiko* (the largest of all taiko drums) was rolled onto the stage and a single, muscular man with large *bachi* (drum sticks) and dressed only in a loin cloth beat out various rhythms with incredible force, the massive pounding reverberating throughout the large hall and producing a truly hypnotic effect. The performance was enthusiastically received by the audience, who repeatedly gave the taiko drummers roaring ovations. I left the hall having become a taiko enthusiast.

Nonetheless, my next encounter with taiko did not occur until several years later when I began my fieldwork among Japanese Americans by attending a meeting of the Nikkei Student Union at UC San Diego. It was the first general meeting of the academic year, and I was surprised to find that it started with a taiko performance. Before the students entered the auditorium for the meeting, they stood outside and watched a small group of mainly Japanese American students from UCSD's Asayake Taiko give a short performance on a small collection of drums. This was the first time that I realized that *Japanese Americans*, not just Japanese from Japan, perform in taiko ensembles as well.

Over the next several months, I quickly discovered that taiko is now everywhere in the Japanese American community. It has spread like wildfire among Japanese Americans in recent decades and is featured prominently in many community events, even if they have nothing to do with music. This includes Day of Remembrance commemorations, Obon and other activities at local Buddhist temples, local Japanese and Asian festivals, community musical and theatrical performances, and meetings and activities on college campuses. There are now numerous community taiko groups and ensembles that consist of mainly Japanese American youth and are often associated with local organizations like Japanese American churches, Buddhist temples, and the JACL. Other taiko groups are based at universities (especially in California) or are independent.

When did Japanese Americans get so interested in taiko? Why have later-generation Japanese Americans embraced it so enthusiastically, and what does it mean for them? How is it part of their revival of ethnic heritage, and what is its relevance for the broader positioning of Japanese Americans in mainstream society?

One of the main reasons why later-generation Japanese Americans have embraced taiko so enthusiastically is that it allows them to recover the ancestral heritage and ethnic identity that have been lost through generations of cultural assimilation. However, the reason taiko makes them feel so connected to their ethnic roots is not because it has been passed down to them from Japan in its original form as an embodied reproduction of an ancient tradition. As is the case with other diasporic, traveling cultures, this traditional musical form has been considerably remade and reinvented as Japanese Americans have appropriated it for contemporary ethnic purposes in their local communities. This illustrates how cultural heritage is not simply based on the persistence and continuity of homeland cultures over the generations, but is also recreated and refashioned by later-generation ethnic minorities. Although taiko is a typical example of embodiment of traditional cultural forms, its performativity also encompasses innovative improvisation as it is constantly exposed to transformations in musical and physical form. In fact, taiko's efficacy as a means of reclaiming ethnic heritage for Japanese Americans lies in its inherently performative nature, since its reconfiguration in the United States allows it to resonate to a greater extent with their current lives and cultural backgrounds.[1]

An Obon festival taiko performance by Naruwan Taiko at the Buddhist Temple of San Diego (photo by author).

Kyo Rei Taiko Kai from the Arizona Buddhist Temple (photo by author).

## The Development of Japanese American Taiko

Taiko has a very long history that goes back thousands of years in Japan, and its origins are shrouded in the mythology of ancient deities, although archaeological evidence suggests it came from China or Korea between 300 and 900 AD. Taiko was part of Japanese imperial court music during the Nara period, was used in war during the feudal era, and has been employed in Noh and Kabuki theater for centuries. Because of its association with the gods since ancient times, it has always been used in Shinto shrines and Buddhist temples as part of religious rituals and ceremonies to invoke the gods, as well as in local festivities such as Obon. In general, taiko provided background music and dramatic ambiance in theater, and during Obon, it was usually played as a solo instrument that beat out the rhythm for dancers. It was never the center of attention as an independent performance.

Taiko ensemble performances (*kumi-daiko*) are a much more recent phenomenon in Japan, where they were started in 1951 by Daihachi Oguchi, a former jazz drummer who created the Osuwa Daiko ensemble. In 1959, Oedo Sukeroku Daiko was formed, which became the first taiko ensemble that toured professionally. Kumi-daiko was further popularized when it was featured in the Festival of the Arts during the 1964 Tokyo Summer Olympics, and a number of local community taiko groups were subsequently created in Japan. In the 1970s, when the Japanese government became concerned with the loss of traditional folk arts, it started to promote and subsidize community festivals, and the subsequent revival of folk traditions in the context of Japanese national identity helped promote the further growth of taiko in the country. In 1969, Tagayasu Den founded the Ondekoza ensemble on Sado Island with a group of youth dedicated to rigorous training and communal living. Ondekoza brought taiko to audiences outside Japan and was the first to tour the United States in 1977. It also led to the creation of Kodo (started by members who split from Ondekoza), which has now become perhaps the most famous taiko ensemble, enthralling audiences worldwide.

The emergence of ensemble taiko drumming in the United States is often associated with the civil rights movement and the political activism of the 1960s and 1970s (Ahlgren 2011: introduction, ch. 1; Asai 1995:438–440; Kobayashi 2006:2–3; Konagaya 2001; Terada 2001:41). A number of prominent figures in the early history of Japanese American taiko were sansei who were involved in the civil rights and Asian American movements, and taiko has occasionally been used in political protest. However, interviews with founding members of the earliest ensembles do not indicate a direct connection between political activism and the creation of taiko groups. Therefore, taiko was related to minority activism only in the sense that it was part of the general ethnic awakening and identity politics of the time and the struggle among Asian Americans to recover and express their cultural heritage and histories.

Taiko was introduced to Japanese Americans by Seiichi Tanaka, a Japanese immigrant, who is known as the "father of North American taiko." Although he initially intended to pursue a martial arts career, he noticed the lack of taiko drums at the San Francisco Cherry Blossom Festival and was inspired to bring the art form to the United States. He returned to Japan to learn taiko from Daihachi Oguchi, the founder of the first kumidaiko group, as well as from other masters. In 1968, he established the first North American taiko group, the San Francisco Taiko Dojo. He then inspired the formation of many other ensembles, eventually teaching thousands of students through rigorous training methods and strict discipline.

In 1969, Reverend Masao Kodani at the Senshin Buddhist Temple in Los Angeles founded Kinnara Taiko, creating an Americanized, hybrid version of taiko that is based on a more informal style of practice and performance and enables broad participation. San Jose Taiko followed in 1973, which was founded by Reverend Hiroshi Abiko, Dean Miyakusu, and Roy Hirabayashi in San Jose's Japantown and has become a leading professional taiko ensemble that incorporates rhythms from various musical traditions. The 1970s saw a continued increase in the number of taiko groups, as well as the spread of taiko to states outside of California, starting with Denver Taiko in 1977, founded at the Tri-State Denver Buddhist Temple. By 1979, there were taiko groups in Utah, Illinois, New York, as well as Vancouver, Canada.

These earliest Japanese American taiko groups were initially influenced by taiko ensembles from Japan, namely Ondekoza and later Kodo, both of which toured the United States, ran workshops, and generated enthusiasm for the art form. They also inspired new taiko groups to form and actively collaborated by sharing knowledge (especially about how to make taikos) and training each other.

Although the number of taiko groups continued to increase in the 1980s, it began to grow exponentially after the 1990s. The earlier ensembles in the 1960s and 1970s were started by third-generation sansei, who continue to be leaders in the taiko community, but the musical form has now been passed down to the fourth-generation yonsei, who have been responsible for its continued expansion and development (Konagaya 2001:166–117). Taiko did not proliferate throughout the Japanese American community until it was taken up enthusiastically by the yonsei, which, again, indicates their considerable interest in reconnecting with their ethnic heritage. In fact, most of the Japanese American youth in local community taiko ensembles today are yonsei. They are also responsible for the growth of collegiate ensembles, especially in California, which started with the founding of the first college taiko group, UCLA's Kyodo Taiko, in 1990. Today, there are dozens of collegiate groups around the country.

Some estimates indicate there are about 150 taiko groups in the United States,[2] although others put the number at 250, 400, or even 1,000 groups.[3] New taiko groups are constantly forming, even as some older ones become defunct, and their number continues to increase each year. Although they are clustered mostly on the West Coast and in Hawaii, others are scattered all across the United States, including states not known for significant Japanese American communities such as Alaska, Minnesota, Nevada, North Carolina, Ohio, and Oklahoma. Even in Phoenix, Arizona, there are no less than *four* taiko ensembles: Kyo Rei Taiko Kai from the Arizona Buddhist Temple, Taka Taiko Gumi from Washington Elementary School, Phoenix Taiko Kai, and Fushicho Daiko. Because of the incredible proliferation of taiko ensembles, they vary widely not only in character, but also in talent and quality.

Although most ensembles consist of amateurs who practice together and put on performances for the local community, there are also a number of professional performing groups, such as the San Francisco Taiko Dojo, San Jose Taiko, On Ensemble, TAIKOPROJECT, and the Kenny Endo Taiko Ensemble. Active collaboration and interaction among the myriad taiko groups continues today through events such as the biennial North American Taiko Conference, the annual Intercollegiate Invitational, the annual Zellerbach International Taiko Festival, and the Los Angeles Taiko Festival, among others.

Taiko is relatively easy to learn since it does not require many years of painstaking music lessons in order to play. In addition, there are plenty of taiko groups and even schools that run workshops, training sessions, classes, and internships in addition to online instruction. Most groups do not require new members to have previous taiko experience or even musical training, nor do they have other prerequisites (Tusler 2003:56). In addition, it is not that difficult to start a new taiko group. Since purchasing taikos from Japan is quite expensive, many North American groups construct their own drums using wine barrels, which makes starting ensembles easier and helps to keep this traditional musical form more accessible.

Most taiko ensembles use *nagado-daiko* (long-bodied drums), a type of *byou-daiko* that is carved from a single log with cowhide drum heads tacked into place. *Nagado-daiko* range from small and medium-sized drums to large *odaiko*, which have heads that are three to six feet or greater in diameter. *Shime-daiko* (rope-tensioned drums) are also used, with sizes again ranging from small to large *okedo*, which can be over ten feet in diameter. Like taiko ensembles in Japan, most Japanese American taiko groups wear loose-fitting, traditional Japanese festival costumes (*happi*), which can include *obi* (sashes worn around the waist) and *hachimaki* (head bands). Ensembles can use other types of percussive instruments such as hand cymbals, small gongs, gourd shakers, rattles, and flutes (*fue*) such as *shakuhachi*. Performances involve highly choreographed and synchronized drumming movements integrated with purely stylistic motions and punctuated by *kiai* (brief shouts or yells). Usually, a group of performers drums in unison, sometimes moving from one drum to another, but there are also solo performances within a group or alone.

## Recovering Ethnic Heritage through Taiko

For many later-generation Japanese Americans, taiko is a means to recover their ethnic heritage. Because it is a quintessentially traditional Japanese musical form that has a long history in Japan, taiko makes them feel connected to their ethnic roots and ancestry. This is one of the dominant motivations among those who join taiko groups and partly explains their growing popularity. According to Steve Okura of UCSD's

Asayake Taiko, "I think taiko is popular among Japanese Americans because it's kind of like going back to your roots. And I think if you're Japanese American, regardless of what generation you are, it's a way to get in touch with your heritage."

Instead of simply listening to Japanese music, later-generation Japanese Americans now have their own musical genre, which they have inherited from their ethnic homeland and incorporated into their own culture as active participants (Powell 2008:909; Yoon 2001:425). In addition, because of taiko's accessibility in local Japanese American communities, they can get in touch with their ancestral heritage without traveling and living in Japan (Powell 2008). This is true not only for those who directly learn and perform taiko, but also for those who attend performances, especially at community events and festivals.

For the third-generation sansei who initially started the taiko movement in the 1970s, the need to reconnect with their ancestral heritage and express their ethnic identity was quite strong (Ahlgren 2011:66; Izumi 2001:40–41; Kobayashi 2006:2; Terada 2001:41). Some of them were definitely inspired by the Asian power and ethnic pride movements of the period. In addition, because of the discriminatory legacy of the internment camps during World War II, which stigmatized people of Japanese ancestry and caused the nisei to assimilate, taiko became a way for the sansei to reclaim a cultural heritage and identity that they had lost over the generations (Terada 2001:40–41). "My parents really wanted my sister and myself to become Americanized," Lesley Hamda of Kinnara Taiko observed. "So we didn't go to Japanese school or anything and I didn't have many Japanese American friends. So I thought that by playing taiko, that would be a way to connect with my heritage."[4] This effort among the sansei to revive ethnic culture and consciousness could cause conflicts with some of their assimilation-oriented nisei parents, as it did in the case of Joyce Nakata Kim, a founding member of Denver Taiko, who recalled:

[My parents] would say, "Why are you going backwards? We wanted you to become Americanized and now you want to get back to all this stuff." . . . And so they totally fought this. You know, they didn't understand it at all. To this day, I don't really know how my parents feel about taiko. I like to think that they're proud. But my dad . . . You know, after I performed, he'd criticize me. So I think that's pretty typical of a nisei man. (JANM interview)

Concerns that Japanese Americans had become overly assimilated were definitely on the minds of the early sansei taiko founders. George Abe, one of the original members of Kinnara Taiko at the Senshin Buddhist Temple, spoke of how the desire to start a taiko ensemble was related to the amount of religious assimilation that had occurred over time at the temple, which made their activities resemble a Protestant congregation. For Kenny Endo, a prominent sansei musician, a year-long stay at a Native American reservation in Arizona where the Poston concentration camp for Japanese Americans was located during World War II inspired him to take up taiko. He observed the closeness of Native Americans to nature and their traditional rituals, which "made me realize how far removed I am from my own culture." As a result, he really wanted to get in touch with his own roots and heritage and became involved in taiko after he returned to Los Angeles (JANM interview).

For some third-generation taiko pioneers, the return to heritage and ethnic roots also meant reconnecting with the first-generation issei by bringing back a lost cultural tradition from their homeland of Japan (Ahlgren 2011:66). George Abe refers to this as "skipping a generation," and explains that "as sanseis, we began to look more not at what the niseis did but what the isseis did. We wanted to communicate with *jichan* and *bachan* [grandfather and grandmother] and found out that there was a very rich culture there that maybe the isseis really didn't transfer [to the niseis] or the niseis didn't pick up" (JANM interview). The first performances of San Jose Taiko were dedicated to the issei as a means of bringing taiko back to them. PJ Hirabayashi, one of the ensemble's founding members, describes the reaction of the issei as follows:

[The] issei [were] crying and then coming up and saying, "Oh, I'm so happy that you are getting in touch with Japanese culture. It makes me very proud." And to hear that made it sound like it's coming from my own grandmother. . . . The sansei were respecting the fact that the issei had come from Japan, and [it] was like we could see our origins there. . . . You can almost see the sense of lineage. (JANM interview)

The taiko movement that was started by the sansei continues to be relevant to fourth-generation yonsei today, motivating them to remain ethnically engaged through the art form. For instance, according to Kelsey Fujita:

> As a yonsei . . . playing taiko has such deep meaning to me that is related to my background. For me, playing taiko is closely related to and intertwined with my Japanese American identity. American taiko flourished during the Civil Rights Movement and . . . it was a new outlet for empowerment and community strength during the redress movement [for the wartime internment of Japanese Americans]. (Quoted in Carle 2008:13)

In fact, some fourth-generation Japanese Americans who grew up in mainly white neighborhoods were enrolled in taiko groups by sansei parents who were worried that they had lost touch with their ethnic heritage (Powell 2008:905).

## Remaking Taiko Traditions in the United States

It is important to note that taiko as performed in the United States appeals to later-generation Japanese Americans searching for their ancestral roots not because it is a faithful reproduction of the Japanese original. As an ancient Japanese musical form, it is definitely steeped in tradition. However, it has also been considerably modified in the United States, resulting in a new, remade tradition of Japanese American taiko. This is why taiko is such an effective means to enact ethnic ancestry: it provides a compelling connection to an ancestral past while remaining relevant to the present.

Taiko is an appropriate means to interrogate the concept of tradition, since much of its attraction to Japanese Americans comes from the fact that it appears to be so quintessentially traditional—that is, a cultural form inherited from the distant past. Although cultural traditions are often understood to have been passed down from the past relatively unchanged, it is quite clear that they have been constantly altered and remade over time (Handler and Linnekin 1984). In fact, Charles Briggs (1996:435) cites an entire line of scholars who have argued that all traditions are created and recreated in the present and thus reflect current agendas and projects instead of some inherited cultural essence of a bounded group.

Therefore, what makes something traditional is not unaltered continuity with past forms or its persistence through long periods of history. A tradition can be defined as any cultural practice that has been around for some time and has gained some respect and authority as a result. As one perceptive taiko blogger notes:

> "Tradition" is just something that you or your group has done for a time. Do you bow as a group before practice? That's a tradition. Do you warm up as a group? That's a tradition, too. Do you have an annual concert or always play at a certain festival? Tradition. . . . The longer your group has been around, the more traditions it will have.[5]

All traditional musical forms like taiko are inherently performative and are products of innovative modifications and transformations of earlier traditions in response to current circumstances. Performativity is thus not incompatible with tradition, but essential to it. According to Millie Creighton, "the validity of tradition . . . also implies the possibility of doing something different and innovating with creative ideas supplied by traditional motifs. So tradition is not frozen in past forms" (2007:223). As professional taiko musician Kenny Endo puts it, "My thing is using tradition as a basis of innovation . . . as a foundation—it's been a great way to create new music for this art." Likewise, Yuji Kimura from Denver Taiko observes that "in addition to being very traditional, [taiko]'s also very creative. And you can blend those two together. And so you can honor and you can respect the past, but you can also add your own creativity" (JANM interviews).

In this way, traditions are constantly remade and "invented" in the present and involve some break and discontinuity with the past.[6] There is no singular "tradition" per se, only multiple ones with some being older while others are newer. As noted earlier, although the use of taiko in religion, festivals, and theater is an ancient tradition in Japan, kumi-daiko is a relatively recent tradition that dates back only to 1951. Japanese kumi-daiko itself is a remade tradition that represents a distinct break from the past in that it involves a new form of ensemble drumming, in contrast to the previous use of taiko as mainly a solo instrument (Bender

2012:5; ch. 4), and it makes taiko the primary instrument at the center of the musical performance instead of background percussion or accompaniment in dance, dramas, festivals, or religious ritual. In addition, Japanese kumi-daiko is based on choreographed and stylistic movements (Yoon 2001:421) that did not exist in earlier taiko traditions, and it often modifies old folk rhythms.

When this kumi-daiko tradition from Japan was remade by later-generation Japanese Americans in the United States as a newer tradition, additional changes were introduced, producing a further historical discontinuity with the past. Recreated in an entirely new American social context, taiko was not passed down through the generations in the United States from the issei to the nisei and then to the sansei. Taiko drums were indeed brought by some issei immigrants to the United States in the early twentieth century, but they saw only limited use in Buddhist temples during Obon festivals and in some martial arts dojos. In addition, the incarceration of Japanese Americans during World War II, which disrupted and scattered their ethnic community, meant that taiko drumming was largely forgotten and not passed down to second-generation Japanese Americans (Konagaya 2001:142).[7] Instead, taiko was suddenly discovered by the sansei starting in the late 1960s when Seiichi Tanaka, who immigrated to the United States from Japan, introduced it. Kinnara Taiko, the first taiko group founded by Japanese Americans, got started when they started jamming on a taiko at their Buddhist temple, which had been put away after the Obon festival.

Therefore, instead of one taiko tradition, we have multiple layers of tradition that have existed for different lengths of time and are reconfigurations of earlier traditions. Japanese kumi-daiko is a relatively newer tradition that modified an ancient taiko tradition, and Japanese American taiko is in turn a modification of the Japanese kumi-daiko tradition.

Although all traditions have been constantly changed and remade, older ones are often considered more "traditional" than recent ones. As a result, newer traditions can attempt to establish a connection with older ones in order to gain greater authority and legitimacy by claiming to be directly inherited from the past. This is shown by Seiichi Tanaka, who returned to Japan to study with Japanese kumi-daiko groups before he helped develop Japanese American taiko and who therefore continues to be the standard-bearer of "traditional" taiko in the United States.

However, other newer traditions acknowledge a discontinuity with the past and emphasize how they have reshaped earlier traditions in response to contemporary social circumstances. In other words, they are conscious of their new and remade condition and may not even consider themselves to be "traditional" per se. This is the case with many Japanese American taiko players, who often claim that their taiko is not "traditional." As Tom Sumimoto, one of my interviewees noted, "The way we play and the music we play, almost nothing is really traditional, like from way back. A lot of it is really new."

"It was all made up. There is nothing traditional about it at all," admitted Reverend Mas Kodani, the founder of Kinnara Taiko (JANM interview). Johnny Mori, another founding member of Kinnara, elaborated:

Japanese American taiko had no roots whatsoever in Japan, nothing at all. Basically, we sat around and said, "Are we making this thing up?" and Reverend Masao said, "Yeah, we're just making this up." And I go, "This has no connection [to Japan]?" . . . And he said, "Nope." (Cited in Powell 2012a:108).

The search for ethnic heritage among later-generation Japanese Americans through taiko is thus not so much about reproducing past forms of Japanese tradition as it is about producing new ones in the present. Performativity is essential to the recovery of ethnic traditions since they are not simply passed down unaltered from the ancestral homeland, but adapted to the contemporary social conditions under which Japanese Americans live in the United States. As a number of scholars have noted, Asian American cultural practices are "partly inherited, partly modified, as well as partly invented" (Lowe 1996:65; see also Espiritu 1994:264; Tuan 2001:128–129). Such remaking of homeland cultures through performativity is an integral part of the recovery of ethnicity among later-generation minorities such as the Japanese Americans because it increases their personal connection to the performance and produces a greater sense of ownership of their cultural heritage. In fact, taiko is part of Japanese American ethnic heritage precisely because it is a new tradition remade in America. If it were simply a replica of taiko as performed in Japan, it would be a *Japanese* ethnic tradition and heritage, not a Japanese American one.

## Making Drums and Music

The significant differences between the Japanese American kumi-daiko tradition and its counterpart in Japan begins with the drums themselves. In contrast to Japanese taiko ensembles, which purchase drums from professional manufacturers (Creighton 2007:214–215), most Japanese American groups make their own taikos out of wine barrels since it is prohibitively expensive for them to buy drums from Japan. Kinnara invented this innovative method to make drums, which involves sanding down and painting wine barrels, soaking cowhides, pulling the skin over the barrel (initially with car jacks and ropes and then with hydraulic jacks), and then tacking them into place. Although there was much trial and error in the beginning, this method of constructing drums was improved over time and widely shared among the early taiko groups. Today, older taiko ensembles continue to actively share their knowledge with newer groups that are still experimenting and not yet adept at building drums. Currently, there are instructions on the Internet about how to make taikos, as well as retailers that sell wine barrels, cowhides, tacks, handles, and other accessories needed to build drums.

In addition to playing on self-made instruments, American taiko groups do not simply perform preexisting pieces/songs, but also compose their own music. This is true even among community taiko groups. According to Deborah Wong (2005:85), original compositions by taiko groups often become signature pieces and are usually not played by other groups. Indeed, only a few individually composed works are in the public domain, and even these are often arranged and played differently by different groups.

Although the music composed by Japanese American taiko ensembles is often based on traditional patterns of Japanese drumming, it also incorporates rhythms from jazz, rock, hip-hop, blues, and Afro-Caribbean, Latin, Brazilian, and African music and shows the influence of the multicultural musical environments in which ensemble members have been raised (Tusler 2003:85). In addition, some ensembles have combined taiko with various types of Western instruments, such as electric guitars, saxophones, keyboard synthesizers, Western drum sets, violins, and bagpipes (Izumi 2001:43; Tusler 2003:45). Taiko players such as

Kenny Endo have performed with jazz musicians, symphony orchestras, and other percussionists such as conga drummers.

As a result, Japanese American taiko music is quite different from that of Japan, where pieces are based mainly on folk music and generally do not incorporate non-Japanese musical styles and instruments. In fact, most amateur Japanese ensembles do not compose their own music; rather, they adapt local folk rhythms (Bender 2012: ch. 4) and play classical repertoires with traditional ways of drumming (Asai 1995:441; Izumi 2001:43). Although Japanese professional ensembles such as Kodo do compose their own pieces and incorporate motifs and instruments from other parts of Asia, they continue to be mainly inspired by Japanese folk music and generally do not use Western instruments and musical forms (Bender 2012:21–22, chs. 2, 3).

Japanese American taiko players often speak about the differences between their brand of taiko and the Japanese version. According to Tom Sumimoto, a UCSD student who used to be part of a community taiko group: "When you see taiko in Japan, it's just like playing traditional kinds of songs. Whereas taiko here is different. Even my taiko group, from the 1970s, had mixed [musical] styles and they were proud of that. It's like using whatever song that has influence."

"Most Japanese American groups are very progressive and have a totally new sound and throw in jazz, hip-hop, Cuban, Brazilian music, like pop groups," Steve Okura of Asayake Taiko explained. "There are Japanese taiko groups [from Japan] that come and perform here in a totally different, traditional style. Taiko has grown from something that was strictly Japanese to a really international art form."

The distinctiveness of Japanese American taiko becomes especially apparent when ensembles in the United States encounter Japanese taiko players or perform in Japan. During Kinnara Taiko's early years, taiko players from Japan had trouble accepting the group's style because it was so different from traditional Japanese taiko. Johnny Mori recounted the reaction of Seiichi Tanaka when he first came to observe Kinnara practicing. Tanaka reportedly said: "You're kind of being disrespectful to the drum. You're playing on these wine barrels. What you're playing is not Japanese traditional rhythms. Nothing about it is Japanese." This is what made Johnny realize that they were playing a distinctive style of "Japanese American taiko."[8] When San Jose Taiko first toured Japan in 1987 as a mature professional ensemble, they were well received, but realized that they were playing a unique musical style different from the Japanese. PJ Hirabayashi describes her experiences as follows:

> We went to Nagasaki where we stayed with Ondekoza [the famous Japanese ensemble] for a few weeks and played with them in a joint performance. It was in Japan where we played juxtaposed to Ondekoza when we realized, "Wow, we are really different." . . . So coming back home after that experience . . . we realized it empowered us to say, "We definitely have a voice. We definitely have a unique identity in musical expression that stands alone from Japanese taiko." (JANM interview)

### Drumming to Have Fun

In addition to developing different types of drums and music, North American taiko ensembles have a distinctive style of performing, emphasizing theatrical dance-like moves and employing types of body movements not used by Japanese groups (Izumi 2001:43). "I think taiko here is more diverse and a lot of it is more visual," Tom Sumimoto observed. "Like a lot more dancing and stuff like that. It's kind of flashy and you show off the moves." In addition, there seems to be more improvisation in both physical movements and musical forms than typically found in Japanese taiko performances.

Another characteristic of the performance style of a number of American taiko groups is that they appear to be really having fun playing taiko and often perform with happy and even joyful expressions and smiles on their faces. In interviews and on blogs and websites, taiko players repeatedly emphasize how taiko is "really fun," "great fun," "a lot of fun," "so much fun," "so enthusiastic, fun, and joyful," and so on. Likewise, Steve Okura felt that one of the reasons he took up taiko was to "have fun as much as possible." According to one blogger, "I'm glad that kumidaiko was created, because that means I get to have fun hitting drums and being active. I use taiko very much as an activity to simply have fun, and I'm not one to be bogged down by the history or details."[9] San Jose Taiko is especially noted for appearing to really enjoy playing taiko for audiences. In fact, their professional performance style is described by their members as very fluid, dance-like, and "happy" (Powell 2012b:131).

In stark contrast, Japanese taiko groups generally perform with serious and disciplined facial expressions and demeanors. Such differences become readily apparent when American and Japanese taiko groups practice or perform together. For instance, Tagayasu Den, who founded Ondekoza in Japan, characterized San Jose Taiko as "sunshine taiko" (JANM interview with PJ Hirabayashi), while Mas Kodani of Kinnara Taiko, which practiced with Ondekoza from Japan, said, "They are the exact opposite of us. I remember one time, they said 'Our taiko is serious taiko and your taiko is fun taiko'" (JANM interview). According to George Abe, Ondekoza was so serious and almost robotic in demeanor that "one of the things we began asking them was, 'You guys never smile on stage. How come?'" (JANM interview).

This contrast in performance styles is certainly noted by Japanese taiko players who have seen Japanese American taiko ensembles. For instance, Motofumi Yamaguchi of Kodo recalled: "Our narrow perspective was that taiko was something that you played seriously. But after seeing their [American] taiko, we realized it is OK to play in that way. . . . But for us, it is difficult to beat the drum and smile like that at the same time."[10]

## Social and Gender Dynamics

Not only have later-generation Japanese Americans created a distinctive style of taiko performance, they have modified the social organization of ensembles as well. Taiko groups in Japan, especially professional ones like Kodo, are hierarchically ordered and instruction is based on a traditional Japanese master-apprentice system (Bender 2012: ch. 4; Creighton 2007). In contrast, Japanese Americans have adopted a more egalitarian ensemble structure, again reflecting the influence of their American upbringing and democratic ideologies. Although some American taiko ensembles are organized in hierarchical *sempai/kohai* (senior/junior) relationships, they are generally not seriously enforced (Tusler 2003:90–93). Other ensembles explicitly reject hierarchies and make a self-conscious effort to maintain equality in status.

For instance, according to George Abe, Kinnara Taiko does not enforce formal discipline in its ensembles and does not have a mentor/mentee or disciple relationship or even teachers per se (JANM inter-

San Jose's "fun taiko" (photo provided courtesy of San Jose Taiko; photo credit: Higashi Design).[11]

views). San Jose Taiko is also based on a nonhierarchical model of organization (Kobayashi 2006:2) and views Japanese traditional social
structures as potentially limiting to individual development (Ahlgren
2011:74). As PJ Hirabayashi explained, the ensemble wanted to create a
system that was fairly horizontal and did not have teachers (JANM interview). Leadership and operational responsibilities are shared equally
among group members and decisions are made by consensus. During
performance, all members have opportunities to play the most desirable

Kodo's "serious taiko" (photo provided courtesy of Kodo Taiko; photo credit: Takashi Okamoto).

or challenging parts, which discourages the emergence of star performers who are superior to others (Ahlgren 2011:74–75).

In terms of gender relations, American taiko groups are also composed differently from Japanese ones, again reflecting an Americanized, egalitarian ethos. Partly because taiko requires physical stamina and endurance, it is a highly masculinized performance in Japan and historically, it was quite rare for women to play taiko (Bender 2012:144–

145). Leading Japanese professional ensembles are dominated by men, and opportunities for women to perform have been limited (Bender 2012:2, 155–157; Kobayashi 2006:2; Wong 2000:73). Amateur taiko groups also maintain the gendered differences of professional groups (Bender 2012:165), although women do sometimes perform in female-only ensembles. Indeed, while the current number of women taiko players in Japan may be equal to, if not greater than, that of men (Bender 2012:144), they are not as prevalent nor as prominent as in American groups (Wong 2000:73).

In contrast, women have performed in American taiko ensembles from the very beginning and have significantly outnumbered male taiko players according to most estimates (Ahlgren 2011:13). As a result, it is not unusual to see ensembles where a majority of performers are women. When Japanese American taiko groups interacted with Japanese ones like Kodo in the 1970s, they would ask the Japanese players why there were no women in their group. In addition, gendered inequalities are generally avoided in organization and in performance in American taiko groups. For instance, in San Jose Taiko, women and men equally share leadership as well as all other responsibilities, and both play strenuous pieces and large drums (Ahlgren 2011:74–75).

Although male taiko players in the United States seem to have a positive opinion of gender equality in their ensembles (Carle 2008:54), this does not mean that women are completely free from sexist objectification by men. Women can be desired precisely because of their essentialized femininity in what is still viewed as a masculine activity. The former director of UCSD's Asayake Taiko spoke frankly to me about this dilemma:

> As a guy, I fought for the inclusion of more women into the group because then, more guys come to watch our performances! I could get into a lot of trouble for saying that because that's exotifying [women]. But it's really hard because if you have women in a taiko group, you kind of want them to sell the fact that they're women. And our performance director would say things like, "If you're a girl, you have to do *kiai* [shouts] in a high pitch to sound more feminine." So women have to ask: by doing this, am I exotifying myself and my sexuality? And how do I play taiko in a way that doesn't promote something like that?"

## The Embodiment and Performativity of Taiko

In many ways, later-generation Japanese Americans have remade and recreated Japanese taiko in the United States and produced a new Americanized taiko tradition that is a product of their own history and musical and cultural backgrounds. However, such dynamic reworking of past forms is not simply about changing instruments, performance styles, and gender dynamics. It is also embedded in the act of performance itself. Japanese American taiko allows for improvised modifications and spontaneous innovations enacted through the body during performance, which constantly transforms both choreographic and musical structure.

In fact, taiko is a classic example of embodiment, which is a phenomenological approach that examines how cultural forms are inscribed upon, inculcated in, and experienced through the body. Learning to play taiko is a highly embodied process and skills are acquired primarily through physical bodily movements, rather than through mental and intellectual processes (the mind). Moreover, as George Abe of Kinnara emphasizes, taiko pedagogy is based not so much on explicit verbal instructions and explanations, as on the emulation of bodily practices, which he associates with a Buddhist desire to produce implicit understanding while remaining vague and mistrusting excessive clarity (JANM interview).

In this sense, taiko is an illustration of Merleau-Ponty's (1962) phenomenology, which collapses the Cartesian mind-body dualism by emphasizing how perception and consciousness are produced through corporeal practices and movements instead of being divorced from them. For example, San Jose Taiko emphasizes "the spiritual unity of the mind and body" (Powell 2012b:135). The spirituality of taiko is connected to the *ki* (spirit or energy) that arises from within the body's *hara* (abdomen) and is experienced physically as it flows through the body and is transferred via the *bachi* (sticks) to the drums to produce sound (Powell 2012b:135; Tusler 2003:76–80).

However, classic analyses of embodiment often remove intentionality and agency from bodily practice. According to Bourdieu (1977: ch. 2), embodiment is occurs outside of explicit awareness and intentionality. The habitus is inculcated and internalized through repetition and reiteration of bodily practices (such as through exercises, rituals, games, and mechanical learning) which leads to practical mastery and skills without the process becoming explicitly conscious. Since practices are produced through habitual unawareness, we are left with subjects who simply embody and reproduce prescribed forms through force of habit and rarely attain the level of discursive consciousness necessary to challenge the received social order.

Likewise, embodiment for Foucault (1979) involves the subjugation of the body to minute disciplinary practices and techniques (including the repetition of basic exercises that control corporeal movements and actions) within the context of institutional power, resulting in docile subjects and bodies.

In some ways, taiko performers resemble docile subjects constituted by the habitual and disciplinary processes of mechanical embodiment. Much of taiko training does involve imitation, rote learning, and repetitive drilling, since proper physical technique and form (*kata*) is necessary to harness the spiritual energy emanating from the body as well as the drums and to produce aesthetically stylized, choreographed movements designed to please the audience (Powell 2008:914, 2012b:125, 130–131; Tusler 2003:71–76; Williams 2013:27–28). Nonetheless, such disciplinary and iterative pedagogies that imprint prescribed forms onto the body through reflexive habit rarely become so totalizing and all-encompassing that they eliminate the possibility of agency and innovative practices that can ultimately reconfigure received cultural forms.

Even the most ritualized, embodied musical practices like taiko incorporate performative elements within predetermined routines. We must distinguish between *performance*, which is any public, cultural display enacted for an audience (Schieffelin 1998:199–200), and *performativity*, which involves innovation, improvisation, and the modification of prescribed forms through individual agency (Noland 2009; Powell 2008:915–916; Schieffelin 1998:200, 204). When taiko is actually performed, players do not simply mechanically embody and reproduce preexisting movements or musical structures; rather, they create intentional, transformative interventions.

Indeed, all embodied, ritual performances involve agency and transformative potential. According to Carrie Noland (2009), the movement and gestures of performances may be inscribed and constrained by habitus, but subjects can also experiment in their motor decisions and alter the rhythms and sequences in ways that challenge dominant cultural meanings. As Judith Butler argues in her theory of performativity (1990, 1996), the iterative nature of gender performances destabilizes prescribed identities and categories and prevents them from becoming essentialized and fully constituted by society. Instead, their constant repetition always leaves room for variation, subversive possibilities, and necessary failures and reconfigurations. For Noland, the performative agency that generates variations in established forms is based on the sensory experience of bodily movement and can range from intentional to involuntary. By repeating gestural routines, subjects can become aware of the body's capacity to perform in innovative ways and alter prescribed forms. However, in other cases, the subject may remain largely unaware of such modifications.

Nonetheless, it is important to realize that performative agency *always* involves active awareness and intentionality. Subjects do not exercise agency if they intend to simply reproduce received cultural forms in their practices and change is simply a product of the unintended consequences of their actions, mistakes, or inability to execute proper form.

American taiko is especially notable because of the ability of performers to spontaneously innovate and actively improvise during highly choreographed performances through the process of repeated embodiment. Physical movements in taiko do not always strictly follow established *kata*, but also involve a process of performative embodiment as new bodily movements are constantly invented and intentionally incorporated by players into traditional movements. This is especially the case with stylistic movements done for aesthetic purposes, such as twirling drumsticks in different ways between beats, whereby performers create their own signature moves. Therefore, although *kata* is based on rote and mechanical inculcation of habitus onto the body in ways that are seemingly less subject to consciousness awareness, distinct moments of intentional improvisation still occur even in highly ritualized and choreographed types of embodiment.

In addition to this type of performative embodiment, taiko incorporates performativity in musical form. Not only do American taiko groups produce original compositions and rearrangements of previous ones; their performances also feature moments of intentional musical improvisation on the part of individual drummers, who play solos while the rest of the ensemble provides the background rhythm. San Jose Taiko is the most known for employing this type of musical performativity. The act of solo improvisation can involve combining and rearranging predetermined rhythms in novel ways or varying or lengthening certain rhythmic phrases (Tusler 2003:87). Solos can be prepared and practiced in advance, but are also spontaneously improvised during the act of performing depending on the whim of the drummer, the tempo of the song, or the energy of the group at any given moment. This enables individual performers to actively display personal rhythms and styles of movement within and across certain pieces (Powell 2008:918).

Eventually, these experiments and improvisational changes introduced during performance can become incorporated as permanent parts of a taiko composition and subsequently be taught to and practiced by others (Powell 2008:918–919), thus transforming the original cultural form. In this way, taiko performances are a balance between prescribed bodily and musical forms and performative possibilities based on individual agency. Therefore, Japanese Americans have not only modified taiko as performed in Japan, but also injected an inherent dynamism whereby taiko is constantly remade by individuals in the spontaneous act of performance.

## Conclusion

This chapter has attempted to capture this contemporary performativity inherent in diasporic cultures. The search for ethnic roots among diasporic descendants such as later-generation Japanese Americans involves not just the inheritance and reiteration of an ancient tradition from their ethnic homeland but also its active recreation in the present. By appropriating the musical tradition of taiko from their ethnic homeland, later-generation Japanese Americans have been able to reclaim a cultural heritage that has been lost over the generations. Insofar as taiko was suddenly discovered by the sansei and considerably remade and reinvented in the process of being incorporated into Japanese American communities, it shows how cultural discontinuity is an inherent part of ethnic heritage, which is never an unbroken traditional homeland culture persisting through the generations. While remaining faithful to some aspects of traditional Japanese taiko, Japanese Americans have introduced significant changes, ranging from making their own drums to incorporating Americanized cultural influences into their music, performance styles, and the organization of their ensembles. Such performative transformation of cultural traditions is quite evident among diasporic peoples, who recreate homeland cultures in new social contexts in different countries. In addition, although performances like taiko are based on the embodiment and reiteration of prescribed musical and physical forms, they are still subject to individual reworking through innovations and improvisations. Such spontaneous modifications are intentional acts of agency that can eventually become part of formal musical and choreographic structures, injecting another level of performativity into Japanese American taiko.

Therefore, the recovery of ethnic heritage among later-generation Japanese Americans is not so much about the reproduction of past traditions, but the active production of new ones. In fact, all traditions are inherently performative since they are constantly remade and "invented" in response to current circumstances; none is inherited unchanged from the past. Instead of a single Tradition, what we have are different layers of tradition that have existed for varying lengths of time. Nonetheless, older traditions often position themselves as more "traditional" and authoritative whereas newer traditions, such as Japanese American taiko, may not even see themselves as really traditional. As a result, the taiko tradition that later-generation Japanese Americans have recovered is considerably modified from the original Japanese version. However, this is what makes it such a compelling way to reconnect with their ethnic ancestry. Through such dynamic remaking of homeland cultures, taiko becomes part of their own ethnic heritage instead of a mechanical reenactment of an antiquated cultural inheritance that feels alien to them.

Finally, it is important to remember that taiko is about the revival not just of Japanese American cultural heritage, but also of their ethnic communities, which have experienced a decline in social cohesion since World War II. As Steve Okura put it, "The Japanese American community needs all the help it can get. And if taiko is such a strong source of unity that brings a lot of cultures together, it can only empower that community." Founded in local Buddhist temples, Japanese American churches, and various other community organizations, grass-roots ensembles play a vital role in strengthening local communities through various organizational and outreach activities. It has also been able to galvanize Japanese Americans by bringing together audiences for performances and also serving as a source of collective identity and solidarity. Most importantly, because of its cultural vitality and popularity among fourth-generation yonsei, taiko helps involve Japanese American youth in community activities, from which they have become increasing disengaged in recent years. In this way, taiko also helps counter not only the loss of cultural heritage that resulted from the wartime incarceration of Japanese Americans, but also the decline and fragmentation of their communities instigated by their post-internment dispersal and increasing social assimilation.

7

# Performative Authenticity and Fragmented Empowerment through Taiko

## Tradition and Authenticity

As discussed in the previous chapter, cultural traditions from the ethnic homeland are constantly reconfigured not only though time but also through space. Recreated in the present, such traditions travel across national borders through the diaspora and are appropriated and remade by co-ethnics in other countries. In addition to being subject to the contingencies of history and different social contexts, musical traditions such as taiko are also constantly reworked through individual performativity, which introduces innovations that transform originally inherited forms.

However, if traditions never remain the same but are always in flux, the issue of cultural authenticity arises. This is especially the case for taiko, which has spread throughout the Japanese diaspora, which consists of Japanese descendants (*nikkei*) scattered across the Americas. As it has traveled from the ethnic homeland and been remade in numerous countries, many different versions of taiko have been created that are embedded in various social and historical contexts. So are certain taiko traditions more authentic than others? Are older cultural traditions perceived to be more authentic than newer ones because of their greater historical continuity with the past? For diasporic descendants like the Japanese Americans, are traditions that closely resemble cultural forms from the ethnic homeland considered to be more authentic? If so, is their attempt to reconnect with their ancestral heritage by completely recreating and reinventing homeland traditions tinged with a nagging sense of insincerity and falsehood?

Issues related to tradition and authenticity are definitely on the minds of Japanese American taiko drummers, as indicated in interviews and online blogs. If Japanese American taiko is "all made up" and "there is nothing really traditional about it at all," as the founders of Kinnara Taiko freely admit, how can it feel ethnically authentic? "Because taiko has developed into a Japanese American kind of westernized art, it gives you the *illusion* of getting in touch with your roots," Steve Okura of Asayake Taiko observed. Nonetheless, if later-generation Japanese Americans are seeking to truly recover the ethnic roots and ancestry that they have lost over the generations, taiko performances cannot feel fabricated and inauthentic.

As a result, there are some Japanese American taiko players who attempt to achieve a certain cultural authenticity by drawing from taiko as practiced in the Japanese homeland. However, authenticity is not simply based on the unchanging nature of cultural traditions or their ability to provide a direct link to an ancient and pristine past. Instead, the remaking of traditional taiko among later-generation Japanese Americans also produces a type of *performative authenticity* that makes taiko resonate with their current lives and feel more real. Therefore, the nostalgic yearning for ethnic heritage involves both recovering the past as well as reconstituting it in the present. Taiko's performative authenticity is quite empowering on a personal level, allowing Japanese Americans to display ethnic and gender identities that challenge and undermine demeaning stereotypes of Asian Americans. However, despite its subversive potential, taiko's reception by American audiences reproduces Orientalizing discourses that racially essentialize Japanese Americans as the exotic, Asian Other and is rather disempowering at the collective level.

## Authenticity, Origins, and Homeland

Authenticity is a sense of genuineness or realness (Erickson 1995, Steiner and Reisinger 2006:299), which is usually based on a connection with historical origins (Linnekin 1991:446). Since authenticity is associated with the preservation and persistence of traditional forms, contemporary cultural performances that faithfully reproduce what was originally practiced in some distant past are often understood to be more authentic. As some scholars note (Chhabra, Healy, and Sills 2003:703; Taylor 2001:14–15), past research on tourism regarded what is staged, performed, and recreated as distorted and modified social constructions and thus fake and inauthentic deviations from the real (MacCannell

1973). As a result, the remaking of traditional forms implicitly becomes associated with a lack of authenticity. In fact, Eric Hobsbawm (1983:8) contrasts invented traditions with "genuine traditions" that apparently have an unbroken continuity with the past and have not been recreated or remade, implying that the former are inauthentic. In contrast, Richard Handler and Jocelyn Linnekin argue that since all cultural traditions constantly change and are thus symbolic constructions, there are no genuine and spurious traditions and that instead, "authenticity is always defined in the present" (1984:286).

More recent research has moved away from realist conceptions of authenticity based on objectivist assessments about whether cultural practices accurately reflect original forms (Kim and Jamal 2007:183; Wang 1999:351). Instead, it has emphasized authenticity as a subjective, experiential state, referred to as "existential authenticity" (Erickson 1995; Kim and Jamal 2007; Steiner and Reisinger 2006; Wang 1999). Authenticity becomes a process of self-realization and identity-formation depending on whether cultural performances feel genuine and real to those participating in them. As shown in heritage tourism, the search for authentic experiences often involves delving into the distant past in order to return to cultural origins where one's true self and identity can apparently be found (Chhabra 2003; McIntosh and Prentice 1999; Steiner and Reisinger 2006:309; Taylor 2001). Tourists see heritage sites and cultural practices as more or less authentic depending on how closely they believe they reproduce conditions from the past (Waitt 2000; Chhabra 2003).

In this sense, authenticity becomes an object of nostalgic desire, a longing for a more traditional past that has disappeared due to the apparent ravages of modernity. In this sense, the search for ethnic heritage among Japanese Americans is also an attempt to reconnect with an authentic cultural past that has been lost because of generations of assimilation in the United States. Nostalgia is predicated on loss, since one can yearn only for something that has disappeared or is in danger of disappearing. It is precisely the cultural assimilation of later-generation Japanese Americans that produces a nostalgic desire to recover a cultural heritage that can form the basis for ethnic authenticity.

Insofar as authenticity is rooted in the distant past, older cultural traditions have a greater claim to authenticity than newer ones because of their presumed connections to origins. As a result, they often become the basis for the experience of ethnic heritage. For diasporic groups that have been scattered around the world, time itself is mapped onto space, so that the ethnic homeland is seen as the source of ethnic authenticity and heritage because it is where cultural traditions originated in the past. Newer cultures in the diaspora are thus positioned as less authentic, or even inauthentic when compared to those of the homeland. As Joni Jones points out (2002:12), the hyphen (for peoples labeled "Asian-American" or "Japanese-American") creates a sense of inauthenticity, so that their diasporic cultures are perceived as derivative modifications of the original and thus less genuine than the cultures of Asians and Japanese (Wong 2005:88).

In this context, Japanese Americans, especially the yonsei, look to their ancestral homeland of Japan as the place of origin where authentic ethnic traditions from the past can be found. They judge cultural practices as more or less genuine based on whether they resemble those in the ancestral homeland, a tendency also found in other Japanese American community activities, such as beauty pageants.[1] As Angela Ahlgren indicates, those engaged in taiko are no exception: "North American taiko players, regardless of their own connection to the Japanese diaspora, look to Japan as an artistic homeland, a source of authenticity, and a site of inspiration" (2011:61).

This is aptly illustrated by Seiichi Tanaka, the Japanese immigrant regarded as the "father of North American taiko." Before he introduced taiko to the United States, he first returned to Japan to train with kumidaiko masters in his homeland. Subsequently, his San Francisco Taiko Dojo ensemble and school adopted the Japanese repertoire and performance style, are organized according to traditional Japanese hierarchical relations, and use "genuine" taiko drums from Japan. Tanaka also employs very disciplined and rigorous training methods and intensive physical conditioning (which he refers to as "no pain, no gain") akin to those of Japanese professional taiko ensembles. Former students recall his training as exhausting, grueling, and painful.

Because Tanaka is associated with older taiko traditions from the original homeland, he has become the arbiter of authenticity in America and "affirms that having roots in Japanese taiko should be the criterion that distinguishes 'real' or 'genuine' taiko" (Ahlgren 2011:26, 70–71; Konagaya 2001:119–120). As Deborah Wong observes:

[Tanaka's] teaching style is considered particularly rigorous, and American taiko players think of any training with him as a mark of authority. Although he is not regarded as the *only* source of "authentic" taiko in North America, his lineage carries a particular weight even though it is not always explicitly recognized as a link to Sukeroku [one of the original Japanese taiko groups that he trained with]. (2005:80; emphasis in the original)

Thus, for instance, a prominent New York taiko group's affiliation with Tanaka and Japanese taiko ensembles like Kodo is seen as a link to Japan and gives the group an aura of authenticity (Yoon 2001:424). Since older traditions (kumi-daiko in Japan) are often considered more "traditional" than recent ones (kumi-daiko in the United States), the latter often claim a connection with the former in order to gain greater authority and authenticity.

In addition, a number of Japanese American taiko players have gone to Japan and lived there for an extended period of time to study taiko from the original source, which gives their playing authentic credibility (Carle 2008:19). The most prominent example is Kenny Endo, a well-known taiko musician. As a result of Tanaka's vast influence as well as those who have studied in Japan, virtually all North American taiko groups owe a tremendous musical and stylistic debt to Japanese professional taiko groups, especially Sukeroku (Wong 2005:85).

However, not all Japanese American taiko players are concerned about authenticity. Some well-known taiko ensembles such as Kinnara, On Ensemble, and TAIKOPROJECT see themselves as more "progressive" and do not claim any connection to Japan or to traditional Japanese taiko. Instead, they pride themselves for being innovative by actively incorporating rhythms, instruments, and performing styles that move away from Japanese ones. One blogger has weighed in on comments posted about cultural tradition and authenticity in taiko by declaring that he does not care much about the issue because he is simply playing taiko to have fun. "If you get too obsessed about authenticity, it becomes restrictive and takes the fun out of it," he opined.[2]

In fact, there is some tension between taiko players who are supportive of the more progressive groups and those who are self-professed traditionalists and judge taiko groups based on a scale of relative authenticity where Japan continues to be the benchmark for what is considered real, "traditional" taiko. Steve Okura of UCSD's Asayake Taiko described his view of the issue in this manner:

> I have pretty mixed feelings about the issue of "diluting" the original Japanese culture. Some people feel taiko should be strictly Japanese and that there are certain styles that are traditional and they try to focus on those. . . . I think taiko has to be inclusive of other cultures, because for me, it has grown from something that was strictly Japanese to really an international art form. But there are those with classical training, who are like, "I grew up this way. Taiko *should* be this way."

In fact, the more progressive and innovative groups can receive criticism and pressure from others for not being sufficiently "authentic" and "traditional," although such concerns seems to be somewhat waning recently. This was initially a source of tension between Seiichi Tanaka and Kinnara Taiko. As described in the previous chapter, when Tanaka first saw Kinnara members practicing, he claimed that that they were not playing real Japanese taiko at all. He did not want them to use the word "taiko," but instead to refer to what they were doing as "drumming" (JANM interviews). Roy Hirabayashi also had to deal with such issues when San Jose Taiko was first forming:

> So I think San Jose Taiko's style of music became a very world musical form. . . . [We] really incorporated a lot of different things. We got into trouble early on because people, the traditionalists, were complaining that you can't use a tambourine with taiko or a cowbell. That's not taiko. People were kind of getting down on us for that kind of stuff. (JANM interview)

The irony of this nostalgic yearning on the part of some Japanese Americans for an authentic tradition of taiko from their ancestral homeland is that the ensemble taiko tradition in Japan is itself relatively new, as noted in the previous chapter, and predates the Japanese American taiko tradition by only about twenty years. Moreover, Japanese kumidaiko is a radically remade tradition and has little resemblance to the taiko of old Japan. In fact, Japanese taiko ensembles themselves do not make any specific claims to an inherited, ancient tradition (Bender 2012: ch. 4). This again indicates how the ethnic homeland, solely because of its privileged status as the place of ancestral origin, becomes the arbiter of authenticity, even if its cultural traditions are very recent and not very "traditional" per se. In diasporic contexts, space becomes a greater determinant of what is considered authentic than time.

## Performative Authenticity

The search for ethnic authenticity and heritage does not simply involve nostalgically reaching out to the homeland and to the past. Although cultural performances that seemingly reproduce older cultural traditions from the country of ancestral origin can be subjectively experienced as more authentic than newer traditions remade in the diaspora, this is not always the case. More recent traditions can sometimes feel more real and authentic than those inherited from the distant past because their improvisational nature and possibilities for innovation make them more relevant to individuals' contemporary histories, identities, and cultures. Because of the performative agency inherent in newer, recreated traditions like Japanese American taiko, they can be adapted to current conditions and therefore resonate with personal experiences and concerns to a greater extent, therefore making them feel more real and genuine.[3] According to Tom Sumimoto, a University of California at San Diego student who used to be part of a community taiko group, "I think taiko is a good example of how Japanese culture progresses and is changed over time by people who sustain it into the future. You're not forced to stick to a regressed tradition, but you can keep changing and adapting it."

I use the term *performative authenticity* to refer to the feeling of genuineness produced by the innovative and adaptable nature of remade traditions. Innovation and change are not incompatible with authenticity (Johnson 2008:125) since it is precisely discontinuities with the past that can be the basis for the subjective experience of authenticity. In fact, the mechanical re-enactment of outdated, past traditions from another time or country, which have little relevance to people's contemporary cultures and identities, can reinforce feelings of estrangement and alienation. In such cases, individuals may simply go through the motions to faithfully replicate these ancient cultural forms, but do not realize their true selves through such rote practices, leaving them feeling inauthentic and false.

Therefore, despite being a substantial modification of the original Japanese version, Americanized taiko still feels very authentic to later-generation Japanese Americans. Just because a tradition is recent and "invented," it is not necessarily experienced as fake and inauthentic. Instead, the performative and innovative nature of American taiko makes it feel more attuned to their personal lives and current circumstances in ways that seem more genuine.[4] "I don't see how you can be a purist with taiko," Mas Kodani remarked. "It's made up. And if it's authentic, it's made up of where you come from. [We] were raised in a different musical background, so it has to be this way" (JANM interview). PJ Hirabayashi spoke about her experiences as follows:

> For me, the realness factor of American taiko was that taiko in America allowed me to experience and understand my identity as a Japanese American. . . . American taiko was *very real*, an instrument of expression that unleashed our historical oppression in America. We were able to openly celebrate our diversity while reverberating joy and empowerment for all to see. (Quoted in Carle 2008:23–24; emphasis in the original)

The modern, performative authenticity of taiko is one reason for its appeal among Japanese American youth. Taiko is often described by fourth-generation yonsei as "cool," "hip," "flashy," "trendy," and even "sexy," words that would never be used to describe other types of classical Japanese music or traditional art forms, indicating how its performativity resonates with their current lives and identities as modern youth.

Therefore, the experience of ethnic authenticity is not always based on unaltered, past traditions inherited from the ethnic homeland but can arise precisely from their performative and remade nature. Performativity also shifts the authority over authenticity from the homeland to diasporic descendants, who are able to adapt traditional homeland cultures for contemporary purposes. For example, when PJ Hirabayashi initially studied taiko with Seiichi Tanaka, she quickly realized that she would never be able to play the instrument like a Japanese person does in Japan. This empowered her to develop a more personally authentic taiko style that was relevant to her own musical background and sensibilities. According to her, "Our music has to be a reflection of who we are, our expression, our voice, our creativity, our stories, our experiences" (quoted in Powell 2008:917). According to Angela Ahlgren, "Rather than measure themselves against an elusive, yet seemingly fixed, quality of Japaneseness, San Jose Taiko sought to create their own authentic practice. . . . Their adopting the term 'Asian American taiko' was in part a way to forge their own authenticity, based on their own experiences as Asians in the U.S. " (2011:69–70)

Likewise, although American ensembles generally do not play on "authentic" drums imported from Japan, this does not make their music feel any less genuine. On the contrary, because Japanese Americans construct their own drums, they are more personally and spiritually connected to the instruments, which can produce a more real and authentic musical experience (Konagaya 2001:120). The fact that they also compose their own pieces inspired by their American musical backgrounds and even make their own *happi* outfits further enhances the performative authenticity of their brand of taiko.

Because of its performative flexibility, taiko feels more authentically real for later-generation Japanese Americans than other traditional Japanese art forms such as flower arrangement, classical dance, tea ceremonies, and calligraphy, which seem to involve the mechanical reproduction of staid and antiquated traditions. A number of women taiko players have mentioned that they have never felt any enthusiasm or personal connection with these traditional Japanese activities. "I couldn't get into classical dancing," PJ Hirabayashi remarked. "I could not get into flower arranging or tea ceremony. It was just not me" (JANM interview). Another female taiko player had a similar experience: "When I had to grow up, I took *odori* [traditional Japanese dancing]. And I just remember having to put on the kimono and get my hair done, and I just felt this was so unnatural. This is not me" (quoted in Izumi 2001:45). In contrast, when they first saw or tried taiko, it immediately spoke to their hearts and cultural sensibilities in a much more direct way.

This performative authenticity of taiko is ultimately the reason for its effectiveness as a means to reconnect with ethnic heritage and roots. Instead of experiencing taiko as an ancient tradition from a distant land, later-generation Japanese Americans have taken possession of it as part of their own contemporary ethnic backgrounds and histories in ways that feel more pertinent and real (Konagaya 2001:121).

Although existential authenticity has been conceptualized as a nostalgic longing for a traditional past and a reaction against the changes of modernity (Kim and Jamal 2007:189, 194; Wang 1999:360–361), authenticity should not always be opposed to modernity. Some traditions like taiko have an inherent dynamism which makes them compatible with the perturbations of modernity, and therein lies their authenticity as experience. Indeed, the performative authenticity of taiko arises from its apparent fusion of tradition and modernity as past cultural forms are reshaped in the present (Clifford 2004:156–159). On the surface, taiko appears to be the epitome of Japanese tradition, with drums, costumes, and music that resemble ancient Japan and its old-fashioned festivals. As Steve Okura described it, taiko is "seemingly so traditional and primitive" and it provides a nostalgic connection to the past. Yet, at the same time, it can also be modernized through innovation and performativity to bring it up to date with the contemporary world. For Japanese Americans, therefore, taiko speaks to their modern lives while allowing them to remain in touch with traditional culture and ethnic ancestry.

Ultimately, the authentic experience of ethnic heritage and roots depends on a delicate balance between tradition and modernity, past and present. If a cultural performance is too rigidly tied to antiquated and ancient traditions and has nothing to do with the modern world, individuals will not feel any genuine affinity to it. On the other hand, if a cultural performance is too innovative and provides no link with past forms of tradition, it feels fabricated and fake vis-à-vis the tradition and cannot become a source of ancestral heritage. As a result, Kenny Endo argues that all performative innovations must be based on an older, traditional foundation: "If you have no foundation, no basis [in tradition], and you start creating something new from there, it's going to lack authenticity as well as quality" (Wong 2005:88). The dynamic balance between tradition and modernity is the essence of ethnic authenticity, which involves performative cultural experiences that are relevant for the present but remained cloaked in the nostalgia of the past.

## Performativity and Personal Empowerment

Performativity does not simply reconfigure cultural traditions and allow people to nostalgically reconnect with ethnic heritage and roots. It also has broader social ramifications, since all cultural performances engage audiences and thus have public effects. As a performance, taiko has also become a form of personal empowerment for Japanese Americans, which enables them to challenge the ethnic and gender stereotypes through which Asian Americans have been commonly represented. In fact, Min Zhou and Jennifer Lee (2004:17) claim that the production of Asian American youth culture is partly an attempt to counteract racial stereotypes. This illustrates how the performative authenticity of remade traditions can serve a double function: while allowing Japanese Americans to reconstitute the past as a source of genuine cultural heritage, the nostalgic longing for an authentic ethnicity also enables them to contest how they have been falsely constituted in the present by displaying the true nature of their ethnic (and gender) identities through their performances.

As Judith Butler emphasizes (1990, 1996, 2010), performativity has the potential to subvert and reconstitute hegemonic ethnic and gender categories. Performativity theory is in some ways an alternative to the social overdetermination found in classic structuralist and poststructuralist theories, which view the subject as being so thoroughly constituted by culture, hegemonic discourses, and relations of power that resistance and transformation through agency and practice become nearly impossible. In contrast, Butler's notion of performativity shifts the emphasis away from the determinism of prescribed structures and hegemonic categories and stresses their active production through iterative practices. Gender categories and identities are performatively constituted because normative and essentialized conceptions are constantly destabilized and reconfigured through their constant repetition, which introduces the possibility of variation, subversion, and the failure to reproduce prescribed injunctions and ideals. Therefore, gender categories and identities are never fully constituted since their coherence is constantly contested and never fixed. By stressing that there is no "I" that precedes performative enactment but that identity is an effect of performances,

Butler perhaps ascribes too much agency to individuals to create themselves through their reiterative acts.

As a cultural performance, taiko has the potential to disrupt prevailing ethnic and gender categories because its power, loudness, and masculine physicality allow later-generation Japanese Americans to subvert the ways in which they have been stereotypically represented as passive and docile model minorities. The performativity of taiko confers upon them the power to constitute authentic ethnic and gender identities on their own terms and present them to their audiences.

However, the performative authenticity and personal empowerment embedded in taiko are not simply a product of their reiterative nature, but are further accentuated when taiko is enacted in the United States, in completely different racial and ethnic contexts than in Japan. Taiko does not appear radical or transformative in Japan, where it is connected to the revival of ancient festival traditions and is becoming increasingly standardized for nationalist purposes (Bender 2012: ch. 7). However, it takes on new meanings in the United States, where it becomes a way to defy ethnic stereotypes that do not exist in Japan. Its repetitive nature enhances these subversive possibilities because the new performative meanings are repeated over and over and thus literally hammered home, so to speak.

Therefore, the performative agency of cultural traditions is enhanced when they are taken up by diasporic subjects in other countries and enacted outside the original sociocultural context of the ethnic homeland. This is why a nostalgic yearning for an authentic ethnic tradition ironically empowers Japanese Americans to contest conventional ethnic and gender stereotypes in the United States.

Empowerment refers to the ability of individuals or groups to control and influence social outcomes through active participation (Cole 2006:95–97; Fetterman 2005:72; Sofield 2003:79; Zimmerman 2000:43, 48). The concept is often applied to local communities and organizations in anthropological studies of power and development (James 2000; Werbner 2000), research and intervention programs (Fetterman 2005; Zimmerman 2000), cultural tourism research (Scheyvens 1999; Sofield 2003), and studies of ethnic and indigenous minorities (Gaidzanwa 2000; Sofield 2003:86-90). Empowerment can occur among individuals, organizations, or communities (Zimmerman 2000) and can be psychological, social, economic, or political in nature (Scheyvens 1999). I find it useful to distinguish between *personal empowerment* at the individual, psychological level, and *collective empowerment* at the social group level.

## Defying Asian American Stereotypes

Japanese American taiko players often feel personally empowered through their performances, which are not only a source of self-esteem and cultural pride, but also a way of defying ethnic stereotypes. Because taiko is loud, physically demonstrative, and visually stunning, it counteracts a number of dominant images of Asian Americans, who have often been rendered politically and socially invisible and silent, their voices excluded from mainstream society (Zhou and Lee: 2004:19). In contrast, taiko draws attention to Asian Americans and demands that they be seen and heard (Yoon 2001:418, 424). In this sense, taiko performances have the potential to be ethnically subversive, unlike Japanese tea ceremonies, flower arrangement, and calligraphy, which value silence and refined body movements (Konagaya 2001:117).

A number of Japanese Americans spoke about how taiko challenges prevalent stereotypes of them as quiet, hardworking model minorities who are submissive and not confrontational (see also Terada 2001:41). When asked about what Kinnara Taiko was reacting against, George Abe answered as follows:

> I think the idea of the "model minority" as hardworking, sharp, intelligent, but quiet. . . . So people kind of step on you, but you remain quiet about it. So I think finding a voice was important for us. To find that, "Hey, we're not all quiet. Some of us are wild. Some of us . . ." We need to be loud. We need to make demands. We need to be heard. (JANM interview)

Such meanings of taiko are also connected to the activism and political movements of the 1960s and 1970s to which it partly traces its origins. Therefore, taiko personally empowers later-generation Japanese Americans to explore and express a more positive and genuine ethnic identity.

In addition, the remaking of taiko by Japanese Americans as a joyful and fun performance, in contrast to the serious and disciplined manner in which it is played in Japan, also counters popular stereotypes of Asians as stoic and unemotional (Powell 2008:912–913, Yoon 2001:424–425). Finally, since taiko is a very masculine type of performance that requires considerable strength and stamina, it may also be a way for Asian American men to counteract images that portray them as effeminate, small, and weak (Konagaya 2005:134–135). "Because of images of Asian men as kind of wimpy with really flimsy physiques, to be able to play taiko is very empowering," Steve Okura noted. "A Japanese American [playing taiko] is buff, and especially on those huge odaiko drums—just railing on those. You've got to have good muscles and endurance to keep that up. So yeah, there's definitely an empowering feeling from that."

## Contesting Gender Stereotypes

However, the potential for taiko to subvert conventional stereotypes is most salient for women taiko drummers, who frequently emphasize the personally empowering nature of their performances. Undoubtedly, this is one of the reasons for taiko's appeal to women in the United States where over 60 percent of all taiko players are estimated to be female (Ahlgren 2011:13; Izumi 2001:45; Tusler 2003:119–121).

A number of female taiko players have spoken directly about how their performances, which involve strength, physicality, loud drumming, and full-throated shouts, challenge the demeaning and constraining stereotypes to which they are subject. For instance, Linda Uehara Hoffman, a founding member of Katari Taiko in Canada, observed that

> for those people who had never performed, especially the women, [taiko] was a way to be a role model for other Asian women. It was a way to break the stereotype of submissive, passive Asian women or the whorish, heart of gold, erotic, sexy Asian women. You know, because nobody is going to take you on, if you're standing up there swinging a stick, hitting the drum really loud. No one is going to say, "Cutie pie," right? (Quoted in Kobayashi 2006:3).

Because the silencing of Asian Americans in mainstream society is more prevalent for Asian women than it is for men, the sheer loudness of taiko performances is especially empowering for women. "I don't know if this is what all women feel, but it's the empowerment that you feel when you hit the drum and the sound of it comes out and it's so loud," Michelle Fujii, a former member of San Jose Taiko, explained. "It just makes you feel that you're not a hidden voice in the society" (quoted in Tusler 2003:121). "We wanted to hit hard, we wanted to make lots of noise to show an image of women being loud and powerful," Linda Uehara Hoffman emphasized (quoted in Terada 2001:53).

Therefore, through the performative authenticity of taiko, Japanese American women are personally empowered to defy derogatory images of Asian women by showing people who they really are. Such subversive gender implications are not as prevalent among taiko ensembles in Japan, where women are not as prominent or are in more of a subordinate role vis-à-vis men. As a result, taiko has not challenged traditional patriarchal gender norms in Japan (Bender 2012:145), which again demonstrates how taiko's potentially transformative impact on normative gender ideologies arises when it is practiced in the different gendered context of the United States, where it can take on new political meanings.

Men also noted the personally empowering effects of taiko for women. According to Steve Okura, "You have the stereotype of Asian women as soft and submissive and quiet and traditional. So with taiko, there's this feeling of: 'Look, I'm a girl, but I have just as much empowerment as a guy. I can bang on drums just like them.'"

Nonetheless, it is important to recognize that taiko is personally empowering for women because it is still viewed through a dominant, masculine lens. In other words, women can defy restrictive, feminine stereotypes through taiko precisely because of its association with male strength and power. By engaging in a masculine activity, they demonstrate how women can be just as strong as men, thus showing how their relative power is derived from an accepted state of male hegemony. As one female taiko player notes, "I represent a female Asian body that is strong, that young girls like me may look at it and go, 'wow, she can do that, she can kiai [shout], she can even be really strong as guys'" (quoted in Terada 2001:53–54).

Therefore, although taiko was not introduced to the United States for the purpose of disrupting and challenging stereotypes of Asian American men and women, this has become one of its important performative consequences which enables Japanese Americans to explore and project an alternative self-image that makes them feel more real and genuine. In this way, a longing for ethnic roots and authenticity through taiko has taken on a subversive edge in the United States because of the particular ethnic and gender dynamics of American society, which contrast with those of Japan. Therefore, ethnic nostalgia can become potentially counterhegemonic when it travels through the diaspora, which partly accounts for the continued popularity of taiko in the United States.

## Racialization, Orientalist Discourses, and Collective Disempowerment

Although empowerment has become a popular buzzword with positive connotations of social justice and equity (Henkel and Stirrat 2001:178; Sofield 2003:111), it is not as liberating as usually assumed. Often, the literature implies that *personal* empowerment naturally leads to *collective* empowerment of communities, and vice versa (Sofield 2003:100; Zimmerman 2000:46, 48–50). However, empowerment at the personal and collective levels does not always correspond. This is especially the case with ethnic performances such as taiko, where collective outcomes depend on audience receptions and understandings. Despite the fact that taiko feels *personally* empowering to many Japanese Americans, it does not *collectively* empower them as an ethnic group because it ends up reinscribing Orientalist discourses among audiences.

Japanese American taiko players may personally revel in the performative authenticity and empowering agency of their art form as a means to convey a distinctive identity that subverts and challenges dominant ethnic and gender stereotypes. However, because of the ambiguity of music as a form of communication, performers do not have control over the reactions and interpretations of audiences, who ultimately determine the social impact of the performances. Therefore, the audience does not always receive the performers' intended message (Wong 2000:67–68) and instead understands the performance in a manner that reinforces preexisting hegemonic perceptions, thus limiting its subversive possibilities and resulting in rather disempowering consequences at the collective level. This ultimately fragments the empowering potential of taiko for Japanese Americans.

Audience reception is especially important since taiko performances are quite popular among the general public, and they are sometimes sold out. Audiences consist not only of Japanese Americans and other Asian Americans, but of substantial numbers of Americans who are not of Asian descent, especially whites. Although this is quite welcome, it may also produce a disconnection between performers and audience, who may differ in their view of what taiko means and what is being conveyed during the performance.

Later-generation Japanese Americans have actively remade and claimed ownership of taiko by producing a unique, Asian American musical genre that has become part of their ethnic heritage and history in the United States. For them, taiko represents their past ethnic struggles for acceptance in an American society that has often racialized and excluded them as the perpetually foreign, Asian Other. However, when American audiences attend concerts by taiko ensembles, they often mistakenly assume that they are watching *Japanese* performers from Japan. This is because taiko as a visual spectacle appears very "Japanese" to them: performers who usually look Asian playing drums that resemble those from ancient Japan while wearing very traditional Japanese costumes. Although a number of prominent professional ensembles are named after the cities where they originate (San Jose Taiko, San Francisco Taiko Dojo, and so on), many taiko groups have Japanese or partly Japanese names and also play pieces that have Japanese titles.

In addition, audiences are often not sophisticated enough to recognize that American taiko groups have incorporated Western musical rhythms into their pieces and developed their own performative style that is different from that of Japanese groups. Although I have attended both Japanese American and Japanese taiko performances, I have been unable to clearly distinguish between the two musical styles. Even Kenny Endo, who became a prominent taiko musician, thought that the first taiko group he ever saw (San Francisco Taiko Dojo) was from Japan and was told only later that they were mainly a sansei group (JANM interview).

A number of Japanese American taiko players were clearly aware of how their performances are being misread by audiences. "When Americans go see a taiko performance, I don't think they are aware that it's actually a Japanese American group," Steve Okura observed. "Unless they are some kind of taiko aficionado, they'll definitely think, 'Oh, this is some Japanese group from Japan.'"

Similarly, PJ Hirabayashi and other taiko performers note how audience members sometimes speak to them using Japanese words, ask whether they are from Japan or whether they speak any English, and are surprised to hear they are actually Americans of Japanese descent (see also Ahlgren 2011:119–120; Tusler 2003:101–102). Even when ensembles introduce themselves to audiences in fluent English and have white American members, certain audience members may still assume they are a Japanese taiko group (Ahlgren 2011:119–120; Yoon 2001:432).

Therefore, taiko in the United States seems to exacerbate the American tendency to conflate Japanese Americans with Japanese immigrants from Japan as audiences often believe they are listening to exotic and ancient music from a distant, foreign land. In this manner, as Paul Yoon (2001:432) points out, Japanese Americans may be unintentionally "re-Orientalizing" themselves. Instead of challenging and contesting Asian American stereotypes, they may be inadvertently reproducing Orientalist discourses that racially essentialize them as cultural foreigners irrevocably tied to exotic Asian homelands. Asian Americans may see taiko performances as empowering, but non-Asians can shift easily into an Orientalist gaze (Wong 2000:72).

As a result, the performative authenticity of taiko is not communicated to many audiences and undermined in the act of reception. This miscommunication between performers and audience members seems to lie in the inherent and ambiguous duality of Japanese American taiko that straddles both the modern and the traditional. For Japanese Americans, taiko feels authentic because they have remade and Americanized a Japanese tradition in ways that speak to their modern lives and allow them to display their true ethnic identities and defy conventional stereotypes. However, audiences do not notice these modern, performative innovations and simply focus on the traditional, Orientalist aspects of the performance. They embrace taiko as authentic because it apparently connects them to an ancient and traditional Japanese art form that has apparently survived unchanged to this day. As Angela Ahlgren (2011:135) notes, audiences are disappointed when they see white taiko members playing in an ensemble, because the performance appears less authentic and "Oriental" to them, indicating how authenticity is read by audiences in a racial manner.

Such Orientalist portrayals are especially apparent when taiko is appropriated by Hollywood and mainstream mass media and therefore taken out of the hands of Japanese Americans. One example is the 1993 movie *Rising Sun*, a crime drama that occurs in the offices of a Japanese corporation based in the United States (Terada 2001:50; Wong 2000). Toward the beginning of the movie, images of powerful male taiko players from San Francisco Taiko Dojo and their thunderous drumming are intermixed with a steamy sex scene between a man presumed to be Japanese and a white woman, whom he apparently murders during sexual intercourse. The scene not only uses Japanese American taiko to promote familiar Orientalist fantasies, but engages in rather blatant racial stereotyping, invoking images of the yellow peril (in the form of sexually menacing Japanese men) during a time when the United States was seriously afraid of Japanese economic supremacy.

Another prominent example is a popular 2006 Mitsubishi car commercial featuring sexy female taiko players from TAIKOPROJECT, UCLA's Kyodo Taiko, and Koshin Taiko who are scantily clad in red, Asian-looking outfits. Framed by dramatic pyrotechnic displays, they beat out thunderous rhythms in an explosion of sound and motion. According to Steve Okura of Asayake Taiko, "People complained that not only were they exotifying taiko, but also erotifying it too." Despite their problematic nature, such mainstream cultural representations and appropriations of taiko are becoming increasingly prevalent as taiko music is featured in more Hollywood movies, amusement parks such as Disney's Epcot Center, popular music bands, Las Vegas shows, popular sporting events, and even video games.

Moreover, this tendency is exacerbated by some taiko groups that dabble in a bit of self-Orientalization in order to draw attention to their ensembles and attract audiences. As Steve Okura admitted:

> It's really hypocritical to perform at some of these events because essentially, what you're selling is Japaneseness. That's what the Caucasians who put on these events are saying: "There's a Japanese group who respect Japan." Even if this is not what we are, you kind of get more exposure by hyping the Japanese aspect of it.

The websites of various taiko groups also promote such images by featuring Japanese characters and backdrops and including pictures of Asians drummers wearing traditional outfits. Their descriptions of taiko and its history can also invoke exotic images of a mysterious Orient by emphasizing the spirituality of taiko and its association with supernatural powers, spirits, religious rituals, and primitive folk arts in ancient Japan. By promoting their ensembles in ways that reinforce such Orientalist discourses, some Japanese Americans may partly undermine their own efforts to develop and perform innovative musical styles as well as ethnic and gender identities that challenge popular stereotypes.

In contrast, certain taiko groups like San Jose Taiko explicitly avoid such Orientalizing histories when portraying taiko on their websites. Instead, they emphasize the history of their ensembles in the United States, Asian American history, or their distinctive style of music. Self-avowedly progressive taiko groups like On Ensemble and TAIKOPRO-JECT do not cover any history and simply mention how they blend traditional Japanese drumming with modern musical styles.

Nonetheless, because the exotic foreignness of taiko attracts audiences in search of Japanese "authenticity," even these ensembles are sometimes promoted in ways that invoke common Orientalist sensibilities in order to increase their popularity. Thus, for example, while San Jose Taiko explicitly avoids exotic images about Japan, when the ensemble tours nationally, agents and marketers capitalize on the increasing commercial appeal of Asia by selling the group to audiences as authentically Japanese and from "over there," rather than as an Asian American ensemble from San Jose, California. They have also pressured the ensemble to change its name to "something Japanese." According to founding member Roy Hirabayashi, "They're trying to represent us as a group from Japan. . . . And then the audience kind of thinks that's what we are, when we really feel that we're trying to present a more American or Asian American perspective to what taiko's all about." Likewise, the ensemble is portrayed in promotional materials as playing ancient and exotic traditional Japanese music (Ahlgren 2011:99–101). Such propaganda is equivalent to the erasure of the history of taiko in the United States as a struggle for Asian American empowerment and distinctive musical expression.

Therefore, despite personally empowering attempts by Japanese American taiko players to subvert hegemonic ethnic representations through their performativity, such efforts do not lead to collective, *political* empowerment that challenges and subverts white-dominated racial formations that exclude Asian Americans as culturally foreign, subordinate groups that are not really American. Instead, by reinforcing Orientalist discourses about Asian Americans, taiko seems to promote their ethnic subjection as the exotic, Asian Other and reproduces the hierarchical racial order in collectively disempowering ways.

In this sense, it is interesting to compare taiko with the martial arts. Both are steeped in Asian tradition and ancient history, involve powerful physicality as well as spirituality (*ki*), emphasize similar embodiment and proper form (*kata*), are performed in front of audiences, and have expanded to non-Asians around the globe. Like taiko, the martial arts are personally empowering, especially for female participants, and defy common stereotypes of Asian Americans as quiet, weak, and passive. Nonetheless, its increasingly popularity among the American public and appropriation by Hollywood has led to collectively disempowering, Orientalist stereotypes of Asian men as martial arts experts who possess a mysterious, inscrutable power or, as one of my interviewees put it, "weird small men who are somehow super strong." It may be instructive for taiko players to reflect on this legacy of the martial arts as they attempt to project authentic performances and identities in order to ensure that pernicious stereotypes of the Asian kung fu master are not replaced by Orientalist images of the drum-beating Asian.

## Beyond the Japanese American Community: The Ethnic and Global Expansion of Taiko

While Japanese Americans have not always effectively conveyed their performative authenticity to audiences nor successfully escaped racially essentialized perceptions that conflate their version of taiko with ancient Japan, their musical genre is rapidly expanding, both ethnically and globally, leading to new possibilities in artistic innovation and self-expression. Taiko has now spread well beyond the Japanese American community, and an increasing number of Americans of other ethnicities are embracing taiko and joining ensembles. These include other Asian Americans, but also non-Asian Americans as well. All of the prominent taiko ensembles now have substantial numbers of non-Japanese American and even Caucasian performers, and a good number of taiko groups can no longer be characterized as Japanese American.

Some taiko groups have become quite pan-Asian as growing numbers of Chinese Americans, Korean Americans, and even Filipino and Vietnamese Americans participate. As a result, taiko has become somewhat synonymous with Asian American identity and culture (Terada 2001:45–46; Yoon 2001). Some ensembles such as Soh Daiko of New York consist of mainly non-Japanese descent Asian Americans. In addition, the number of white American taiko players is increasing, and some taiko groups consist mainly of non-Asians, such as St. Louis's Osuwa Daiko and Phoenix Taiko Kai. Therefore, taiko may go the way of jazz and eventually become disconnected from its Japanese American and even Asian American roots and become a general musical genre shared by many ethnic groups (Ahlgren 2011:127).

There seems to have been some initial resistance among Japanese Americans to the ethnic expansion of taiko (Creighton 2007:209), and there are reportedly certain taiko groups that will not accept those who are not of Japanese ancestry (Carle 2008:31). Steve Okura noted that there is a huge tension in his UCSD group between those who want to keep taiko Japanese American and those who support greater ethnic inclusiveness. However, it seems that most Japanese Americans have become receptive to non-Japanese American members in their ensembles (Tusler 2003:108). "I think as taiko grows and expands out of the Asian American community, as it expands out of the Japanese American community, there's going to be some uneasiness because it was so important as a way of establishing our cultural identity," says Shoji Kameda of On Ensemble. "The history of taiko will be inextricably bound to the history of Asian America and no one can ever take that away. . . . But we have to be secure enough in ourselves to let go of control."[5]

A number of Japanese Americans who acknowledge the increasingly multiethnic nature of taiko emphasize that these new taiko players must respect the instrument and understand the history of taiko. "I'm very mixed about this because I see both sides," Steve Okura admitted.

> I think if you're going to play taiko, please be respectful of the culture and the roots of it. If that's the case, I think that would be the greatest thing in the world. But I went to the culture show at Loyola Marymount and they had a mainly white/Latino taiko group that was pretty bad. I mean,

people were having fun, which is great. But they were screwing up and just banging on things. I thought that was kind of disrespectful.

On the other hand, as taiko is increasingly taken up by other Asian Americans and Americans from other ethnic groups, this may encourage further innovation and new musical forms since these taiko players will be even further removed from the original Japanese taiko tradition. For instance, one non-Japanese descent taiko player says, "We can create our own style and not be bogged down with 'this is how you should do it' mentalities that can be a part of Japanese culture" (Johnson 2008:125). Indeed, Soh Daiko, a pan-Asian taiko ensemble, has already incorporated Chinese culture and Korean music into their performances (Yoon 2001:429–430).

In addition to its ethnic expansion in the United States, taiko is also becoming increasingly international, and indeed, global. Initially, it seems the international growth of taiko occurred mainly within the Japanese diaspora, expanding to Japanese Canadians, Japanese Brazilians, and other Japanese descendants in South America. However, taiko has now grown beyond the geographical and ethnic confines of the Japanese diaspora to countries not known for any significant Japanese descent populations, including Germany, the United Kingdom, the Netherlands, Belgium, Sweden, Spain, Italy, Ukraine, Australia, New Zealand, Singapore, and Malaysia, all of which have taiko groups.[6]

## Conclusion

As demonstrated by taiko, the search for ancestral roots among Japanese Americans is also a search for ethnic authenticity. However, the recovery of an ethnic heritage that feels genuine involves both reaching out to the past and reconfiguring it in the present. Since the ethnic homeland, the original source of ancient traditions, is positioned as more culturally authentic than the diaspora, Japan has become a place of nostalgic desire for a number of Japanese Americans where true taiko can be found. Although kumi-daiko in Japan is also a recently remade tradition, some American taiko ensembles claim greater continuity to the ancestral Japanese past and greater authenticity. This has produced some tension with more "progressive" and Americanized taiko groups, which do not position themselves in terms of cultural authenticity.

In fact, the performance of cultural heritage and ancestry does not have to closely resemble traditional cultural practices inherited from the homeland for it to be experienced as ethnically authentic. On the contrary, newer, "invented" traditions that are remade in the present can feel more real and genuine because they are constantly reshaped according to contemporary ethnic contexts, making them more personally relevant and meaningful compared to rote reenactments of outdated cultural practices. Ultimately, the ethnic authenticity of taiko for Japanese Americans is found in the contemporary performativity inherent in the embodiment of reconstituted traditions. Performative authenticity shifts cultural authority from the ethnic homeland to descendants in the diaspora. However, because taiko appears very traditional and ancient on the surface, it provides a nostalgic connection to ancestral roots while allowing Japanese Americans to innovate and recreate the musical form to make it part of their own contemporary American ethnic background and culture. A fusion of tradition and modernity based on both continuity with and discontinuity from the past explains taiko's efficacy (and popularity) as a means to recover ethnic heritage in a manner that feels truly authentic.

The performative authenticity of taiko also personally empowers Japanese Americans to constitute and display their ethnic and gender identities to the American public in ways that undermine how Asian Americans have been stereotypically seen. By reshaping past traditions, they also reconstitute themselves in the present, potentially challenging dominant ethnic and gender representations. This performative power of traditional cultural practices emerges not simply because of their repetitive nature. Instead, cultural forms acquire an agentive intentionality as they travel from the homeland through the diaspora and are enacted under novel circumstances in different places, where they counter ethnic hegemonies that did not exist in the country of origin. In this manner, ethnic nostalgia for traditional cultural heritage can become political and subversive.

However, despite the stereotype-busting performance style of Japanese American taiko, it is not collectively empowering since it often reproduces Orientalist discourses among audiences who are drawn to its exotic and mysterious foreignness and cannot tell the difference between Japanese American culture and the traditional culture of ancient

Japan. Although taiko is authentic to Japanese Americans because they have modified past traditions for their own purposes, it is authentic for audiences because it appears to connect them to an unaltered, traditional past from a faraway land. Therefore, what is personally empowering can become quite disempowering at the collective, ethnic level by subjecting Japanese Americans to white-dominated racial hierarchies that marginalize them as culturally foreign. As taiko gradually enters the mainstream, it may increasingly feed such Orientalist imaginations and fantasies, seriously fragmenting its empowering and counterhegemonic potential and leading to the erasure of the distinctive history of ethnic struggle and recognition among Japanese Americans.

Nonetheless, taiko is spreading to other ethnic groups in the United States as well as to other countries, creating new possibilities for further innovation and performativity as taiko is remade in disparate ethnic and national contexts. Although taiko was initially employed by Japanese Americans to explore and assert a specific identity and ethnic heritage, it is now becoming a means for peoples of various nationalities to express a global identity as human beings of the earth (Creighton 2007:203). There seems to be something primeval about taiko that may account for its universal appeal. In addition to the relative simplicity of the instrument and its primordial, thundering beats, it has a fundamental connection to the earth, since the drums are made out of elemental materials from nature—namely, wood from trees, the hides of animals, and metal from the ground. Taiko in this manner seems to embody the rhythm of the earth. According to Mark Miyoshi, the taiko drum maker,

> I believe that these drums have the power to change the world and to help people. What I'm hoping . . . is that people can use . . . that power that they have in their relationship with the drum, to think about the larger world and what can be done and needs to be done. And that spirituality, that kind of power and strength, can change the world. And that's the kind of change we need in this world today. (JANM interview)

# Diasporicity and Japanese Americans

## Japanese Americans in Diasporic Context

Although Japanese Americans in the past have been analyzed in nationalized contexts as an ethnic minority (Fugita and O'Brien 1991; Matsumoto 2014; Okamura 2014; Spickard 1996; Tamura 1994; Yoo 2000; Azuma 2005), they are also part of a diaspora of Japanese descendants who are dispersed throughout the Americas.[1] Because of substantial migration from Japan to the Americas from the 1880s until World War II and smaller emigration flows in the postwar period, there are now significant populations of Japanese descendants living outside the ethnic homeland in both North America (mainly in the United States and Canada) and South America, especially in Brazil and Peru, but also in Argentina, Paraguay, and Bolivia. There are also small populations of Japanese descendants in Mexico and Central American countries.

Indeed, peoples of Japanese descent living outside of Japan (known as *nikkei* or *nikkeijin* in Japanese) have entered the literature on diasporas. The various communities of nikkei, scattered primarily throughout the Americas, are now collectively known as the "Japanese diaspora" (Adachi 2006b; Creighton 2010; White 2003), and its population has actually been estimated at three million people worldwide (Adachi 2006a:1; Sheffer 2003a:105). The Japanese diaspora now appears on lists of the world's major diasporas and has also been mentioned in general discussions of diasporas (Brubaker 2005:3; Butler 2001:201; Cohen 1997:22, 28, 178; Sheffer 2003a:1, 105). There is even a journal called *Pan-Japan: The International Journal of the Japanese Diaspora* and an international symposium on the "nikkei diaspora" was held in Japan in March 2010.

This chapter explores Southwest Japanese Americans in diasporic context and the extent to which their social relations are transnationally embedded within this broader diasporic community of Japanese descendants scattered across the Americas. In fact, Asian Americans are increasingly being analyzed in transnational and diasporic contexts (Lee

2005; Okamura 2003; Parreñas and Siu 2007). Although Sau-Ling Wong (1995) criticized the transnational turn in Asian American Studies as an act of depoliticization that elides the long history of Asian American resistance against racial and socioeconomic inequalities in the United States, it is important to remember that local ethnic contexts are inextricably connected to transnational and diasporic projects. For instance, the marginalization and exclusion of racialized minorities in local societies can cause them to seek supranational forms of diasporic belonging. As a result, lack of assimilation and discrimination in host societies is understood to be part of the diasporic condition (Brubaker 2005:6; Cohen 1997:186; Faist 2010:13; Parreñas and Siu 2007:13; Safran 1991:83).

Although this book has examined Japanese Americans primarily in the national context of the United States, their search for ethnic heritage, which is conditioned by their racialized minority status in American society, has a transnational dimension that has produced a multiplicity of homeland-diaspora relations across the generations. Therefore, even an apparently localized issue such as the ethnic identity of a minority group cannot be understood in a strictly national perspective since it involves affinities and practices that transnationally engage distant homelands in a diasporic context. The second-generation shin-nisei have maintained transnational lives based on affiliations with their parents' country of origin whereas the fourth-generation yonsei have developed a sense of ethnic heritage by recovering cross-border ties with the ancestral homeland that have been lost over the generations. In addition, there is the question of whether Japanese American ethnic identities involve any affiliations with other Japanese-descent nikkei living in the diaspora. As a result, an analysis of Japanese American ethnicity that is restricted to the nation-state may not capture the multifaceted nature of their ethnic relations and consciousness, which can spill over national borders. However, do such transnational ethnic affinities make Japanese Americans diasporic?

## Diasporicity

Numerous researchers have noted a dramatic expansion in the meaning and application of the concept of diaspora in recent decades (Adachi 2006a:2; Brubaker 2005:2; Butler 2001:189–190; Faist 2010:12; Shuval

2000:42; Safran 1991:83; Tölölyan 1996:3). Diasporas are now understood to include not only the forced dispersal of persecuted peoples such as the Jews, Armenians, Palestinians, and Africans (that is, "victim diasporas") but also the voluntary scattering of populations around the world for economic, business, colonial, and political reasons (Bruneau 2010; Butler 2001:199; Cohen 1997:28–29, 180-184; Faist 2010:12; Tölölyan 1996:12; Van Hear 1998:6).In fact, the concept of diaspora seems to have proliferated to such an extent that it is often used to refer to any territorially dispersed population with a homeland, as a number of scholars have noted (Braziel and Mannur 2003:2–3; Brubaker 2005:2; Dufoix 2008:34). Some migrant groups that are not widely dispersed but reside predominantly in one or two countries, such as Mexicans, Cubans, and Haitians in the United States, are sometimes understood to be diasporic as well (Berg 2011; Clifford 1994: 312, 314; Laguerre 1998; Sheffer 2003b:25; Safran 1991:90; Smith 2003). There are even references to political, gender, and musical diasporas (Brubaker 2005:2). Although a broader and more inclusive application of the concept of diaspora is to be welcomed, its over-enthusiastic and somewhat indiscriminate application to almost all migratory groups must be avoided (Braziel and Mannur 2003:2–3; Brubaker 2005:2–4; Tölölyan 1996:10). If everything is ultimately diasporic, then nothing is really diasporic, and the term eventually loses its meaning and ability to differentiate between different types of migratory groups (Brubaker 2005:2–4).

A number of scholars have therefore advocated a more restricted and limited definition of the term in order to better distinguish between migrants who are diasporic and those who clearly are not (Brubaker 2005:2–4; Butler 2001:194; Cohen 1997:187; Paerregaard 2010:94–95; Safran 1991:83; Tölölyan 1996:10, 30). However, the original definitions of diaspora offered by Robin Cohen (1997:22–26), William Safran (1991:83), and Khachig Tölölyan (1996) consisted of extensive lists that contained anywhere from six to nine criteria or characteristics (Bruneau 2010:36–37). Since even the most classic diasporic populations do not meet all these criteria (Clifford 1994:305–306), we are still left with a conundrum: which (and how many) of these fundamental characteristics must a migratory or ethnic population have in order to be considered diasporic?

More recently, scholars have attempted to whittle down these definitional lists to a few (usually three) essential elements that constitute diasporas. They agree that diasporas are ethnic groups that have dispersed to two or more countries and have retained some actual or imagined connection to their original homelands (Butler 2001:192–194; Brubaker 2005:5–6; Faist 2010:12–13; Parreñas and Siu 2007:1; Van Hear 1998:6). However, beyond migratory dispersal and homeland (which are part of all definitions of diasporas), there is less agreement on what the third essential criterion of diasporas should be. Those mentioned are: (1) transnational social relationships among the geographically dispersed ethnic population across national borders; (2) a collective diasporic consciousness and identity; and (3) marginalization and lack of assimilation to the host society.

So which of these is the third essential component that constitutes diasporas? Any choice we make among these three options seems rather arbitrary and subject to the preferences and interests of individual researchers. Nonetheless, without a third essential definitional component, the concept of diaspora would remain too vague and apply to most of the world's migrant and ethnic groups, which are often dispersed to more than one nation-state and retain some affiliation to a homeland. Even if we were to agree on the fundamental characteristics of diasporas, such definitional approaches eventually lead to exclusionary intellectual debates about which migratory ethnic groups are diasporic and which are not, as a number of scholars have noted (Clifford 1994:304–306; Dorais 2010:94; Klimt and Lubkemann 2002:146). My previous work argued that Japanese Americans are not part of a diaspora based on a three-part definition (Tsuda 2012a; 2012b). Others claim that Japanese-descent nikkei communities dispersed across the Americas are diasporic (Adachi 2006a; White 2003).

The oft-asked question, "Is such-and-such group a diaspora/diasporic?" is the wrong question to ask. Instead of conceptualizing diaspora as an objective social state (which exists, or does not exist), I suggest we understand it as a relative condition of *diasporicity* wherein some ethnic groups are more diasporic than others. The diasporicity of an ethnic group is defined by its relative degree of embeddedness in transnational social relations and affiliations with both the ethnic homeland and dispersed co-ethnic communities in the diaspora located in other countries. The concept of diasporicity is thus grounded on the most constitutive element of diasporas: migratory dispersal from the ethnic homeland and the transnational communities it subsequently produces when scattered populations develop and maintain social connections and identifications with each other across national borders. Diasporas as transnational communities resemble a wheel with the homeland at the center and the various overseas diasporic communities on the circumference with the spokes representing their ties to the homeland and the wheel rim representing their connections to each other. Usually, centripetal homeland connections and attachments of diasporic communities are more prevalent and dense than lateral ones across the diaspora. Nonetheless, such lateral transnational connections between dispersed ethnic groups are an equally important part of diasporic analysis.

My use of "diasporicity" to refer to the relative strength of a dispersed ethnic group's transnational relations and identifications is different from how it is employed in the literature, where the term is synonymous with diasporas or the diasporic condition in general (Brubaker 2005:4; Dorais 2010:94; Lubkemann 2013).[2] As a theoretical move, my definition of diasporicity avoids exclusionary debates about whether or not an ethnic group is diasporic, which depends on different definitions adopted by individual researchers and is intellectually not very productive. Instead of such either/or propositions, diasporicity assumes that all geographically dispersed ethnic populations are diasporic to some extent and simply examines their level of diasporicity. Even within one dispersed ethnic group, diasporicity can vary over time and among individuals because of differences in age, gender, and generation.

Apart from casual references to the "diasporic experiences of Japanese Americans" (Igarashi 2001:228) and brief discussions of them in the context of diasporas (Bhatia and Ram 2001; Tölölyan 1996:22–23; Takamori 2011:43, Ch. 4), I am not aware of any extensive analyses of their diasporicity. It is also interesting that Japanese descendants living outside the United States in Latin America are often considered part of a diaspora (Adachi 2006b; Lesser 2007) whereas Japanese Americans are never analyzed in diasporic context.

Although they are members of a Japanese diaspora, Japanese Americans do not manifest a high level of diasporicity in their transnational ethnic relations, which is an indication of their general integration and cultural assimilation to mainstream American society. However, like other diasporic groups, they have much stronger social connections to their ethnic homeland than they do to other Japanese descent communities in the Americas. This chapter examines their diasporic social linkages both with Japan and with other nikkei in the diaspora.

## The Japanese Diaspora

Japanese have been emigrating from the homeland for well over a century and have scattered to various countries around the world mainly for economic reasons (thus, it is classified as an economic or labor diaspora; Cohen 1997:178). Substantial Japanese emigration to the Americas started around the 1880s, initially to North America (mainly to the United States but also to Canada) and lasted for several decades. Emigration to Latin America began in the early 1900s (predominantly to Brazil, but also to other South and Central American countries) and continued into the 1960s. Many of these emigrants, who were from Japan's poor, overpopulated rural areas, went to the Americas to fill labor shortages as agricultural workers. Although they initially intended to be only migrant sojourners, most of them settled permanently. During the period of Japanese colonialism before World War II, Japanese emigrants also dispersed throughout the Japanese empire to various countries in Asia (especially China and Korea) and to the Pacific Islands mainly as agricultural settlers, capitalists, and administrators. However, most of them repatriated to Japan at the end of World War II along with the Japanese military.

In the postwar period (beginning in the late 1960s), Japanese again began emigrating from a now economically prosperous Japan as businessmen, professionals, and students initially to the United States and Europe, and then to other countries around the world. However, the postwar emigration of highly skilled Japanese has been relatively limited in number and a majority of them reside abroad only temporarily. As a result, the Japanese diaspora is now becoming older and consists mainly of Japanese descent nikkeijin of the second, third, and fourth generations.

Despite their broad migratory dispersal from the Japanese homeland, the nikkei communities found primarily in the Americas are no longer very diasporic because their centripetal transnational ties to Japan have generally weakened, and they have not developed notable lateral ethnic connections and affiliations with each other (Okamura 1998:24; White 2003:316). Unlike newer, first-generation diasporas, these dispersed populations of Japanese descendants are generations old and have as-similated to their respective host societies, which has led to the attenuation of their transnational ethnic connections.

As an economic "diaspora," the nikkei in the Americas do not share a strong historical memory of past persecution and traumatic migratory dispersal (unlike classic victim diasporas) nor has there been any collective political mobilization across borders (such as to establish or support a beleaguered homeland) that would help keep the diasporic community more cohesive over time. In addition, they do not share a common language like the Filipino, Indian, or Arab diasporas, and are divided among English, Portuguese, and Spanish speakers. Japanese is spoken only by a limited number of first-generation issei and some second-generation nisei and is rapidly disappearing as a common language that unifies the diasporic community. Likewise, the nikkeijin do not have a strong religious faith as a basis for ethnic solidarity across national borders, in contrast to Jewish, Muslim, or Hindu diasporas.

## Transnational Connections to the Ethnic Homeland

Although centripetal homeland connections tend to be much stronger for most diasporic peoples than lateral connections to co-ethnics in other countries, most Japanese Americans, as part of an older diaspora, seem to have a somewhat weak homeland diasporicity. Their cultural and social assimilation to mainstream America over the generations has attenuated their transnational ties to the ethnic homeland (Spickard 1996:152; Tölölyan 1996:22–23).

Most Japanese Americans I interviewed had visited Japan sometime during their lives. However, only a small number had lived there for more than a few months or had enduring transnational attachments to their ancestral homeland. In fact, seventeen out of my sample of fifty-five interviewees had never even visited Japan. Among this group, about half had no real intention of doing so because they felt no personal connection to their ethnic homeland. The other half who planned to visit Japan in the future wanted to do so for mainly professional and business reasons.

Of those interviewees who have visited Japan, a number of them had done so only briefly, as tourists. Although their vacations left them with quite positive impressions of their ethnic homeland as discussed earlier (see also Tsuda 2009: ch. 9), in most cases, such short visits, generally in group tours with other Americans or Japanese Americans, have not led to long-term, transnational contact with the country or with Japanese in Japan. It is significant that relatively few of the Japanese Americans who visited Japan exclusively as tourists actually met with their Japanese relatives. Most of those who did are prewar second-generation nisei (the third-generation sansei and fourth-generation yonsei generally lost contact with their Japanese relatives a long time ago), and none of them stayed in touch with their relatives after their trip.

Only about one fifth of my interviewees have lived in Japan for longer periods of time. Most of them went there as exchange students during college (usually for one semester or a year) or earlier in their lives, while a few worked, taught, or conducted research in Japan. As a result, only a small number of Japanese Americans in my interview sample (about 10 percent) have some type of sustained transnational commitment to Japan. Some of these individuals have lived in Japan for extended periods and continue to be engaged in the country (or planned to live there in the future). Others, who have taken short trips to Japan at various times in their lives, plan to continue doing so in the future; they also stay in touch with Japanese relatives, friends, or acquaintances. Among this group of Japanese Americans who have active transnational relations with Japan, all except two are postwar shin-nisei, whose strong connections to their ethnic homeland arose mainly because of their Japanese parents. The others are a prewar nisei who had been sent back to Japan for his education by his parents (that is, a *kibei*) and a yonsei who is married to someone living in Japan.

It is important to remember that the diasporicity of any ethnic group constantly changes over time. Therefore, it also needs to be historicized as well as analyzed in terms of generation. As Clifford (1994:306) observes, diasporas can "wax and wane in diasporism" at different times in their history depending on changing social circumstances (see also Dorais 2010). In addition, diaspora studies need to be more aware of how the strength of transnational connections to both the homeland and co-ethnics in the diaspora depends on generational status. In general, research on diasporas has not paid sufficient attention to how diasporic experiences vary from one generation to another. Mette Berg's (2011) work on Cubans in Spain is one of the few studies that explicitly examines historical generational differences among diasporic peoples.

When examining the historical and generational variables that affect diasporicity, we must be wary of commonsense assumptions that diasporicity gradually wanes over time as a diaspora ages and its population gradually shifts from the first to the second and eventually later immigrant generations (Esman 2009:10). In the case of Japanese Americans, their diasporic history has not followed a linear temporality where their transnational connections to the ethnic homeland progressively weaken because of increased assimilation over the generations. Although there was a decline in homeland connections from the first to the second prewar generations, this initial weakening of homeland diasporicity has been somewhat reversed in recent decades by the more recent generations of Japanese Americans who have experienced an ethnic reawakening, as shown in previous chapters.

For a few decades after the Japanese initially immigrated to the United States in the late nineteenth and early twentieth centuries, the first-generation issei stayed in close touch with Japan and continued to hope that they would one day return to their homeland. The Japanese government created institutions to manage and support emigration and overseas communities, and the issei (and even the second-generation nisei) maintained their connections to Japan through consulates, newspapers, Japanese schools, ethnic and prefectural organizations, and short-term trips (Azuma 2005; Ueda 2002).

However, diasporic ties to the ethnic homeland considerably weakened among the prewar second generation, despite the fact that a limited number of them were sent to Japan for their education (the kibei). While this attenuation was part of a process of cultural assimilation and social integration into mainstream American society, as mentioned in Chapter 1, the internment experience and World War II severed many of the remaining ties between Japan and Japanese-descent communities in the United States. It also caused many nisei to culturally assimilate and deemphasize their ethnic heritage in order to demonstrate their loyalty to America. As a result, relatively few of them were able or willing to develop transnational relations with Japan. Although most of the prewar nisei in my interview sample had visited Japan briefly as tourists and even met their Japanese relatives, none, apart from the kibei, has remained in contact with their relatives or has any sustained transnational involvement in their ethnic homeland.

In contrast to the prewar nisei, the postwar third generation experienced an ethnic awakening as youth in the 1960s and 1970s, when ethnic activism was growing and the Asian American movement was seeking a return to cultural roots and heritage. However, this awakening seems to have been limited and did not generally involve living in Japan and developing active transnational relationships with the country and therefore did not lead to a notable increase in homeland diasporicity (see Chapter 3). In general, as the political radicalism of the period subsided over the years, the sansei seemed to continue the assimilative trajectory of the nisei, especially as they grew older. Very few of those in my interview sample have any notable transnational connections to Japan or express a current desire to recover their ancestral roots. Moreover, a majority of them has never even been to Japan. As a result, the sansei generally conduct their lives exclusively in an American ethnic and cultural context.

However, a resurgence of homeland diasporicity has occurred in recent decades among youth from the fourth generation and the postwar second generation. As discussed in Chapter 5, the yonsei have reactivated transnational cultural and social ties to Japan in an effort to reconnect with their ethnic heritage. In fact, almost all of my fourth-generation interviewees had lived in Japan recently, with a few others planning to do so in the near future, a proportion that is much higher than among even the postwar shin-nisei.

Homeland diasporicity has also been strengthened in recent decades through the emergence of the postwar second-generation shin-nisei, who have remained transnationally engaged with Japan (Chapter 2). Unlike the yonsei, who must actively create their diasporic ties to Japan (a "forged transnationalism"), the homeland diasporicity of the shin-nisei persists from their transnational parents. A number of my shin-nisei interviewees have lived and worked in Japan, and several have professional careers related to their ethnic homeland. Even those who have not lived for a notable period in the country have visited it at various times throughout their lives because of the influence of their parents, and they generally remain connected to their relatives and other Japanese.

Therefore, although centripetal diasporic attachments to ethnic homelands are often associated with social exclusion and lack of assimilation of ethnic minorities in the host society (Clifford 1994:307–308; Faist 2010:13; Safran 1991:96; Shuval 2000:44), homeland diasporicity is not incompatible with assimilation (Glick Schiller 2005:160–161, 167; Parreñas and Siu 2007:14; Shuval 2000:46). This is especially the case in inclusive, multiethnic countries where even assimilated ethnic minorities may be encouraged or pressured to maintain their ethnic heritage through transnational attachments to the homeland. In the case of the yonsei, it is precisely their full assimilation in a multicultural America that motivates them to reconnect with the ethnic homeland. The shin-nisei are also culturally assimilated, but this does not preclude their simultaneous diasporic engagement with Japan because of their bilingualism and biculturalism.

In addition to generational differences, homeland diasporic commitments can also vary considerably over the individual's life course. It is not a coincidence that the shin-nisei and yonsei generations, who consist mainly of youth, have the highest levels of homeland diasporicity. As noted earlier, for Asian Americans, and perhaps for other minorities, youth is a time for cultural heritage exploration and ethnic identity development (especially for those who are college students), compared to their childhood, when they faced greater assimilationist and Americanization pressures. Likewise, the third generation's attempt to revive ethnic roots decades ago also occurred when they were youth and were influenced by the ethnic politics of the time.

However, as the shin-nisei and yonsei grow older, their diasporic attachments to Japan may attenuate as they become busy with their professional careers and family lives. Although most of the yonsei in my interview sample have reconnected with Japan and their cultural heritage, it is somewhat doubtful that this homeland diasporicity will persist into their adult lives. Most have lived only briefly in Japan on college study abroad programs with other American students (with whom they mainly interacted), and although they did socialize with Japanese students, they generally did not establish long-term friendships with them (partly because of the language barrier). Nor did the yonsei visit their ancestral relatives back in Japan (their families lost touch with relatives in Japan long ago), although one of them did find the village where she believes her ancestors originated. As a result, most have not remained transnationally engaged in Japan after returning to the United States, nor do they have plans to work or live there in the future or to pursue careers that are directly related to Japan. Consequently, the study abroad experiences of yonsei during college may simply end up being a once-in-a-lifetime opportunity to live in their ancestral homeland and explore their ethnic roots. Therefore, the shin-nisei, who have been connected to their ethnic homeland since childhood through their parents, may be the only generation of Japanese Americans that maintains enduring if not lifelong transnational relations with Japan. As indicated in the conclusion of Chapter 2, the older shin-nisei I interviewed have careers related to Japan or planned to remain involved in the country in the future.

In sum, although there has been a resurgence of transnational homeland engagement among recent generations of Japanese Americans, it seems to be confined mainly to youth and does not seem to last throughout the life course in a number of cases. This is another reason why the homeland diasporicity of Japanese Americans remains somewhat weak in general. The newer Japanese expatriate communities consisting of businessmen and professionals are much more diasporic than the older Japanese American communities, since they tend to maintain strong linkages to Japan during their lives abroad. It is also not surprising that the children of these Japanese expatriates who settle permanently in the United States (the shin-nisei) may be the only ones who have enduring transnational commitments to Japan. In this sense, the newest generations in a diaspora tend to be the most diasporic.

## Lateral Transnational Connections to Other Nikkei in the Americas

The literature on diasporas places heavy emphasis on centripetal connections to the homeland and does not seriously examine lateral transnational ties among co-ethnic populations in the diaspora. Studies that analyze both types of diasporic transnationality are quite rare (Paerregaard 2010). Although homeland diasporicity is usually much stronger, we must also consider lateral transnational connections and identifications among dispersed ethnic populations since they are an integral part of diasporas (Butler 2001:207; Clifford 1994: 206; Tambiah 2000:172) and make them different from other migratory groups. Like diasporic peoples, all migrants have left their homelands and remain attached to them, but since they are not characterized by geographical dispersal, they do not have transnational relations with co-ethnics scattered in other countries. Therefore, the significant difference between diasporas and other migratory ethnic groups is not simply their ongoing or reawakened attachment to the homeland and its ancestral culture, as some authors claim (Shuval 2000:46). If we do not pay equal attention to lateral diasporic connections among dispersed ethnic populations, we lose what diasporicity is all about.

Given that Japanese Americans have low homeland diasporicity, it is not surprising that their lateral transnational ethnic linkages to other Japanese-descent nikkei communities in the Americas are even weaker. The majority of my Japanese American interviewees had never met or associated with Japanese descendants from other countries and their awareness of their nikkei counterparts in Latin America was quite low. Even though lateral transnational ethnic ties are weaker for most diasporas, the general absence of such diasporicity among Japanese Americans is quite notable.

In some cases, when the members of an ethnic group scatter to various countries to form diasporic communities, they simply maintain the social connections they originally had with each other back in the homeland (Dorais 2010). In other cases, such transnational ethnic linkages are actively created and developed after migratory dispersal by scattered diasporic populations. In the case of Japanese immigrants in the Americas, however, such lateral ethnic ties did not really exist from the beginning nor were they developed after immigration (White 2003).

It seems that the Japanese emigrants who dispersed to different countries in the Americas developed their ethnic communities in separate national contexts without much interaction among them except for a very limited amount of subsequent migration within South America, especially from Peru to Argentina, Bolivia, and Paraguay (Masterson 2004:42), and the internment of over two thousand Japanese Latin Americans (mainly Japanese Peruvians) in the United States during World War II. In addition, Japanese emigration to various regions in the Americas occurred during different time periods. Most Japanese emigration to North America took place during the first two decades of the twentieth century. However, when the United States prohibited further Japanese immigration starting with the "Gentlemen's Agreement" in 1908 and culminating in the Oriental Exclusion Act of 1924, the migrant flow was diverted to South America. Therefore, the bulk of Japanese emigration to Brazil (and Peru) occurred during the 1920s and 1930s. Much of Japanese emigration to Paraguay and Bolivia took place after this period and continued into the 1960s, although there was limited emigration to Brazil at this time as well. Postwar Japanese emigration to North America of high-skilled professionals and students did not begin until after the 1960s. Because different groups of Japanese emigrated to separate countries at different times, the issei immigrant settlers who dispersed across the Americas probably did not have preexisting social relationships with each other and also found it difficult to develop cross-border diasporicity later on.

In fact, only *two* of the Japanese Americans I interviewed (out of my sample of fifty-five) had sustained social relations with nikkeijin living in other countries in the Americas. One is a nisei born in Mexico but raised in the United States who has Japanese Mexican friends he continues to visit. The other is actively involved in the Pan-American Nikkei Association Conventions. Two other Japanese Americans have relatives in Mexico and Brazil, but are no longer in touch with them. None of my other informants has any meaningful diasporic connections to other nikkei in the Americas.

However, a limited number of Japanese Americans have had brief encounters with other nikkei while traveling or living abroad in the past. Four met Japanese Brazilians (two of them in Japan and two during trips to Brazil), and three met Japanese Mexicans. Most of these encounters were no more than short conversations (partly because of the language barrier in most cases). Only three of my interviewees have ever encountered any Japanese Canadians abroad, and only one has had any substantial interaction with them (at a conference). One of my informants has met Japanese descendants in Europe.

Since most Japanese Americans have lost much of their ethnic heritage because of generations of assimilation in the United States, those who meet other nikkeijin while abroad experience more national cultural differences than ethnic commonalities as Japanese descendants, making it difficult to develop diasporic ethnic ties with them. Of course, the language barrier is the primary cultural obstacle, and a number of Japanese Americans have noted their inability to communicate with the Latin American nikkeijin. A young sansei mentioned the sheer ethnic strangeness of encountering people who look Japanese speaking in foreign languages:

> So I was walking around Mexico City during my vacation, and I run into this Japanese guy and he's speaking Spanish like crazy! I was like, "Woa!" It totally tripped me up. It's just kind of funny because you wouldn't expect it. Whenever you run into someone of your own culture abroad, you try a bit harder to relate to them, but you're still in a weird, foreign country.

However, even when limited communication is possible, my Japanese American interviewees feel that the Latin American nikkei are essentially people of a foreign nationality, and they have not developed any diasporic ethnic affinity with them based on their common Japanese ancestry. This was true even of Christine, who is one of the most cosmopolitan of the Japanese Americans I spoke to (she has lived in Panama, speaks fluent Spanish, and knows some Portuguese). Although she did not meet any Japanese descendants in Panama, she did interact with Japanese Brazilians while traveling in São Paulo:

> It was American versus Brazilian. I mean, I guess I felt some connection just because I knew we had some common ancestry. But there were cultural differences definitely. They don't see things from a U.S. point of view. I got the sense they are fully integrated in Brazil. They dress like Brazilians and their way of life is totally Brazilian. They go by Brazilian time, and show up half an hour late!

"It was just the same as being exposed to a Mexican, period," said a sansei who encountered Japanese Mexicans in Mexico. "Or the same as meeting foreigners from Spain or Guatemala, or from any other country for that matter."

In general, however, a majority of my Japanese American interviewees have never had any contact with Japanese descendants from other countries. In fact, about a fifth of these individuals were not even aware that other nikkei communities existed. For instance, Kate Nishimoto said, "I know nothing about other Japanese descendants around the world. Absolutely nothing. In fact, I thought the Japanese had only migrated to the U.S." Another interviewee reasoned that since Latin American countries are poorer than the United States, there must not have been much economic incentive for Japanese to migrate to that region. Others, like Dan Matsushita, did not know about nikkeijin communities elsewhere, but figured that if so many Japanese had immigrated to the United States, they might have gone to other countries as well:

> I know nothing about Japanese in Latin America. Nothing. I'm really surprised to hear there's a big population of Japanese descendants in Brazil. But I figure, if there are Japanese Americans, there might be Japanese Brazilians. Hey, there may be Japanese Lithuanians for all I know! If I heard about them, I'd be like, "OK, that's fine, I don't care." Growing up in Southern California, nothing surprises me anymore.

Other Japanese Americans who have never interacted with Latin American nikkeijin have at least heard of them, though they still know very little about their Latin American counterparts. Some are vaguely aware that there are large Japanese descent communities in South America, but have no further knowledge of these communities. Several do have some specific information about Japanese Brazilians, including their current ethnic return migration to Japan (partly because among these were college students who had read my book on the subject in their classes!). The rest had heard only about the former infamous Peruvian President, Alberto Fujimori (although there was some confusion about which South American country he had been president of). In fact, a number of my Japanese American informants had first become aware of Nikkei in South America when they heard news of Fujimori. A few others knew about the internment of Japanese Peruvians in the United States, and several had learned about Japanese Latin Americans in college classes, read about them in the Japanese American Citizens League (JACL) newsletter, or heard about them through other Japanese American organizations. Most of the Japanese Americans in this group are aware of only the Japanese Brazilians and Peruvians, and almost no one knew anything about other Latin American nikkei communities.

I was rather surprised that substantial numbers of Japanese Americans (over a fourth of my sample) had never even heard of Japanese Canadians, although they generally knew of the large Chinese immigrant communities in Canada. When I broached the subject, I received a number quizzical responses such as:

> "Japanese Canadians? Now, that's a completely new concept for me."
> "I didn't know Japanese went up there."
> "Japanese Canadians? So do they live on the west coast of Canada or something?"
> "I've never heard of them. But I would like to meet one. I like Canadians!"

On the other hand, those who did know about the Japanese Canadians generally had a somewhat greater awareness of their ethnic counterparts to the north that those to the south. Most mentioned that the Japanese Canadians had also been interned in concentration camps during World War II, and a few others knew about specific nikkei communities or individuals in Canada.

## A Diasporic Revival? Recent Attempts to Develop Transnational Ethnic Connections

The relative lack of interaction among Japanese Americans with other nikkeijin communities does not mean there have been no attempts by Japanese descendants in the Americas to build lateral ethnic ties across national borders to strengthen their diasporicity. As shown by the revival of homeland ties by the yonsei, diasporic connections are not only based on the persistence of the transnational connections of the migrants who initially dispersed from the ethnic homeland (compare with Dorais 2010). They can be reactivated and developed by later generations of diasporic descendants. As Creighton observes (2010:134), while nikkei communities in the Americas have historically not had much contact with each other, in the last ten to twenty years, lateral diasporic ethnic networks have begun to emerge. For instance, the Japanese American National Museum (JANM) in Los Angeles has made a notable effort to expand beyond Japanese American issues by running a "Discover Nikkei" project, which has a website about nikkei in other parts of the world with interviews, news, events, information, audio-visual materials, and a global online community. It has also recruited scholars to work on the International Nikkei Research Project, which resulted in two scholarly volumes (Hirabayashi, Kikumura-Yano, and Hirabayashi 2002; Kikumura-Yano 2002).

The most prominent example of diasporic ethnic networking among nikkeijin communities is the Pan-American Nikkei Association (PANA) Convention, which brings together people of Japanese descent from throughout the Americas every two years. The convention's workshops and presentations emphasize the importance of promoting lateral trans-national ethnic and professional connections and developing a common Nikkei identity among Japanese descendants in the Americas (Creighton 2010; Takenaka 2009). The PANA conventions seem less interested in building a diasporic community by reestablishing centripetal homeland connections to Japan (Hirabayashi and Kikumura-Yano 2002; Takenaka 2009:1331, 1333). PANA was created in 1981 mainly through the initiative of Latin American Nikkei with the collaboration of the Japanese American Citizens League (Creighton 2010:136–137; Takenaka 2009:1332). According to Ayumi Takenaka (2009), Nikkei leaders involved in PANA were concerned that their ethnic communities were threatened by increasing assimilation, intermarriage, and a weakening of ethnic identity and participation. For them, the development of transnational ethnic networks (especially between South American and North American nikkei) has become a way to reinvigorate nikkei communities that have had little awareness of each other (Creighton 2010:139).

However, the impact of PANA (and other diasporic nikkei projects) seems quite limited. Although the PANA conventions have been held every two years since 1981 in various countries in the Americas, they draw only a few hundred participants, most of whom are community leaders or are affiliated with various local nikkei organizations. Others are well-to-do nikkeijin (including businessmen and professionals interested in networking) who can afford the travel costs and registration fees (Takenaka 2009:1325, 1338). Takenaka (2009:1329) reports that most of the 150 Japanese descendants that she has interviewed over the years have never participated in PANA. Among my sample, there is one Japanese American (who is a prominent community leader and journalist) who actively attends (and reports on) the PANA conventions, but almost all of the others I spoke to are not even aware of PANA's existence.

Participation in other nikkei diasporic activities also seems very low. Only one of my Japanese American informants is aware of JANM's "Discover Nikkei" project because she used to work at the museum. The global online community of nikkeijin on the project's website has only 143 members, 98 of whom live in the United States (64 in California). As White notes (2003:216), attempts to strengthen diasporicity among nikkei organizations across the Americas have not generated any real or sustained connections. It seems that the efforts of later-generation Japanese Americans to explore their ethnic heritage by visiting Japan has been much more diasporically significant than attempts by organizations to build lateral diasporic ties between nikkei communities in the Americas.

As is the case with other diasporas, it is usually the ethnic leaders and elites (including businessmen, professionals, and scholars) who are most active in transnational diasporic community-building and consciousness-raising, while the rest of the community is much less engaged. In the case of the Japanese diaspora, however, even the numbers of nikkei leaders who are involved in developing diasporic ethnic networks across borders seem to be quite limited. None of the leaders of the JACL in San Diego or Phoenix (or the Japanese American Historical Society of San Diego) show any awareness of nikkei diasporic efforts; instead, they are focused exclusively on local and sometimes national issues. Therefore, it is not surprising that the rest of the Japanese American community does not have social linkages to, or much interest in, other nikkeijin in the Americas. In this sense, the level of diasporicity between Japanese Americans and other nikkeijin seems particularly low.

## Conclusion

This chapter has cautioned against both expansive and restrictive approaches to diasporas. On the one hand, there is a tendency to conceptualize diasporas so broadly that virtually any migratory group becomes diasporic. As a result, the term loses its conceptual utility and becomes mainly a rhetorical device. In contrast, restrictive definitional approaches that list essential characteristics of a diaspora can lead to exclusionary consequences since certain dispersed ethnic populations possess these qualities while others do not.

Instead, I have suggested we analyze diasporas not as an objective state of being, but simply as a relative condition of diasporicity based on the transnational social consequences of geographical dispersal from the homeland. "Diasporicity" refers to the extent to which dispersed ethnic groups are transnationally engaged with each other and with the ethnic homeland. Since the level of embeddedness in cross-border ethnic networks varies, some ethnic groups are more diasporic than others. We also need to pay more attention to lateral transnational ethnic ties among people scattered in the diaspora instead of focusing only on their transnational attachment to the homeland (as most studies have done). Although centripetal homeland ties are usually more prominent for most diasporic groups, if they do not also have lateral transnational connections, they begin to resemble ordinary migrant groups that do not have much diasporicity. Finally, since the strength of transnational diasporic linkages fluctuates over time, they must be historicized across the generations and over the life course.

As part of an older diaspora of Japanese descendants scattered throughout the Americas, Japanese Americans no longer have a high level of diasporicity. Since most of them are generations old, their ancestral bonds to the ethnic homeland have attenuated over time. Although transnational linkages to Japan were the strongest among the first-generation issei, generations of cultural and social assimilation among prewar nisei and sansei have led to a considerable weakening of their homeland diasporicity. Nonetheless, diasporic histories do not always follow linear trajectories, as shown by the reactivation of homeland ties among both the recent generations of yonsei, who have reached out to the ancestral homeland as part of their ethnic revival, and the postwar shin-nisei, whose parents are members of the recent Japanese business and professional diaspora.

Therefore, the progressive assimilation of ethnic minorities over time does not preclude diaporic possibilities. However, it is also important not to exaggerate this recent resurgence of homeland diasporicity among the yonsei since it may be limited to a one-time study-abroad opportunity in Japan. Not only are such recent revivals of diasporicity confined to certain segments of the Japanese American population; they also seem to be occur mainly among youth and not last throughout the lifecycle. Only the shin-nisei, who are generally bicultural and the most diasporic among all Japanese Americans, seem to have enduring transnational relations with the homeland.

Lateral transnational connections with other nikkei communities are even weaker among Japanese Americans. Because of the different historical timing of Japanese migration to various countries in the Americas, the scattered Japanese immigrant communities never built significant ethnic networks with each other. Therefore, very few Japanese Americans have any sustained diasporic relations to their nikkeijin counterparts in other countries, and some of them are not even aware of the existence of other Japanese-descent communities. Meanwhile, the prominent national cultural differences that have emerged among the nikkei because of generations of assimilation make it difficult for later-generation Japanese Americans to develop transnational diasporic connections. Most Japanese Americans who actually encounter nikkei in other countries experience more cultural alienation than mutual ethnic understanding. Recent attempts by nikkei across the Americas to build transnational ethnic networks through their organizations have had very limited impact so far.

Although diasporic histories do not track neatly with progressive rates of assimilation over time, there may be an important distinction to be made between older and newer diasporas. Newer diasporas composed mainly of first-generation migrants tend to have the most active and cohesive transnational ethnic connections and higher levels of diasporicity. In contrast, some older diasporas have weaker diasporicities, especially if they have become well-integrated into the nation-states in which they reside, and no longer have active transnational commitments either to their ancestral homelands or to co-ethnics living in other countries.

# Conclusion

## *Japanese American Ethnic Legacies and the Future*

This book has illustrated the continuing relevance of ancestral heritage among ethnic minorities such as the Japanese Americans who have been in the United States for generations. Regardless of whether they are in active search of their heritage and homeland, ethnic ancestry continues to inform the identities and daily experiences of Japanese Americans living in the American Southwest. Therefore, heritage cultures are not simply important for newly arrived and still unassimilated immigrants and minorities. They remain quite relevant for older ethnic minorities like Japanese Americans as well. However, significant variations in the experience and practice of ethnic heritage have emerged among them according to generation.

For ethnic groups like the Japanese Americans whose ancestors immigrated to the United States during a limited time period, generations not only indicate relative distance from the original immigrants but also correlate with specific historical and age cohorts. Therefore, members of one immigrant generation have experienced the same formative historical events during their childhood and youth, and these can have a lifelong influence on their ethnicity. By examining the experience of ethnic heritage by generation, this book has also analyzed the impact of different historical periods on Japanese Americans.

The prewar second-generation nisei, who came of age during World War II, were racialized as "enemy aliens" because of their Japanese ancestry and suffered from severe discrimination and persecution. In response, they distanced themselves from Japan and their ethnic heritage, emphasizing their racial citizenship and nationalist loyalties as culturally assimilated Americans. Subsequently, a limited amount of postwar immigration from Japan produced two separate historical generations within the same second immigrant generation. The prewar and postwar nisei had divergent historical experiences, which have produced very different ethnic outcomes. Unlike their prewar predecessors, the postwar shin-nisei have embraced the current multicultural and pro-Japanese climate, taken advantage of opportunities to travel to their ethnic homeland, and become bilingual, bicultural, and transnational in an era of globalization.

The third-generation sansei have inherited the assimilative legacy of their prewar nisei parents and have become further integrated into mainstream American society through socioeconomic mobility and intermarriage. Having grown up in an assimilationist era, they have lost touch with their ethnic heritage and feel completely Americanized. In contrast, the fourth-generation yonsei in my research sample have recovered their lost heritage culture as well as transnational ties to Japan because of their continued multicultural racialization as culturally different "Japanese" and positive imaginings of their ethnic homeland and its culture. Although they certainly have not reversed the assimilative legacy of the prewar nisei and sansei generations, they are experiencing an ethnic revival. It remains to be seen however, whether such youth engagement in ethnic heritage will be sustained into their adult lives.

The cultural heritage practices of Japanese Americans in the Southwest extend beyond their personal lives and transnational experiences to cultural performances in their communities. Nowhere is this more evident than in their numerous taiko ensembles, which were started by the sansei and have become popular among the yonsei. While appropriating an ancient Japanese cultural form, Japanese Americans have remade and refashioned traditional taiko, producing a performative style that is quite distinct from the one practiced in Japan. Nonetheless, this performativity inherent in Japanese American taiko is what makes such an "invented tradition" feel authentic and relevant to their contemporary lives.

In terms of their overall ethnic trajectory, therefore, Japanese Americans have not followed predictable generational patterns wherein transnational commitments to heritage and homeland weaken over time. It may be no surprise that the shin-nisei are the most connected to their Japanese heritage and language and have developed the most transnationally informed understanding of themselves and their lives. In contrast, their prewar second-generation counterparts are very nationalized and Americanized, and are less engaged in their Japanese heritage compared to the later generations of Japanese Americans. After the shin-nisei, it is not the third-generation sansei who are the most ethnic and transnational, but ironically, the fourth-generation yonsei. And despite their high levels of assimilation and Americanization, the sansei have been more interested in their ancestral culture and acknowledge its impact more than the prewar nisei I interviewed.

It is also important to note that neither the shin-nisei nor the yonsei have developed their ethnic heritage in predominantly local Southwest Japanese American communities. Instead of relying on the apparently derivative culture of the ethnic community, they have gone straight to the "authentic" source of their ancestral culture, which originated in Japan.[1] This includes learning the Japanese language and culture and, most importantly, developing transnational connections to, and living in Japan. Active engagement in ethnic heritage often involves transnational mobility, and almost all of the shin-nisei and yonsei I interviewed had lived in Japan either as ethnic return migrants or as exchange students and visitors.

Like the earlier ethnic persistence and pluralism literature, the current transnationalism perspective also initially positioned itself in opposition to assimilation, emphasizing the continuation of transnational linkages to the homeland and its culture despite the pressures of assimilation. These theories all posit a certain ethnic linearity over time, assuming that ancestral heritages, and the transnational homeland relations that sustain them, gradually weaken across the generations because of the corrosive forces of assimilation. However, the ethnic legacy of Japanese Americans in the Southwest indicates that cultural histories do not always follow such simple trajectories. After the gradual loss of cultural heritage and transnationalism among the prewar nisei and sansei, the most recent generations of Japanese Americans have reversed this trend. Undoubtedly, progressive cultural assimilation and mainstream social integration have not precluded the simultaneous maintenance of homeland cultures and transnational ties. Indeed, assimilation can even instigate a return to ethnic roots under conditions of racialized multiculturalism as seen among the yonsei. Thus, it is more productive to see assimilation and transnational engagement in ethnic heritage as coexisting and mutually constitutive.

The experiences of Japanese Americans across the generations also challenge the common assumption that the ethnic heritage and transnationalism of later-generation minorities is based on the retention and persistence of the original culture and the cross-border connections of their immigrant ancestors (or ethnic replenishment by current immigrants). Ancestral cultures and transnational ties can certainly be inherited from the original immigrants, as shown by the second generation, but they can also be reactivated and forged anew long after they were lost among previous generations, as is the case with the fourth-generation yonsei. Likewise, Japanese American taiko illustrates how the performance and practice of ethnic heritage are not simply based on the continuity of original homeland cultures over the generations, but involve the active appropriation and remaking of ancestral traditions through the forging of new transnational relations by members of the later-generations.

Regardless of the strength of their ancestral heritage, this book has argued for the importance of analyzing Japanese Americans in transnational perspective. Even apparently localized issues related to ethnic identity and minority cultures should not be considered in an exclusively national context, as has often been done for Asian Americans, especially since transnational mobilities and connections are critical for the production of local heritage cultures and identities. In addition to situating Japanese Americans within their transnational relations and migrations to the ancestral homeland, I have also examined them in diasporic context by analyzing their connections to other Japanese descendants living in the Americas (the nikkei). Instead of assuming that all geographically dispersed ethnic groups that remain engaged with their heritage and homeland are equally diasporic, I have found it more productive to analyze diasporicity—the relative strength of an ethnic group's transborder connections and identifications with the homeland and co-ethnics residing in other countries. Although the homeland diasporicity of Japanese Americans has attenuated over time, it varies considerably across the generations and remains stronger than their diasporic connections to other nikkei in the Americas.

## Explaining Ethnic Heritage

The reason the history of Japanese American ethnicity across generations has not followed predictable, linear patterns is that the relative salience of ethnic heritage is ultimately a product of numerous, interacting variables, and not just an ancestral culture and transnational connection to the homeland that has been passed down from previous generations (in progressively weaker form). Each generation of Japanese Americans has negotiated its own ethnic positionality in response to a multitude of historical and contemporary factors. This has caused some generations to be more engaged in their cultural heritage than others in a distinctly nonlinear manner.

There have been numerous theories that attempt to explain the relative strength of ethnic heritage among second- and later-generation ethnic minorities (although they are not presented as theories of ethnic heritage). Transnationalism implicitly points to cross-border connections to the ethnic homeland and transborder mobility as a critical means for retaining ethnic heritage. Although definitely relevant to Japanese Americans, this perspective focuses primarily on first-generation immigrants and does not really explain what causes U.S.-born ethnic minorities to maintain transnational ties and homeland cultures.

Community solidarity/social capital theories generally assume that intact and cohesive immigrant communities and families allow heritage cultures to be retained among the children of immigrants, thus slowing down the assimilative process. This is exemplified by segmented assimilation theory and the notion of selective acculturation discussed in the Introduction. However, older ethnic minorities like the Japanese Americans, who have scattered around the country and live in white suburban neighborhoods, no longer have the ethnic community solidarity that would allow their cultures to endure—and Japanese Americans generally do not rely that much on local ethnic communities to sustain their ancestral cultural heritage.

Discrimination and ethnic marginalization perspectives assume that such experiences can cause minorities to retain their ethnic identities and cultures, as in the well-known concept of "reactive ethnicity" (Portes and Rumbaut 2001: ch. 7; see also Tsuda 2003: ch. 3). However, although minorities can react negatively against discrimination and racism by strengthening their ethnicity, they may also attempt to assimilate and deemphasize their ancestral heritage in order to avoid discrimination, as shown by the prewar nisei described in Chapter 1.

Finally, ethnic replenishment theory argues that current immigrants replenish the ethnicity of later-generation minorities of the same national origin. However, this theory does not apply to minorities such as Japanese Americans who have not experienced a large-scale influx of new immigrants from the ancestral homeland in recent decades. As discussed in Chapter 5, the yonsei seem to experience *panethnic* replenishment from the large numbers of second-generation Asian Americans, who expect Japanese Americans to have retained their heritage culture just as they have. In this case, Asian Americans are not directly replenishing the Japanese ethnicity of the yonsei, in the same way that Mexican immigrants replenish the Mexican ethnicity of later-generation Mexican Americans, for example. Instead, they are simply part of the racialized multiculturalism that pressures Japanese American yonsei to recover their ethnic heritage.

While these theories certainly help explain the relative strength of Japanese Americans' attachment to ethnic heritage to some extent, they miss some critical variables that constitute their ethnicity. In addition, these theories examine only one factor that influences ethnic heritage and do not examine how these factors are related to each other.

This book has focused on the following social variables that explain the importance of minority ethnic heritage: immigrant generation, age, racialization, the positionality of the ethnic homeland, and the prevalence of assimilation or multiculturalism. Immigrant generational status has some obvious impact on ethnic heritage, since greater generational proximity to the original immigrants increases the likelihood that heritage cultures and transnational homeland connections will be retained. This certainly helps explain the strong heritage ethnicity and transnationalism of the second-generation shin-nisei. However, generation is only one causal factor and must be examined along with other variables. For instance, generation does not explain why the prewar nisei did not maintain their cultural background and transnational ties to Japan the way that the shin-nisei have; nor does it explain why the fourth-generation yonsei have a stronger connection to their Japanese heritage and homeland than the third-generation sansei (or the prewar nisei, for that matter).

Age is another important, if not often neglected, factor that strongly influences interest in ethnic heritage. As noted in early chapters, youth of the second generation are still under the cultural influence of their immigrant parents, who are instrumental in encouraging and pressuring them to learn heritage languages and cultures and become transnationally involved with the ethnic homeland through family trips. As they become older and independent of their parents, the incentive to remain connected to their cultural heritage may become weaker. While youth can be a time of ethnic and identity exploration, especially on tolerant college campuses with multiethnic students and study abroad opportunities, as these youth become adults preoccupied with their careers and children, they may show less interest in their ethnic ancestry and have less time to devote to cultural heritage activities and languages as well as transnational homeland ties. This is especially the case if they marry someone from outside their ethnic group.

Therefore, it is no coincidence that the two generations of Japanese Americans that are the most involved with their ethnic heritage, the shin-nisei and yonsei, are both generally around college age and that the two generations that are less, or not at all, involved are elderly prewar nisei and middle-aged sansei. However, even among those of the same age, generational influences continue to have an impact. The reason the shin-nisei are more likely to maintain their cultural heritage and transnational lives into adulthood than the yonsei is that they are generationally closer to Japan because of their immigrant parents.

Racialization has been a constant for Japanese Americans, and its impact on ethnic heritage has been a dominant theme of this book. Regardless of generation, level of assimilation, or historical period, Japanese Americans have always been racialized as ethnically and culturally "Japanese" simply by virtue of their Asian appearance. Nonetheless, the racial meanings associated with Japaneseness have differed depending on the historical period in which different generations of Japanese Americans were raised. During the World War II period, they experienced a negative, discriminatory racialization that discouraged retention of ethnic heritage. In more recent decades, they have experienced a less pernicious and much more positive type of racialization that can encourage the maintenance and recovery of ethnicity.

In terms of the historical factors that produce these different types of racialization, this book has emphasized the positionality of the ethnic homeland and multiculturalism. Attitudes of mainstream society toward the ancestral homeland of ethnic minorities vary from one historical period to another depending on the country's changing position in the global order and international relations. Negative positionality of the homeland can lead to detrimental, discriminatory racialization, which can produce a type of reactive ethnicity among minority individuals in some cases, and assimilative responses in others who attempt to distance themselves from their ethnic ancestry and avoid discrimination. Conversely, historical periods when the homeland is more favorably positioned can lead to more positive racializations that tend to increase and renew minorities' interest in ancestral cultures, therefore promoting ethnic heritage and transnational involvement with the country of ancestral origin.

The historical shift from an assimilationist to a multicultural ideology in the United States has affected the nature of racialization as well. While multiculturalism, unlike assimilation, certainly encourages immigrant-descent minorities to retain and recover their ethnic differences and homeland transnationalism, it can become rather involuntary and somewhat compulsory for racialized minorities. Racialized multiculturalism can impose an expectation of cultural difference on racially visible minorities in societies where ethnic diversity is encouraged. In this sense, both homeland positionality and multiculturalism are related to historical generation, since they constitute the formative environment that shapes the ethnicity of minority individuals when they first come of age.

## Different Generations, Different Ethnicities

The confluence of racialization with the historical factors of homeland positionality, multiculturalism, and assimilation account for the relative significance of ethnic heritage among different generations of Japanese Americans in the American Southwest. The prewar second-generation nisei not only grew up in a historical period when assimilationist ideologies were still pervasive, but suffered from a purely discriminatory and adverse racialization that was related to the negative positionality of Japan and led to their incarceration during World War II. As a result, they asserted their racial citizenship and national belonging as assimilated Americans at the expense of their Japanese cultural heritage and identity. Because of such formative historical experiences, the prewar nisei continue to live in an exclusively nationalized context today and have not transnationally connected with their heritage culture, despite being only one generation removed from the Japanese homeland.

The third-generation sansei, who have a greater generational distance from their ancestral heritage and ethnic homeland, also came of age in the first few decades after World War II when assimilation was still normative and before Japan's international positionality had dramatically improved. Even when they were youth, they did not engage in transnational efforts to connect with their ancestral Japanese heritage, although there was temporary interest in ethnic history and identity as a result of the Asian American movement. As a result, they eventually became disconnected from their cultural heritage. Although their racialization as "Japanese" was no longer as negative as it had been for their nisei parents, they continue to demand that their racial citizenship as assimilated Americans be recognized. However, because the sansei have also been influenced by more recent multiculturalist ideologies and positive understandings of their Japanese ancestry, they claim to have retained favorable aspects of their heritage culture and are proud of being Japanese Americans. In addition, a limited number of sansei youth in the 1970s who had been inspired by the Asian American movement and its return to ethnic roots began the taiko movement, which has now spread among the Japanese American community.

The dynamics of racialization have changed considerably for the two most recent generations of Japanese Americans. Both the second-generation shin-nisei and the fourth-generation yonsei were born and raised in the last few decades and are thus of the same historical generation, although they are generations apart in terms of immigration. Unlike the prewar nisei and sansei, they have come of age under the influence of multiculturalism (as well as globalization) and the currently favorable position of Japan in the international order, and as a result, their continued racialization as "Japanese" is much more positive compared to earlier historical periods. Moreover, this racialization, which now operates in the context of multiculturalism, pressures Japanese American youth to be ethnically different and transnationally engaged with their now favorably-regarded homeland.

Because the shin-nisei are generationally closer to Japan and to their parent's immigrant culture, they have responded to their positive, multicultural racialization by accepting the cultural heritage and homeland transnationalism of their immigrant parents. In contrast, because the yonsei are of considerable generational distance from their heritage and homeland, racialized multicultural pressures have led to concerns about the extent of their overassimilation and loss of a desirable, ancestral culture. As a result, they have reclaimed their Japanese ethnic roots by reaching out to their ethnic homeland and forging transnational ties.

Therefore, although assimilation generally weakens ties to ethnic heritage, especially during historical periods when it is the dominant ideology, it does not always do so, especially when it is combined with other historical factors. As we have seen, the assimilation of later-generation ethnic minorities can actually cause them to yearn for and revive ancestral cultures and heritages, especially in contemporary contexts of racialized multiculturalism and positive imaginings of homeland.

In addition, historical factors explain the divergent responses to racialization among different generations of Japanese Americans. Growing up in what was an assimilationist era when their ethnicity was not favorably regarded because of Japan's negative positionality, the prewar nisei and sansei have tended to assert their racial citizenship as Americans. In contrast, the shin-nisei and yonsei youth tend to respond to their racialization by maintaining or searching for their cultural heritage, especially since they have come of age during a time when the multicultural valorization of ethnic roots and difference has become dominant and Japan and Japanese culture are favorably regarded.

As noted in the Introduction, not only are racialization processes embedded in history; they are also constituted by and reproduce hierarchical racial formations and inequalities. Despite being in the United States for generations, Japanese Americans continue to experience racialized exclusion from the nation-state as cultural foreigners who are not truly American simply because of the way they look. This has led to persisting ethnic discrimination and the denial of full social rights despite their status as culturally assimilated citizens. It also reinforces the dominant racial system wherein whites are positioned at the top of the ethnic hierarchy and have a monopoly over national identity and citizenship, and racialized minorities are positioned as subordinate groups who are regarded as not really American and less than full citizens.

The ways in which Japanese Americans have responded to and contest their racialization vary considerably in their potential to challenge dominant racial formations. The efforts by prewar nisei and sansei to assert their racial citizenship seem to be the most effective in this regard. By demanding that their status as bona-fide Americans be recognized despite their Japanese appearance, they may eventually cause currently monoracial notions of American national identity to be reshaped in more inclusive ways, which may eventually reorder racial formations, so that whites no longer have exclusive control over Americanness and the full privileges of citizenship. In fact, the struggle for racial citizenship among prewar nisei in response to their discrimination and incarceration during World War II was critical for their greater acceptance in mainstream society and their subsequent socioeconomic mobility in the postwar period. This helped mitigate their racial subordination and improved the standing of Japanese American nisei and their descendants in the American racial order (albeit at the expense of producing new and problematic ethnic stereotypes about model minorities).

In contrast, the persistence of the Japanese heritage culture among the shin-nisei and attempts to actively recover it among the yonsei may inadvertently reproduce hegemonic racial formations that forever tie Japanese Americans to a foreign culture and homeland and marginalize them as outsiders. This is especially the case with taiko performances, which have become quite popular among Asians and non-Asian Americans alike. Although taiko is personally empowering because it allows individual Japanese Americans to publicly defy ethnic stereotypes, its collective reception by white audiences is rather disempowering and accentuates their Orientalization as peoples with exotic and ancient cultures from the Far East.

## The Future of the Japanese American Community

### Community Decline

According to the U.S. Census, the total population of Japanese descendants is still quite substantial. In 2014, it was 1,374,825, having increased from 1,148,932 in 2000. However, this population includes those who are only partially of Japanese descent. Those who chose "Japanese alone" on the census are only 759,056 in number and have been declining since 1990, when the figure was 847,562. Moreover, this population of monoracial Japanese descendants includes 302,685 individuals who are

foreign-born, some of whom are probably temporary business expatriates and students who will eventually return to Japan. This means that
*only 477,525* are U.S.-born individuals of monoracial Japanese descent,
which is the population of second- to fourth-generation Japanese
Americans mainly represented in my research sample. This number will
continue to decline because of increasing rates of intermarriage among
Japanese Americans, which is now at 70 percent (Iijima Hall 2008:45).

Given the declining numbers of Japanese Americans, what does the
future have in store for their ethnic community? This is not simply an
academic question, but an issue that has been on the minds of many of
my interviewees as well as students at the Nikkei Student Union's "culture forums" at the University of California at San Diego. They are well
aware that the Japanese American community continues to shrink and
weaken, worry about its future cohesion and vitality, and wonder how
long their organizations and cultural activities will persist. As one yonsei aptly put it, "We are a dying race." Several interviewees felt Japanese
Americans are starting to resemble white ethnics who have lost their
identities and communities. "I think we are going the way of previous
ethnic groups," one of them observed. "It's like with the Irish. You talk
to them and it's like, 'Yeah, I have grandparents who are Irish.' But I
don't think they relate very much to it at all." Others believe that Japanese Americans will eventually blend into the mainstream population
through intermarriage.

Because of these circumstances, researchers have marveled at how
the Japanese American community endured and persisted for generations, as noted in earlier chapters. Interestingly, a couple of my interviewees observed that the internment experience has helped keep the
Japanese American community together over time because it is an issue
with which they have been able to identify. It has also had a galvanizing
effect, as shown by the successful redress movement. In effect, past persecution and discrimination can contribute to the maintenance of ethnic
communities, cultures, and identities. (O'Brien and Fugita 1991:102–112).
For instance, the Japanese American Historical Society of San Diego,
which is perhaps the most active and well-attended Japanese American
organization in the city, would not have existed without the internment.
Founded by a group of elderly prewar nisei who had been interned in
the same concentration camp, it continues to address the internment

experience. As noted in earlier chapters, negative racialization can lead to racism and discrimination, but it can also keep minority communities intact for longer periods.

Nonetheless, some of my interviewees feel that the past cannot keep Japanese Americans together forever. They believe that Japanese Americans have moved well beyond internment and redress and are no longer subject to serious discrimination, and that there are currently no pressing civil rights issues to galvanize the community. Instead, they are socioeconomically successful and no longer need or are interested in their ethnic communities. This was also the dominant theme of the Nikkei Student Union's skit discussed in Chapter 5, which lamented the decline of the ethnic community and expressed hope that young Japanese Americans would not sacrifice their heritage for the sake of socioeconomic success and assimilation.

Japanese American organizations are especially feeling the effects of a shrinking and weakening ethnic community. Not only have past Japan-towns long since disappeared, Japanese American organizations continue to experience declining membership, while being unable to attract significant numbers of Japanese American youth to their activities and events (Montero 1980:43; Spickard 1996:159). One sansei JACL board member in Phoenix remarked: "We need to get programs started to bring these younger people in. That is the future. If not, the community will die out in a generation. It won't be around for my kids." While anywhere from 43 to 50 percent of Japanese Americans were estimated to be involved in some kind of Japanese American organization from the 1960s to the 1980s (Montero 1980:43; O'Brien and Fugita 1991), I suspect the percentage today is dramatically smaller. For instance, among my sample of interviewees, only those whom I recruited through local Japanese American organizations are involved in the ethnic community; almost none of the others are actively involved (although some had been more active when they were children because of their parents). Although Japanese Americans tend to become disengaged from the local ethnic community once they move away for college and begin pursuing careers, there is a tendency among some of them to become reengaged once they have children, since they want their offspring to remain connected with their ethnic heritage (Kitano 1993:115; Tuan 2001:110, 112, 123).

Nonetheless, all of the leaders of the Japanese American organizations I spoke with are quite concerned about the future. This was especially the case with the Japanese American Citizens League. Although its finances and membership rolls remain substantial, fewer and fewer members are actively involved. In fact, even the president of the San Diego chapter characterized JACL as a "dying organization." He noted that there are no longer many Japanese American civil rights issues to fight for compared to the past and that Japanese Americans are no longer interested in political activism. "A lot of us are very comfortable with where we are because we are professionals with good pay, nice offices, and everything," he noted. As a result, JACL has become more focused on pan-Asian American civil rights in order to remain relevant. He explained as follows:

> We're becoming more Asian American because of our role as the oldest Asian American civil rights organization and the needs of the broader [Asian] community. We know hate doesn't recognize the distinction between different groups. So considering what we do, I think we need to be more Asian American in that sense. . . . We haven't actively recruited [other Asian Americans], but we have actively networked. When someone from another Asian group is a victim of a hate crime, we are quick to step up and offer our assistance and our background. We were also the first to stand up when Arabs were detained after 9/11. We reminded people of the Japanese American interment and said, "Hasn't the U.S. government learned anything from it?"

Ironically, JACL's pan-Asian outreach had actually alienated some of my interviewees in San Diego, who feel that the organization is no longer engaged with local Japanese American communities.

Although the Japanese American Historical Society of San Diego is considerably more popular than JACL in San Diego and many people show up to its events, the organization's board members are almost all elderly (only one is middle-aged), and they are quite concerned that younger Japanese Americans are not interested in the community's history. As mentioned in Chapter 1, their well-attended annual meeting consisted mainly of elderly and middle-aged members with relatively few youth, who mainly accompanied their older parents.

Membership issues are a concern even for the popular Nikkei Student Union at the UC San Diego. One board member spoke to me about how the student organization has to actively publicize in order to recruit members, because there are not many Japanese American students anymore and even they are not always interested in Japanese American organizations. As a result, their club has become heavily dependent on non-Japanese American students, who are now half of its membership. "It's different for the Korean American Student Association," he explained. "They don't have to ask for people to come, and they don't have to reach out to non-Koreans. People just come because there are so many [Korean Americans] and that's their place."

Needless to say, today's Japanese American youth are the future of the ethnic community. In this sense, the revival of ethnicity among the yonsei will help forestall the gradual erosion of the Japanese American community, at least for another generation. The popularity of taiko among the yonsei has increased their interest in the local Japanese American community, since many of its organizations have taiko groups that attract these youth. Their frequent and popular performances certainly draw audience members from the community. Therefore, taiko has become a common ethnic activity that has helped bring together a fragmented and declining community. The former president of UC San Diego's Asayake Taiko even expressed the hope that taiko would keep the Japanese American community alive in spirit even if its actual members dwindle. "The hard-core Japanese American community that is working hard to keep the past alive is eventually going to die out," he remarked. "But it's my hope that it can still live through taiko. Hopefully, down the line, if you really want to study taiko and you're not Japanese American, you'll still have to study the Japanese American culture because a lot of its past is expressed through the music, the traditional folk songs. This might not be true, but I hope it will be."

The future of the Japanese American community is also in the hands of shin-nisei youth. Although Japanese immigration to the United States since 1965 has been relatively modest, it will continue into the foreseeable future, and a number of these immigrants will have children and settle permanently in the United States. Thus, although the number of shin-nisei is still rather small, it will continue to grow. Because the prewar nisei are passing away and the sansei will also do so in the next several decades, the shin-nisei may eventually become the largest generation of Japanese Americans. In fact, they may already outnumber the yonsei, if only those of complete Japanese descent are counted.

The shin-nisei have not been part of the traditional Japanese American community, and based on my limited sample, few seem actively involved or have any interest in Japanese American organizations. Even the Japanese American members of the Nikkei Student Union are predominantly yonsei. Nonetheless, the shin-nisei represent a new lineage of Japanese Americans. Although a good number will intermarry, some will also marry Japanese Americans or Japanese from Japan. If there is any notable population of new third-generation *shin-sansei* in the future, they will undoubtedly follow a different ethnic trajectory from the older sansei generation who are the descendants of prewar Japanese immigrants.

### Biracial Happa and Japanese American Ethnicity

Because Japanese Americans have been in the United States for a long time and currently have a 70 percent intermarriage rate, a good proportion of the Japanese-descent population is now of mixed-heritage. Close to 45 percent of the 1,374,825 Japanese descendants in the United States are of mixed heritage and are often referred to as *happas*, an ethnic term that originated in Hawaii.[2] Because most Japanese Americans intermarry with whites, many of the happas are half Japanese and half white (King-O'Riain 2006:42–45).

The number of biracial (as well as increasingly multiracial) Japanese descendants will grow in the future. Some of the sansei and many of the yonsei are happas. In addition to the high Japanese American intermarriage rate, a good number of current Japanese immigrants who settle in the United States will probably intermarry. Of the 302,685 foreign-born Japanese living in America, 67.5 percent are women. Although some have undoubtedly accompanied Japanese husbands to the United States, a good number of them are single and are likely to marry non-Japanese, mainly white men. Their children will then become biracial second-generation happas. In fact, there is already a growing number of shin-nisei happas.

Given the large and increasing numbers of happas, they will be important for the future of Japanese Americans (King-O'Riain 2006:45).

Do they have ethnic experiences that resemble monoracial Japanese Americans of their generation and do they even identify as "Japanese American"? Since I interviewed only a small number of biracial Japanese descendants and my sample is quite skewed, I can make no generalizations about them. However, it is instructive at the end of this book to examine their ethnic consciousness and the extent to which they consider themselves part of the Japanese American community.

Five out of the six biracial Japanese descendants I interviewed are half Japanese and half white, and by coincidence, four of them are generationally shin-nisei on the Japanese side of their family (one parent, usually their mother, is from Japan). The other two are a half-white/half-Japanese man of the third generation and a half-Filipina/half-Japanese woman of the fourth generation. Two of the shin-nisei happas do not fit the general profile of shin-nisei who are completely of Japanese descent. They do not speak any Japanese, do not feel attached to their Japanese heritage, and have not been to Japan. However, one expressed interest in visiting the country and did mention that she is proud of her partial Japanese ancestry. In contrast, the other two shin-nisei happas have had experiences more similar to their Japanese American shin-nisei counterparts in terms of ethnic heritage. One of them speaks some Japanese, had accompanied her father to Japan a number of times, and feels some connection to the country. The other actually lives in Japan (she is married to a Japanese man), is fluent in Japanese, and is quite proud of being half Japanese.

My third-generation happa interviewee also somewhat resembles his Japanese American sansei counterparts in terms of the way in which he relates to his ethnicity. Although he is of course completely Americanized, he is quite proud of his partial Japanese heritage and claims to have inherited positive aspects of Japanese culture. Likewise, the Filipina/Japanese fourth-generation woman resembles yonsei Japanese Americans. Having studied Japanese in college and spent a year in Japan through a study abroad program, she feels quite connected to her Japanese heritage (at least when she was younger), and is also very active in the local Japanese American community. I also spoke with a biracial white/Japanese fourth-generation boy (who accompanied his sansei mother when I interviewed her). His mother was encouraging him to explore his Japanese heritage, and he is a member of a local taiko group. He also expressed interest in Japanese culture, as well as visiting and living in Japan in the future. In fact, he told me he wished he were 100 percent Japanese descent and wanted to marry a Japanese American girl!

Thus, four out of my six biracial interviewees have had ethnic experiences that are similar to those of Japanese Americans of their generation who are of complete Japanese descent. It is very interesting to note that they have stronger Japanese facial features than my two other biracial interviewees and are seen by others as being half Japanese, or not completely white. This indicates that racialization continues to be important for constituting the ethnicity of even biracial individuals (Spickard 1989:115–116). The two happa who have little connection to their ethnic heritage do not have noticeable Japanese facial features and can generally pass as white. Both of them told me that other people (especially whites) simply assume they are white; one never mentions his partial Japanese ancestry unless asked. It is only close acquaintances who start to notice, after about a month, that he may not be 100 percent white.

Regardless of their appearance and affinity to their Japanese ancestry, none of my biracial Japanese/white interviewees identifies as "Japanese American." "Japanese American to me is someone who is full-blooded Japanese and raised in America," one of them remarked. "So it would be a misnomer to call myself that." Nor do they identify by generation (shin-nisei, sansei, yonsei). This is true even for the four biracial interviewees who look more Japanese. For the three biracial Japanese/white individuals who have a stronger Japanese appearance, other people could tell they are ethnically different (that is, not completely white) by appearance and often wondered about their background. When asked, they tended to identify themselves as "half Japanese," thus emphasizing the side of their identity that is more ethnically marked, or as "half Japanese, half white." In fact, the sansei happa man actually described his ethnicity to others as "Japanese." The two happas who look white also identified as "half Japanese/half white." A couple of my biracial interviewees identify as "happa," but only to other Japanese Americans and Asians who are familiar with the term. However, one interviewee (who looks quite white) did not even know what happa means!

Of all my biracial interviewees, only the Japanese/Filipina woman, Barbara Kitamura, identifies as "Japanese American." She passed as Japanese American in my interactions with her in the local community and did not mention that her mother is Filipina until one third of the way into our interview. Barbara told me she identifies as Japanese American to other Japanese Americans and does not disclose her Filipina heritage to them. Everyone in the community assumes she is Japanese American because of her Japanese last name, and she generally mentions her Filipina background only to Filipinos. She feels that Japanese Americans (including her grandmother) have prejudices against Filipinos, which is why she does not identify as half-Filipina in front of them.

Most of my biracial interviewees have never been involved in the Japanese American community (see also Spickard 1989:112–113). The only exceptions are Barbara and the sansei happa man who had attended events at the local Buddhist temple when he was young (but he is no longer involved with the community). It is not that the happas feel excluded from the Japanese American community; they simply do not have much interest in it. This may be because most of them are of the shin-nisei generation on the Japanese side of their families, and shin-nisei in general are disconnected from the Japanese American community. In the past, some members of the Japanese American community had trouble accepting happas (Spickard 1989:117, Takahashi 1997:209), but today, most seem to openly welcome them, especially given the declining numbers of Japanese Americans (King-O'Riain 2006:96–97). However, I generally did not encounter many happa at Japanese American community events, and those who did attend were children who came with their families.[3] I also saw only a limited number of happa students at UC San Diego's Nikkei Student Union. In fact, there used to be a Happa Club at the university, but it had been defunct for a number of years by the time I conducted fieldwork.

*\*\**

Although a number of my Japanese American interviewees are concerned that their community is "disappearing" or "dying," it is safe to say that Japanese Americans are not in any danger of ethnic extinction, despite their shrinking population and the continued scattering and erosion of their ethnic community. While it is true that the number of Japanese Americans of complete Japanese descent will continue to decline, the general Japanese-descent community remains quite large. However, it is becoming increasingly diverse, not just in terms of generation, but also in terms of racial and ethnic composition. In the future, "Japanese Americans" will increasingly consist of people like the shin-nisei and the happas, who have not been part of the traditional ethnic community. Even if many of them do not strictly identify as Japanese Americans, this simply indicates that the boundaries of the Japanese-descent community in the United States are becoming wider and more porous. This, in turn, may lead to more inclusive understandings of what it means to be "Japanese American," which are not limited simply to those who trace their ancestry exclusively to prewar Japanese immigrants (Spickard 1996:160; Yamashiro 2008:259–260).

The true significance of this increasing diversity among Americans of Japanese ancestry will not be known for another several decades. However, the present and future status of their ethnicity is significant not only for peoples of Japanese descent in the United States. Ultimately, it reflects the future ethnic trajectory of newer Asian American groups, which now outnumber the Japanese Americans.

# NOTES

1 This is the year when the Immigration and Nationality Act of 1965 was enacted. The act abolished previous national origins quotas and enabled large numbers of Asians to begin immigrating to the United States on employment visas and for the purposes of family reunification.

2 Although there was some immigration of Chinese and Filipinos during this period, the vast majority of them arrived in the United States after 1965.

3 They were brought to the United States by American military personnel serving in Japan during the post–World War II American occupation.

4 The exceptions are Yanagisako (1985), who focuses narrowly on kinship, and King-O'Riain (2006), whose book is limited to beauty pageants from the perspective of multiracial contestants. Jonathan Okamura (2008, 2014) has published on contemporary Japanese Americans in Hawaii.

5 These were the two largest groups of Asian Americans at the time along with Filipino Americans.

6 These figures include those who chose "Japanese alone," "Korean alone," or in combination with other racial/ethnic ancestries. It also includes both U.S. and foreign-born individuals.

7 I did not interview any Japanese Americans whom I would consider members of the working class or upper class members of the super-rich elite.

8 This was also true for earlier European-origin ethnic groups, whose ancestors mainly immigrated during a circumscribed period of time (Alba and Nee 1997:833; Waters and Jiménez 2005:121). Generational distinctions become less salient for ethnic groups that have a long history of immigration.

9 One notable exception is Tomás Jiménez's (2010) study of later-generation Mexican Americans.

10 Studies that have some coverage of the contemporary status of Japanese Americans either do not mention the shin-nisei or do so only briefly (e.g., Kitano 1993; O'Brien and Fugita 1991; Spickard 1996; Takahashi 1997). Yonsei were included in the research sample for Tuan's (2001) book and Okamura has written briefly on yonsei experiences and yonsei activists in Hawaii (2008:138–144, 2014: ch. 7). The only other studies I could find that include significant samples of yonsei are short articles by Hieshima and Schneider (1994) and Wooden, Leon, and Toshima (1988).

11 Someone of the 2.5 generation would have one parent who is a first-generation immigrant and another parent who is second generation. Likewise, someone of the 3.5 generation would have one parent who is of the second immigrant generation and one parent who is third generation.

12 Yamashiro (2008, 2011) ignores generational differences among Japanese Americans in Japan by claiming that most of her interviewees were of mixed generation, which is hard to believe as explained earlier in this chapter. Takamori (2011) gives an overview of different generations of Japanese Americans, but does not analyze how generation affects their ethnic experiences in Japan.

13 The only Japan-towns that remain are in Los Angeles, San Francisco, and San Jose, which are now partly sustained by newer Japanese expatriate business communities.

14 This contrasts with contiguous globalization, which involves the actual physical movement of people, goods, and capital across national borders.

15 This term is taken from Schein (1998).

16 For instance, most Americans believe that all those who trace their ancestry to Europe have always been considered white. They are often not aware that immigrants from southern or eastern Europe during the nineteenth century (for instance) were initially not seen as truly white, but as members of distinctly "darker," "swarthier," or "Slavic" races, and that therefore, the racial category and meaning of "white" was not fixed but has been constantly contested and expanded throughout American immigration history.

17 The next two sections were previously published as an article entitled "Is Native Anthropology Really Possible?" *Anthropology Today* 31, no. 3 (2015): 14–17. Reprinted with permission from John Wiley and Sons.

## CHAPTER 1. THE PREWAR NISEI

1 For instance, in San Diego and Phoenix, the JACL youth group went defunct many years ago.

2 The founding historian of JAHSSD was a local city college faculty member.

3 The only exception I have come across is van Niekerk's study examining differences in socioeconomic mobility between second-generation descendants of earlier better-educated Caribbean immigrants and more recent, lower-class Caribbean immigrants in the Netherlands.

4 The few studies of the adult second generation (e.g., Kasinitz et al. 2008) do not compare them to younger age cohorts. Portes and Rumbaut's (2001) study of the second generation does take age differences into account, but it is a longitudinal study that simply tracked one age cohort over time.

5 However, when the 442nd Japanese American Regimental Combat team was training in the deep south during World War II, they were classified as "honorary whites" and told to use white-only facilities and sit toward the front of the bus (Yenne 2007: ch. 6).

6  In this respect, it is important to note that Japanese Americans in Hawaii, who were a much larger proportion of the state's population (close to 40 percent), were not interned during World War II in significant numbers despite their greater proximity to Japan and the fact that Hawaii was the only part of the United States directly attacked by the Japanese.

7  The internment of Japanese Americans has been extensively documented in many historical accounts. For example, see Fugita and Fernandez (2004: ch. 3, 6), Maki, Kitano, and Berthold (1999: ch. 3), Matsumoto (2014: ch. 4), Spickard (1996: ch. 6), and Takezawa (1995: ch. 3).

8  A minority of young nisei men answered "no" to both questions or gave qualified answers. The loyalty questionnaire led to conflicts between Japanese Americans willing to volunteer for the U.S. military versus those who were not. When the draft was instated for Japanese Americans, some of the latter became draft resistors. This became a source of conflict in the Japanese American community which continued after World War II.

9  The U.S. government was actively involved in propaganda promoting the loyalty and heroic exploits of Japanese American soldiers (see Fujitani 2011: ch. 5).

10  However, Ueda (2002:35) does note that nisei of this period had few opportunities to visit Japan.

## CHAPTER 2. THE POSTWAR NISEI

1  Most of my informants spoke of this perception as an ethnic stereotype, but only two were ambivalent about or critical of it.

2  The only exceptions were those who were biracial (and thus of Japanese descent on only one side of the family) and Doug, who was 2.5 generation.

3  Asian American children raised in white suburbs often attempt to assimilate in order to be accepted by mainstream society and may distance themselves from their ethnic heritage. However, as they enter college and immerse themselves in a more ethnically diverse and tolerant environment (which also increases their interaction with other Asian Americans), they often experience an ethnic awakening and interest in exploring their minority identities.

## CHAPTER 3. ASSIMILATION AND LOSS OF ETHNIC HERITAGE AMONG THIRD-GENERATION JAPANESE AMERICANS

1  Perhaps because of their minority status and persecution during World War II, third-generation Japanese Americans did not yet feel as secure compared to majority whites about their place in American society and thus could not assert their ethnic differences without fear of negative repercussions.

2  One of them did feel that their parents wanted them to be proud of their heritage and therefore took them to events in the Japanese American community.

3  The food metaphor refers to those who look "yellow" on the outside but have become assimilated and "white" on the inside.

4 Maeda (2012) analyzes how the Asian American movement also led to interracial coalitions with blacks, Native Americans, and Hispanics as well as international affinities with Third World peoples across the globe.

5 In contrast, one interviewee did not feel she was "a typical American" because she continued to have a strong ethnic minority consciousness and identified with other minorities more than with whites.

6 Even today, the sansei report experiencing less discrimination than the prewar nisei (see also Takezawa 1995:132).

7 Although he regarded the Japanese in Japan in a generally positive manner, he did not like their racism, prejudice, and judgmental nature, nor their history of imperialism.

8 Carol's grandmother accompanied her to Japan and tried to translate. However, the grandmother could not speak much English, so there was still a communication gap. In fact, her relatives found it amusing that the grandmother and granddaughter could not communicate well with each other.

## CHAPTER 4. THE STRUGGLE FOR RACIAL CITIZENSHIP AMONG LATER-GENERATION JAPANESE AMERICANS

1 Portions of this chapter were previously published as an article entitled "'I'm American, Not Japanese!': The Struggle for Racial Citizenship among Later-Generation Japanese Americans," *Ethnic and Racial Studies* 37, no. 3 (2014): 405–424. Reprinted with permission from the Taylor & Francis Group (http://www.tandfonline.com/)

2 Kim (2008: ch. 8) has some examples of how second-generation Korean Americans are seen as foreigners in their daily lives. The only description of the racialization of later generation Asian Americans as perpetual foreigners is Tuan's (2001) book on the subject, but her ethnographic examples of such experiences are limited and are mainly from third generation Japanese and Chinese Americans, although her sample does include the fourth generation as well. The Asian American literature often mentions how Asian Americans are asked, "Where are you from?" or told, "You speak English so well," without further elaboration or discussion of other ways in which they are perceived as foreign.

3 Others who have examined social citizenship also tend to focus on social class issues and social welfare rights (e.g., Barbalet 1993; Dwyer 2004)

4 It seems this does not always produce culturally assimilated subjects since the dual process of self-making and being made involves a subject that submits to power relations but also contests and resists them.

5 For instance, the Brazilian nation is understood to be composed of a mixture of three "founding" races (white, black, Indian), a notion popularized by the famous Brazilian scholar Gilberto Freyre.

6 Some would argue that the racial category of "black" is also defined as American. In fact, black African or Caribbean immigrants are often mistaken as African Americans in the United States.

7 Part of this statement was also quoted in Chapter 1.

8  In daily conversation, I often noticed Japanese Americans describing themselves (or other Japanese Americans) simply as "Japanese," instead of using the more formal term of "Japanese American."

9  They were seen as shorter with darker complexions and distinct facial features and hair color compared to Anglo Americans (Jacobson 1999: ch. 2).

10  Even the Japanese Americans of mixed racial descent I interviewed felt that they are perceived as racially different and are not considered white.

## CHAPTER 5. ETHNIC REVIVAL AMONG FOURTH-GENERATION JAPANESE AMERICANS

1  There was even an article in the *New York Times* entitled "Young Japanese Americans Honor Ethnic Roots" (August 2, 2004).

2  Other Asian Americans (e.g., see Kibria 2002a:92–94; Kim 2008:203; Louie 2004:107) as well as later-generation Mexican Americans (Jiménez 2010:170–171) are also viewed as closely tied to their ancestral heritage and homeland.

3  A few others were somewhat less pessimistic and claimed that Japanese Americans could spread their influence by reaching out to the broader society and understanding themselves better.

4  In fact, the current trendiness of Japanese culture is one reason why a good number of Americans of non-Japanese descent have also become interested in J-pop, study Japanese in college, and visit Japan as exchange students.

5  Some of them participated in the Japanese American community when they returned home to visit their parents during summer or winter breaks.

## CHAPTER 6. JAPANESE AMERICAN TAIKO AND THE REMAKING OF TRADITION

1  This and the next chapter are partly based on interviews with taiko ensemble leaders conducted by the Japanese American National Museum (JANM) for the 2005–2006 exhibition, *Big Drum: Taiko in the United States*. Quotations from these interview transcripts are labeled "JANM interview" and used with the permission of the JANM.

2  See the Rolling Thunder website at www.taiko.com.

3  See the the Japanese American National Museum website at http://blog.janm.org/index.php/2013/07/22/natsumatsuri-taiko/ and the Taiko Center website at http://www.taiko-center.co.jp/english/history_of_taiko.html.

4  From the Japanese American National Museum DVD, *Big Drum: Taiko in the United States* (2005).

5  From the True Taiko Tales website at http://truetalltaikotales.blogspot.com/2012/11/tradition.html.

6  In fact, it is problematic to label certain traditions as "invented" (Hobsbawm 1983) since this implies that some traditions have been recreated and are discontinuous with the past, whereas other (true? real?) traditions apparently have been continuously passed down unchanged from historical times.

7 See also the Taiko Center website at http://www.taiko-center.co.jp/english/history_of_taiko.html.
8 From the Japanese American National Museum DVD, *Big Drum: Taiko in the United States*.
9 From the True Taiko Tales website at http://truetalltaikotales.blogspot.com/2012/04/taiko-community-rant.html.
10 From the Japanese American National Museum DVD, *Big Drum: Taiko in the United States* (2005) ("Kodo in America" segment).
11 Permission to use these photos does not necessarily indicate San Jose Taiko's agreement with the research findings.

CHAPTER 7. PERFORMATIVE AUTHENTICITY AND FRAGMENTED EMPOWERMENT THROUGH TAIKO

1 According to King-O'Riain (2006: ch. 4), Japanese American beauty pageants strongly prefer contestants who look Japanese (versus multiracial) and can demonstrate skill in the Japanese language or culture. In other words, those who resemble Japanese in Japan both racially and culturally are seen as more ethnically authentic Japanese Americans.
2 From the True Taiko Tales website at http://truetalltaikotales.blogspot.com/2012/04/taiko-community-rant.html.
3 As Wang notes (1999:359), creativity can generate a sense of existential authenticity.
4 In fact, those who engage in indigenous or heritage tourism based on staged performances and recreated ethnic festivals often experience them as authentic (Chhabra, Healy, and Sills 2003; Taylor 2001).
5 From the Japanese American National Museum website at http://www.janm.org/exhibits/bigdrum/interviews/taikoproject/
6 Outside of the United States, the countries that have by far the most taiko groups are Canada, Germany, and the United Kingdom.

CHAPTER 8. DIASPORICITY AND JAPANESE AMERICANS

1 This chapter is a substantially modified version of the article "Disconnected from the 'Diaspora': Japanese Americans and the Lack of Transnational Ethnic Networks," *Journal of Anthropological Research* 68, no. 2 (2012): 95–116 (2012). Reprinted with permission from the University of Chicago Press, Copyright © by The University of New Mexico
2 Even when more specific definitions of "diasporicity" are offered, they are quite general. For instance, Stephen Lubkemann (2013) uses "diasporicity" simply to refer to identity discourses among diasporic peoples (see also Klimt and Lubkemann 2002:146, 149). According to Louis-Jacques Dorais (2010:94), diasporicity is the degree to which transmigrants display characteristics that differentiate them from other migrants (and thus make them diasporic).

CONCLUSION

1 The only notable exception is taiko, which most yonsei learn from the local Japanese American community or independent ensembles.

2 Although *happa* technically refers to anyone of mixed-descent, I noticed that Japanese Americans tended to use the term to refer to those who are half Japanese/half white. For instance, one interviewee who was half Japanese/half Filipina was never referred to as a hapa, nor did she use that term for herself.

3 There are whites married to Japanese Americans who come to these community events as well.

# REFERENCES

Abu-Lughod, Lila. 1991. "Writing Against Culture." In *Recapturing Anthropology: Working in the Present*, edited by Richard Fox. Santa Fe, NM: School of American Research Press, 137–162.

Adachi, Nobuko. 2006a. "Introduction: Theorizing Japanese Diaspora." In *Japanese Diasporas: Unsung Pasts, Conflicting Presents, and Uncertain Futures*, edited by Nobuko Adachi. London: Routledge, 1–22.

————, ed. 2006b. *Japanese Diasporas: Unsung Pasts, Conflicting Presents, and Uncertain Futures*. London: Routledge.

Aguilar, John. 1981. "Insider Research: An Ethnography of a Debate. In *Anthropologists at Home in North America: Methods and Issues in the Study of One's Own Society*, edited by Donald Messerschmidt. Cambridge, UK: Cambridge University Press, 15–26.

Ahlgren, Angela. 2011. "Drumming Asian America: Performing Race, Gender, and Sexuality in North American Taiko." Ph.D. diss., University of Texas, Austin.

Akiba, Daisuke. 2006. "Japanese Americans." In *Asian Americans: Contemporary Trends and Issues*, edited by Pyong Gap Min, 2nd ed. Thousand Oaks, CA: Pine Forge Press, 148–177.

Alba, Richard. 1990. *Ethnic Identity: The Transformation of White America*. New Haven, CT: Yale University Press.

————. 1999. "Immigration and the American Realities of Assimilation and Multiculturalism." *Sociological Forum* 14 (1): 3–25.

Alba, Richard, and Jennifer Holdaway. 2013. *The Children of Immigrants at School: A Comparative Look at Integration in the United States and Western Europe*. New York: New York University Press.

Alba, Richard, and Victor Nee. 1997. "Rethinking Assimilation Theory for a New Era of Immigration." *International Migration Review* 31 (4): 826–874.

Anae, Melani. 2010. "Teu Le Va: Toward a Native Anthropology." *Pacific Studies* 33 (2–3): 222–240.

Asai, Susan Miyo. 1995. "Transformations of Tradition: Three Generations of Japanese American Music Making." *Musical Quarterly* 79 (3): 429–453.

Asakawa, Gil. 2004. *Being Japanese American: A JA Sourcebook for Nikkei, Happa ... & Their Friends*. Berkeley, CA: Stone Bridge Press.

Azuma, Eiichiro. 2005. *Between Two Empires: Race, History, and Transnationalism in Japanese America*. Oxford, UK: Oxford University Press.

Barbalet, J. M. 1993. "Citizenship, Class Inequality and Resentment." In *Citizenship and Social Theory*, edited by Bryan Turner. London: Sage Publications, 36–56.

Bauböck, Rainer. 2001. "Cultural Citizenship, Minority Rights, and Self-Government." In *Citizenship Today: Global Perspectives and Practices*, edited by T. Alexander Aleinikoff and Douglas Klusmeyer. Washington, DC: Carnegie Endowment for International Peace, 319–348.

Behar, Ruth. 1996. *The Vulnerable Observer: Anthropology that Breaks Your Heart*. Boston: Beacon Press.

Bender, Shawn. 2012. *Taiko Boom: Japanese Drumming in Place and Motion*. Berkeley: University of California Press.

Berg, Mette. 2011. *Diasporic Generations: Memory, Politics, and Nation among Cubans in Spain*. Oxford, UK: Berghahn Books.

Bhatia, Sunil, and Anjali Ram 2001. "Rethinking 'Acculturation' in Relation to Diasporic Cultures and Postcolonial Identities." *Human Development* 44 (1): 1–18.

Bloemraad, Irene, Anna Korteweg, and Gökçe Yurdakul. 2008. "Citizenship and Immigration: Multiculturalism, Assimilation, and Challenges to the Nation-State." *Annual Review of Sociology* 34: 153–179.

Bonacich, Edna, Sabrina Alimahomed, and Jake Wilson. 2008. "The Racialization of Global Labor." *American Behavioral Scientist* 52 (3): 342–355.

Bonilla-Silva, Eduardo. 2014. *Racism without Racists*, 4th ed. Lanham, MD: Rowman and Littlefield.

Bourdieu, Pierre. 1977. *Outline of a Theory of Practice*. Cambridge, UK: Cambridge University Press.

Boyd, Monica, and Elizabeth Grieco. 1998. "Triumphant Transitions: Socioeconomic Achievements of the Second Generation in Canada." *International Migration Review* 32 (4): 853–876.

Braziel, Jana, and Anita Mannur. 2003. "Nation, Migration, Globalization: Points of Contention in Diaspora Studies." In *Theorizing Diaspora: A Reader*, edited by Jana Braziel and Anita Mannur. Malden, MA: Blackwell Publishers, 1–22.

Brettell, Caroline, and Faith Nibbs. 2009. "Lived Hybridity: Second-Generation Identity Construction through College Festival." *Identities: Global Studies in Culture and Power* 16: 678–699.

Briggs, Charles. 1996. "The Politics of Discursive Authority in Research on the 'Invention of Tradition.'" *Cultural Anthropology* 11 (4): 435–469.

Brubaker, Rogers. 2005. "The 'Diaspora' Diaspora." *Ethnic and Racial Studies* 28 (1): 1–19.

Bruneau, Michel. 2010. "Diasporas, Transnational Spaces and Communities." In *Diaspora and Transnationalism: Concepts, Theories and Methods*, edited by Rainer Bauböck and Thomas Faist. Amsterdam: Amsterdam University Press, 35–50.

Bunzl, Matti. 2004. "Boas, Foucault, and the 'Native Anthropologist': Notes toward a Neo-Boasian Anthropology." *American Anthropologist* 106 (3): 435–442.

Butler, Judith. 1990. *Gender Trouble: Feminism and the Subversion of Identity*. New York: Routledge.

——. 1996. "Imitation and Gender Insubordination." In *Women, Knowledge, and Reality: Explorations in Feminist Philosophy*, edited by Ann Garry and Marilyn Pearsall, 2nd ed. New York: Routledge Kegan Paul, 371–387.

——. 2010. "Performative Agency." *Journal of Cultural Economy* 3 (2): 147–161.

Butler, Kim. 2001. "Defining Diaspora, Refining a Discourse." *Diaspora: A Journal of Transnational Studies* 10 (2): 189–219.

Capo Zmegac, Jasna, Christian Vob, and Klaus Roth, eds. 2010. *Co-Ethnic Migrations Compared: Central and Eastern European Contexts*. Berlin: Verlag Otto Sagner.

Carle, Sarah Anne. 2008. "Bodies in Motion: Gender, Identity, and the Politics of Representation in the American Taiko Movement." M.A. thesis, University of Hawaii.

Castles, Stephen, and Alastair Davidson. 2000. *Citizenship and Migration: Globalization and the Politics of Belonging*. New York: Routledge.

Chan, Sucheng, and Shirley Hune. 1995. "Racialization and Panethnicity: From Asians in America to Asian Americans." In *Toward a Common Destiny: Improving Race and Ethnic Relations in America*, edited by Willis Hawley and Anthony Jackson. San Francisco: Jossey-Bass Publishers, 205–233.

Chhabra, Deepak, Robert Healy, and Erin Sills. 2003. "Staged Authenticity and Heritage Tourism." *Annals of Tourism Research* 30 (3): 702–719.

Clifford, James. 1994. "Diasporas." *Cultural Anthropology* 9 (3): 302–338.

——. 2004. "Traditional Futures." In *Questions of Tradition*, edited by Mark Salber Phillips and Gordon Schochet. Toronto: University of Toronto Press, 152–168.

Cohen, Robin. 1997. *Global Diasporas: An Introduction*. Seattle: University of Washington Press.

Cole, Stroma. 2006. "Cultural Tourism, Community Participation and Empowerment." In *Cultural Tourism in a Changing World: Politics, Participation and (Re)presentation*, edited by Melanie Smith and Mike Robinson. Tonawanda, NY: Channel View Publications, 89–103.

Connor, John. 1974. "Acculturation and Family Continuities in Three Generations of Japanese Americans." *Journal of Marriage and Family* 36 (1): 159–165.

Creighton, Millie. 2007. "Changing Heart (Beats): From Japanese Identity and Nostalgia to Taiko for Citizens of the Earth." In *East-West Identities: Globalization, Localization, and Hybridization*, edited by Chan Kwok-bun, Jan Walls, and David Hayward. Boston: Brill, 203–228.

——. 2010. "Metaphors of Japanese-ness and Negotiations of Nikkei Identity: The Transnational Networking of People of Japanese Descent." In *Japanese and Nikkei at Home and Abroad: Negotiating Identities in a Global World*, edited by Nobuko Adachi. Amherst, NY: Cambria Press, 133–162.

Daniels, Roger. 1988. *Asian America: Chinese and Japanese in the United States since 1850*. Seattle: University of Washington Press.

Dicks, Bella. 2000. *Heritage, Place, and Community*. Cardiff, UK: University of Wales Press.

Dorais, Louis-Jacques. 2010. "Politics, Kinship, and Ancestors: Some Diasporic Dimensions of the Vietnamese Experience in North America." *Journal of Vietnamese Studies* 5 (2): 91–132.

Dufoix, Stéphane. 2008. *Diasporas*. Berkeley: University of California Press.

Dwyer, Peter. 2004. *Understanding Social Citizenship: Themes and Perspectives for Policy and Practice*. Bristol, UK: Policy Press.

Dyson, Michael. 1999. "The Labor of Whiteness, the Whiteness of Labor, and the Perils of Whitewashing." In *Race, Identity, and Citizenship: A Reader*, edited by Rodolfo Torres, Louis Mirón, and Jonathan Xavier Inda. Malden, MA: Blackwell, 219–224.

Eckstein, Susan. 2002. "On Deconstructing and Reconstructing the Meaning of Immigrant Generations." In *The Changing Face of Home: The Transnational Lives of the Second Generation*, edited by Peggy Levitt and Mary Waters. New York: Russell Sage Foundation, 211–215.

Eckstein, Susan, and Lorena Barberia. 2002. "Grounding Immigrant Generations in History: Cuban Americans and Their Transnational Ties." *International Migration Review* 36 (3): 799–837.

Erickson, Rebecca. 1995. "The Importance of Authenticity for Self and Society." *Symbolic Interaction* 18 (2): 121–144.

Esman, Milton. 2009. *Diasporas in the Contemporary World*. Cambridge, UK: Polity Press.

Espiritu, Yen Le. 1992. *Asian American Panethnicity: Bridging Institutions and Identities*. Philadelphia: Temple University Press.

———. 1994. "The Intersection of Race, Ethnicity, and Class: The Multiple Identities of Second-Generation Filipinos." *Identities* 1 (2–3): 249–273.

———. 2003. *Home Bound: Filipino American Lives across Cultures, Communities, and Countries*. Berkeley: University of California Press.

Faist, Thomas. 2010. "Diaspora and Transnationalism: What Kind of Dance Partners?" In *Diaspora and Transnationalism: Concepts, Theories and Methods*, edited by Rainer Bauböck and Thomas Faist. Amsterdam: Amsterdam University Press, 9–34.

Fetterman, David. 2005. "Empowerment and Ethnographic Evaluation: Hewlett-Packard's $15 Million Digital Divide Project (A Case Example)." *NAPA Bulletin* 24: 71–78.

Flores, William. 1997. "Citizens vs. Citizenry: Undocumented Immigrants and Latino Cultural Citizenship." In *Latino Cultural Citizenship: Claiming Identity, Space, and Rights*, edited by William Flores and Rina Benmayor. Boston: Beacon Press, 255–277.

Foner, Nancy. 2002. "Second-Generation Transnationalism, Then and Now." In *The Changing Face of Home: The Transnational Lives of the Second Generation*, edited by Peggy Levitt and Mary Waters. New York: Russell Sage Foundation, 242–252.

———. 2009. "Introduction: Intergenerational Relations in Immigrant Families." In *Across Generations: Immigrant Families in America*, edited by Nancy Foner. New York: New York University Press, 1–20.

Fox, Jon. 2007. "From National Inclusion to Economic Exclusion: Ethnic Hungarian Labour Migration to Hungary." *Nations and Nationalism* 13 (1): 77–96.

Foucault, Michel. 1979. *Discipline and Punish: The Birth of the Prison*. New York: Vintage Books.

Fugita, Stephen, and David O'Brien. 1991. *Japanese American Ethnicity: The Persistence of Community*. Seattle: University of Washington Press.

Fugita, Stephen, and Marilyn Fernandez. 2004. *Altered Lives, Enduring Community: Japanese Americans Remember Their World War II Incarceration*. Seattle: University of Washington Press.

Fujitani, Takashi. 2011. *Race for Empire: Koreans as Japanese and Japanese as Americans during World War II*. Berkeley: University of California Press.

Gaidzanwa, Rudo. 2000. "Indigenisation as Empowerment? Gender and Race in the Empowerment Discourse in Zimbabwe." In *The Anthropology of Power: Empowerment and Disempowerment in Changing Structures*, edited by Angela Cheater. London: Routledge, 118–132.

Gans, Herbert J. 1979. "Symbolic Ethnicity: The Future of Ethnic Groups and Cultures in America." *Ethnic and Racial Studies* 2 (1): 1–20.

———. 1997. "Toward a Reconciliation of 'Assimilation' and 'Pluralism.'" *International Migration Review* 31 (4): 875–892.

Giddens, Anthony. 1984. *The Constitution of Society: Outline of the Theory of Structuration*. Berkeley: University of California Press.

Glazer, Nathan. 1997. *We Are All Multiculturalists Now*. Cambridge, MA: Harvard University Press.

Glick Schiller, Nina. 2005. "Lived Simultaneity and Discourses of Diasporic Difference." In *Displacements and Diasporas: Asians in the Americas*, edited by Wanni Anderson and Robert Lee. New Brunswick, NJ: Rutgers University Press, 159–169.

Gordon, Edmund, and Mark Anderson. 1999. "The African Diaspora: Toward an Ethnography of Diasporic Identification." *Journal of American Folklore* 112 (445): 282–296.

Gordon, Milton. 1964. *Assimilation in American Life: The Role of Race, Religion, and National Origins*. New York: Oxford University Press.

Guarnizo, Luis Eduardo, and Luz Marina Díaz. 1999. "Transnational Migration: A View from Colombia." *Ethnic and Racial Studies* 22 (2): 397–421.

Guarnizo, Luis, Alejandro Portes, and William Haller. 2008. "Assimilation and Transnationalism: Determinants of Transnational Political Action among Contemporary Migrants." In *The Transnational Studies Reader: Intersections and Innovations*, edited by Sanjeev Khagram and Peggy Levitt. New York: Routledge, 118–134.

Guest, Greg, Arwen Bunce, and Laura Johnson. 2006. "How Many Interviews Are Enough?: An Experiment with Data Saturation and Variability." *Field Methods* 2006 18: 59–82.

Haller, William, and Patricia Landolt. 2005. "The Transnational Dimensions of Identity Formation: Adult Children of Immigrants in Miami." *Ethnic and Racial Studies* 28 (6): 1182–1214.

Handler, Richard, and Jocelyn Linnekin. 1984. "Tradition, Genuine or Spurious." *Journal of American Folklore* 97 (385): 273–290.

Hansen, Marcus. 1952. "The Third Generation in America." *Commentary* 14: 492–503.

Harden, Jacalyn. 2003. *Double Cross: Japanese Americans in Black and White Chicago.* Minneapolis: University of Minnesota Press.

Hayano, David. 1979. "Auto-Ethnography: Paradigms, Problems, and Prospects." *Human Organization* 38 (1): 99–104.

Hayashi, Brian Masaru. 2008. *Democratizing the Enemy: The Japanese American Internment.* Princeton, NJ: Princeton University Press.

Henkel, Heiko, and Roderick Stirrat. 2001. "Participation as Spiritual Duty: Empowerment as Secular Subjection." In *Participation: The New Tyranny?*, edited by Bill Cooke and Uma Kothari. London: Zed Books, 168–184.

Hickman, Mary, Sarah Morgan, Bronwell Walter, and Joseph Bradley. 2005. "The Limitations of Whiteness and the Boundaries of Englishness: Second-Generation Irish Identifications and Positionings in Multiethnic Britain." *Ethnicities* 5 (2): 160–182.

Hieshima, Joyce, and Barbara Schneider. 1994. "Intergenerational Effects on the Cultural and Cognitive Socialization of Third- and Fourth-Generation Japanese Americans." *Journal of Applied Developmental Psychology* 15: 319–327.

Hirabayashi, James, and Akemi Kikumura-Yano. 2002. "The Pan-American Nikkei Association: A Report on the Tenth and Eleventh Meetings." *Amerasia Journal* 28 (2): 147–157.

Hirabayashi, Lane Ryo, Akemi Kikumura-Yano, and James Hirabayashi. 2002. *New Worlds, New Lives: Globalization and People of Japanese Descent in the Americas and from Latin American in Japan.* Stanford: Stanford University Press, 19–27.

Hobsbawm, Eric. 1983. "Introduction: Inventing Traditions." In *The Invention of Tradition*, edited by Eric Hobsbawm and Terence Ranger. Cambridge, UK: Cambridge University Press, 1–14.

Hosokawa, Bill. 1992. *Nisei: The Quiet Americans: The Story of a People.* Niwot: University Press of Colorado.

Hurh, Won Moo. 1998. *The Korean Americans.* Westport, CT: Greenwood Press.

Igarashi, Yoshikuni. 2001. "In-Betweens in a Hybrid Nation: Construction of Japanese American Identity in Postwar Japan." In *Orientations: Mapping Studies in the Asian Diaspora*, edited by Kandice Chuh and Karen Shimakawa. Durham, NC: Duke University Press, 228–248.

Iijima Hall, Christine. 2008. "Biracial & Multiracial Issues in Arizona AAPI." In *The State of Asian Americans and Pacific Islanders in Arizona.* APAZI and ASU Asian Pacific American Studies Program report, 44–47.

Izumi, Masumi. 2001. "Reconsidering Ethnic Culture and Community: A Case Study on Japanese Canadian Taiko Drumming." *Journal of Asian American Studies* 4 (1): 35–56.

Jackson, Alecia. 2004. "Performativity Identified." *Qualitative Inquiry* 10 (5): 673–690.

Jacobson, Matthew. 1999 *Whiteness of a Different Color: European Immigrants and the Alchemy of Race.* Cambridge, MA: Harvard University Press

———. 2006. *Roots Too: White Ethnic Revival in Post–Civil Rights America.* Cambridge, MA: Harvard University Press.

James, Wendy. 2000. "Empowering Ambiguities." In *The Anthropology of Power: Empowerment and Disempowerment in Changing Structures*, edited by Angela Cheater. London: Routledge, 13–27.

Jiménez, Tomás. 2010. *Replenished Ethnicity: Mexican Americans, Immigration, and Identity*. Berkeley: University of California Press.

Jiobu, Robert. 1988. *Ethnicity and Assimilation: Blacks, Chinese, Filipinos, Japanese, Koreans, Mexicans, Vietnamese, and Whites*. Albany: State University of New York Press.

Johnson, Henry. 2008. "Why Taiko? Understanding Taiko Performance at New Zealand's First Taiko Festival." *Sites: New Series* 5 (2): 111–134.

Jones, Joni. 2002. "Performance Ethnography: The Role of Embodiment in Cultural Authenticity." *Theatre Topics* 12 (1): 1–15.

Joppke, Christian. 1999. "How Immigration is Changing Citizenship: A Comparative View." *Ethnic and Racial Studies* 22 (4): 629–652.

———. 2004. "The Retreat of Multiculturalism in the Liberal State: Theory and Policy." *British Journal of Sociology* 55 (2): 237–257.

Kanuha, Valli Kalei. 2000. "'Being' Native versus 'Going Native': Conducting Social Work Research as an Insider." *Social Work: A Journal of the National Association of Social Workers* 45 (5): 439–447.

Kasinitz, Philip, John Mollenkopf, and Mary Waters. 2004. "Worlds of the Second Generation." In *Becoming New Yorkers: Ethnographies of the New Second Generation*, edited by Philip Kasinitz, John Mollenkopf, and Mary Waters. New York: Russell Sage Foundation, 1–19.

Kasinitz, Philip, John Mollenkopf, Mary Waters, and Jennifer Holdaway. 2008. *Inheriting the City: The Children of Immigrants Come of Age*. New York: Russell Sage Foundation.

Kasinitz, Philip, Mary Waters, John Mollenkopf, and Merih Anil. 2002. "Transnationalism and the Children of Immigrants in Contemporary New York." In *The Changing Face of Home: The Transnational Lives of the Second Generation*, edited by Peggy Levitt and Mary Waters. New York: Russell Sage Foundation, 96–122.

Kazal, Russell. 1995. "Revisiting Assimilation: The Rise, Fall, and Reappraisal of a Concept in American Ethnic History." *American Historical Review* 100 (2): 437–471.

Kendis, Kaoru Oguri. 1989. *A Matter of Comfort: Ethnic Maintenance and Ethnic Style among Third-Generation Japanese Americans*. New York: AMS Press.

Kibria, Nazli. 2002a. *Becoming Asian American: Second-Generation Chinese and Korean American Identities*. Baltimore: Johns Hopkins University Press.

———. 2002b. "Of Blood, Belonging, and Homeland Trips: Transnationalism and Identity among Second-Generation Chinese and Korean Americans." In *The Changing Face of Home: The Transnational Lives of the Second Generation*, edited by Peggy Levitt and Mary Waters. New York: Russell Sage, 295–311.

Kikumura-Yano, Akemi, ed. 2002. *Encyclopedia of Japanese Descendants in the Americas: An Illustrated History of the Nikkei*. Walnut Creek, CA: AltaMira Press.

Kim, Hyounggon, and Tazim Jamal. 2007. "Touristic Quest for Existential Authenticity." *Annals of Tourism Research* 34 (1): 181–201.

Kim, Nadia. 2008. *Imperial Citizens: Koreans and Race from Seoul to LA*. Stanford: Stanford University Press.

King, Russell, and Anastasia Christou. 2010. "Cultural Geographies of Counter-Diasporic Migration: Perspectives from the Study of Second-Generation 'Returnees' to Greece." *Population, Space and Place* 16 (2): 103–119.

King-O'Riain, Rebecca Chiyoko. 2006. *Pure Beauty: Judging Race in Japanese American Beauty Pageants*. Minneapolis: University of Minnesota Press.

Kitano, Harry. 1969. "Japanese American Mental Illness." In *Changing Perspectives in Mental Illness*, edited by Stanley Plog and Robert Edgerton. New York: Holt, Rinehart and Winston.

———. 1993. *Generations and Identity: The Japanese American*. Needham Heights, MA: Ginn Press.

Kobayashi, Kim Noriko. 2006. "Asian Women Kick Ass: A Study of Gender Issues within Canadian Kumi-Daiko." *Canadian Folk Music* 40 (1): 1–11.

Konagaya, Hideyo. 2001. "Taiko as Performance: Creating Japanese American Traditions." *Japanese Journal of American Studies* 12:105–124.

———. 2005. "Performing Manliness: Resistance and Harmony in Japanese American Taiko." In *Manly Traditions: The Folk Roots of American Masculinities*, edited by Simon Bronner. Bloomington: Indiana University Press, 134–156.

Kondo, Dorinne. 1986. "Dissolution and Reconstitution of Self: Implications for Anthropological Epistemology." *Cultural Anthropology* 1 (1): 74–88.

Kurashige, Lon. 2002. *Japanese American Celebration and Conflict: A History of Ethnic Identity and Festival, 1934–1990*. Berkeley: University of California Press.

Kymlicka, Will. 1995. *Multicultural Citizenship: A Liberal Theory of Minority Rights*. Cambridge, UK: Cambridge University Press.

Laguerre, Michel. 1998. *Diasporic Citizenship: Haitian Americans in Transnational America*. New York: St. Martin's Press.

Lee, Christopher. 2005. "Diaspora, Transnationalism, and Asian American Studies: Positions and Debates." In *Displacements and Diasporas: Asians in the Americas*, edited by Wanni Anderson and Robert Lee. New Brunswick, NJ: Rutgers University Press, 23–38.

Lee, Sangmi. Forthcoming. "Between the Diaspora and the Nation-State: Transnational Ethnic Unity and Fragmentation among the Hmong in Laos and the United States." Ph.D. diss., University of Oxford.

Lesser, Jeffrey. 2007. *A Discontented Diaspora: Japanese Brazilians and the Meanings of Ethnic Militancy, 1960–1980*. Durham, NC: Duke University Press.

Levitt, Peggy. 2001. "Transnational migration: Taking Stock and Future Directions." *Global Networks* 1 (3): 195–216.

———. 2002. "The Ties that Change: Relations to the Ancestral Home over the Life Cycle." In *The Changing Face of Home: The Transnational Lives of the Second Generation*, edited by Peggy Levitt and Mary Waters. New York: Russell Sage Foundation, 123–144.

Levitt, Peggy, and Nina Glick Schiller. 2008. "Conceptualizing Simultaneity: A Transnational Social Field Perspective on Society." In *The Transnational Studies Reader*:

*Intersections and Innovations*, edited by Sanjeev Khagram and Peggy Levitt. New York: Routledge, 284–294.

Levitt, Peggy, and B. Nadya Jaworsky. 2007. "Transnational Migration Studies: Past Developments and Future Trends." *Annual Review of Sociology* 33:129–56.

Levitt, Peggy, and Mary Waters. 2002. Introduction. In *The Changing Face of Home: The Transnational Lives of the Second Generation*, edited by Peggy Levitt and Mary Waters. New York: Russell Sage Foundation, 1–30.

Ling, Susie. 1989. "The Mountain Movers: Asian American Women's Movement in Los Angeles." *Amerasia Journal* 15 (1): 51–67.

Linnekin, Jocelyn. 1991. "Cultural Invention and the Dilemma of Authenticity." *American Anthropologist* 93 (2): 446–449.

Lock, Margaret, and Nancy Scheper-Hughes. 1996. "A Critical-Interpretive Approach in Medical Anthropology: Rituals and Routines of Discipline and Dissent." In *Medical Anthropology: Contemporary Theory and Method*, edited by Thomas Johnson and Carolyn Sargent, rev. ed. New York: Praeger, 41–70.

Louie, Andrea. 2004. *Renegotiating Chinese Identities in China and the United States*. Durham, NC: Duke University Press.

Lowe, Lisa. 1996. *Immigrant Acts: On Asian American Cultural Politics*. Durham, NC: Duke University Press.

Lubkemann, Stephen. 2013. "Diasporicity and its Discontents: Liberian Identity Arguments and the Irresolution of Return (1820–2013)." Paper presented at the African Studies Association 56th Annual Meeting.

Lyman, Stanford. 1970. *The Asian in the West*. Social Science & Humanities Publication No. 4. Reno, NV: Desert Research Institute.

MacCannell, Dean. 1973. "Staged Authenticity: Arrangements of Social Space in Tourist Settings." *American Journal of Sociology* 79 (3): 589–603.

Maeda, Daryl. 2012. *Rethinking the Asian American Movement*. New York: Routledge.

Maki, Mitchell, Harry Kitano, and S. Megan Berthold. 1999. *Achieving the Impossible Dream: How Japanese Americans Obtained Redress*. Urbana: University of Illinois Press

Mannheim, Karl. 1952. *Essays on the Sociology of Knowledge*. New York: Oxford University Press.

Masterson, Daniel. 2004. *The Japanese in Latin America*. Urbana: University of Illinois Press.

Masuda, Minoru, Gary Matsumoto, and Gerald Meredith. 1970. "Ethnic Identity in Three Generations of Japanese Americans." *Journal of Social Psychology* 81 (2): 199–207.

Matsumoto, Valerie. 2014. *City Girls: The Nisei Social World in Los Angeles, 1920–1950*. Oxford, UK: Oxford University Press.

Matsuo, Hisako. 1992. "Identificational Assimilation of Japanese Americans: A Reassessment of Primordialism and Circumstantialism." *Sociological Perspectives* 35 (3): 505–523.

May, Stephen, and Christine Sleeter. 2010. "Introduction. Critical Multiculturalism: Theory and Praxis." In *Critical Multiculturalism: Theory and Praxis*, edited by Stephen May and Christine Sleeter. New York: Routledge, 1–18.

McIntosh, Alison, and Richard Prentice. 1999. "Affirming Authenticity: Consuming Cultural Heritage." *Annals of Tourism Research* 26 (3): 589–612.

Menjívar, Cecilia. 2002. "Living in Two Worlds? Guatemalan-Origin Children in the United States and Emerging Transnationalism." *Journal of Ethnic and Migration Studies* 28 (3): 531–552.

Merleau-Ponty, Maurice. 1962. *Phenomenology of Perception*, translated by Colin Smith. London: Routledge.

Min, Pyong Gap, ed. 2002. *Second Generation: Ethnic Identity among Asian Americans*. Walnut Creek, CA: Altamira Press.

———. 2006a. "Major Issues Related to Asian American Experiences." In *Asian Americans: Contemporary Trends and Issues*, edited by Pyong Gap Min, 2nd ed. Thousand Oaks, CA: Pine Forge Press, 80–107.

———. 2006b. "Settlement Patterns and Diversity." In *Asian Americans: Contemporary Trends and Issues*, edited by Pyong Gap Min, 2nd ed. Thousand Oaks, CA: Pine Forge Press, 32–53.

Montero, Darrel. 1980. *Japanese Americans: Changing Patterns of Ethnic Affiliation Over Three Generations*. Boulder, CO: Westview Press.

Morimoto, Toyotomi. 1997. *Japanese Americans and Cultural Continuity: Maintaining Language and Heritage*. New York: Garland Publishing.

Motzafi-Haller, Pnina. 1997. "Writing Birthright: On Native Anthropologists and the Politics of Representation." In *Auto/Ethnography: Rewriting the Self and the Social*, edited by Deborah Reed-Danahay. Oxford, UK: Berg, 195–222.

Münz, Rainer, and Rainer Ohliger, eds. 2003. *Diasporas and Ethnic Migrants: Germany, Israel, and Post-Soviet Successor States in Comparative Perspective*. London: Frank Cass.

Murji, Karim, and John Solomos. 2005. "Introduction: Racialization in Theory and Practice." In *Racialization: Studies in Theory and Practice*, edited by Karim Murji and John Solomos. Oxford, UK: Oxford University Press, 1–27.

Nakano Glenn, Evelyn. 1986. *Issei, Nisei, War Bride: Three Generations of Japanese American Women in Domestic Service*. Philadelphia: Temple University Press.

Narayan, Kirin. 1993. "How Native Is a 'Native' Anthropologist?" *American Anthropologist* 95: 671–686.

Nelson, Linda Williamson. 1996. "Hands in the Chit'lins': Notes on Native Anthropological Research among African American Women." In *Unrelated Kin: Race and Gender in Women's Personal Narrative*, edited by Gwendolyn Etter-Lewis and Michéle Foster. New York: Routledge, 183–199.

Newton, Barbara, Elizabeth Buck, Don Kunimura, Carol Colfer, and Deborah Scholsberg. 1988. "Ethnic Identity among Japanese-Americans in Hawaii: A Critique of Hansen's Third-Generation Return Hypothesis." *International Journal of Intercultural Relations* 12 (4): 305–315.

Noland, Carrie. 2009. *Agency and Embodiment: Performing Gestures/Producing Culture*. Cambridge, MA: Harvard University Press.

Novak, Michael. 1971. *The Rise of the Unmeltable Ethnics*. New York: Macmillan.

O'Brien, David, and Stephen Fugita. 1991. *The Japanese American Experience.* Bloomington: Indiana University Press.

Ohnuki-Tierney, Emiko. 1984. "'Native' Anthropologists." *American Ethnologist* 11 (3): 584–586.

Okamura, Jonathan. 1998. *Imagining the Filipino American Diaspora: Transnational Relations, Identities, and Communities.* New York: Garland Publishing.

———. 2003. "Asian American Studies in the Age of Transnationalism: Diaspora, Race, Community." *Amerasia Journal* 29 (2): 171–193.

———. 2008. *Ethnicity and Inequality in Hawai'i.* Philadelphia: Temple University Press.

———. 2014. *From Race to Ethnicity: Interpreting Japanese American Experiences in Hawai'i.* Honolulu: University of Hawaii Press.

Omatsu, Glenn. 2000. "The 'Four Prisons' and the Movements of Liberation: Asian American Activism from the 1960s to the 1990s." In *Contemporary Asian America: A Multidisciplinary Reader,* edited by Min Zhou and James Gatewood. New York: New York University Press, 80–112.

Omi, Michael, and Howard Winant. 1986. *Racial Formation in the United States: From the 1960s to the 1980s.* New York: Routledge & Kegan Paul.

———. 2015. *Racial Formation in the United States,* 3rd ed. New York: Routledge.

Ong, Aihwa. 1996. "Cultural Citizenship as Subject-Making: Immigrants Negotiate Racial and Cultural Boundaries in the United States." *Current Anthropology* 37 (5): 737–751.

Paerregaard, Karsten. 2010. "Interrogating Diaspora: Power and Conflict in Peruvian Migration." In *Diaspora and Transnationalism: Concepts, Theories and Methods,* edited by Rainer Bauböck and Thomas Faist. Amsterdam: Amsterdam University Press, 91–107.

Park, Lisa Sun-Hee. 2005. *Consuming Citizenship: Children of Asian Immigrant Entrepreneurs.* Stanford, CA: Stanford University Press.

Parreñas, Rhacel Salazar. 2001. *Servants of Globalization: Women, Migration and Domestic Work.* Stanford, CA: Stanford University Press.

Parreñas, Rhacel, and Lok Siu. 2007. "Introduction: Asian Diasporas—New Conceptions, New Frameworks." In *Asian Diasporas: New Formations, New Conceptions,* edited by Rhacel Parreñas and Lok Siu. Stanford, CA: Stanford University Press, 1–27.

Perlmann, Joel, and Roger Waldinger. 1997. "Second Generation Decline? Children of Immigrants, Past and Present—A Reconsideration." *International Migration Review* 31 (4): 893–922.

Portes, Alejandro. 2003. "Conclusion: Theoretical Convergencies and Empirical Evidence in the Study of Immigrant Transnationalism." *International Migration Review* 37 (3): 874–892.

Portes, Alejandro, Patricia Fernández-Kelly, and William Haller. 2005. "Segmented Assimilation on the Ground: The New Second Generation in Early Adulthood." *Ethnic and Racial Studies* 28 (6): 1000–1040.

Portes, Alejandro, Luis Eduardo Guarnizo, and Patricia Landolt. 1999. "Introduction: Pitfalls and Promise of an Emergent Research Field." *Ethnic and Racial Studies* 22 (2): 217–230.

Portes, Alejandro, and Rubén Rumbaut. 2001. *Legacies: The Story of the Immigrant Second Generation*. Berkeley: University of California Press.

Portes, Alejandro, and Min Zhou. 1993. "The New Second Generation: Segmented Assimilation and its Variants among Post-1965 Immigrant Youth." *Annals of the American Academy of Political and Social Sciences* 530 (1): 74–98.

Potter, Robert. 2005. "'Young, Gifted and Back': Second-Generation Transnational Return Migrants to the Caribbean." *Progress in Development Studies* 5 (3): 213–223.

Powell, Kimberly. 2008. "Drumming against the Quiet: The Sounds of Asian American Identity in an Amorphous Landscape." *Qualitative Inquiry* 14 (6): 901–925.

———. 2012a. "Composing Sound Identity in Taiko Drumming." *Anthropology and Education Quarterly* 43 (1): 101–119.

———. 2012b. "The Drum in the Dojo: Re-Sounding Embodied Experience in Taiko Drumming." In *Thinking Comprehensively about Education: Spaces of Educative Possibility and Their Implications for Public Policy*, edited by Ezekiel Dixon-Román and Edmund Gordon. New York: Routledge, 123–140.

Pyke, Karen, and Tran Dang. 2003. "'FOB' and 'Whitewashed': Identity and Internalized Racism among Second Generation Asian Americans." *Qualitative Sociology* 26 (2): 147–172.

Robbins, Joel. 2004. *Becoming Sinners: Christianity and Moral Torment in a Papua New Guinea Society*. Berkeley: University of California Press.

Robinson, Greg. 2010. *A Tragedy of Democracy: Japanese Confinement in North America*. New York: Columbia University Press.

Roediger, David. 2005. *Working Toward Whiteness: How America's Immigrants Became White: The Strange Journey from Ellis Island to the Suburbs*. New York: Basic Books.

Rosaldo, Renato. 1989. *Culture and Truth: The Remaking of Social Analysis*. Boston: Beacon Press.

———. 1994. "Cultural Citizenship in San Jose, California." *PoLAR: Political and Legal Anthropology Review* 17 (2): 57–63.

———. 1999. "Cultural Citizenship, Inequality, and Multiculturalism." In *Race, Identity, and Citizenship: A Reader*, edited by Rodolfo Torres, Louis Mirón, and Jonathan Xavier Inda. Malden, MA: Blackwell, 253–261.

Rumbaut, Rubén. 2005. "Turning Points in the Transition to Adulthood: Determinants of Educational Attainment, Incarceration, and Early Childbearing among Children of Immigrants." *Ethnic and Racial Studies* 28 (6): 1041–1086.

Rumbaut, Rubén, and Alejandro Portes, eds. 2001. *Ethnicities: Children of Immigrants in America*. Berkeley: University of California Press.

Safran, William. 1991. "Diasporas in Modern Societies: Myths of Homeland and Return." *Diaspora: A Journal of Transnational Studies* 1 (1): 83–99.

Schein, Louisa. 1998. "Forged Transnationality and Oppositional Cosmopolitanism." In *Transnationalism from Below*, edited by Michael P. Smith and Luis Guarnizo. New Brunswick, NJ: Transaction Publishers, 291–313.

Scheyvens, Regina. 1999. "Ecotourism and the Empowerment of Local Communities." *Tourism Management* 20: 245–249.

Schieffelin, Edward. 1998. "Problematizing Performance." In *Ritual, Performance, Media*, edited by Felicia Hughes-Freeland. New York: Routledge, 199–211.

Sheffer, Gabriel, ed. 2003a. *Diaspora Politics*. Cambridge, UK: Cambridge University Press.

———. 2003b. "From Diasporas to Migrants—from Migrants to Diasporas." In *Diasporas and Ethnic Migrants: Germany, Israel, and Post-Soviet Successor States in Comparative Perspective*, edited by Rainer Münz and Rainer Ohliger. London: Frank Cass, 21–36.

Shuval, Judith. 2000. "Diaspora Migration: Definitional Ambiguities and a Theoretical Paradigm." *International Migration* 38 (5): 41–56.

Silbereisen, Rainer, Peter Titzmann, and Yossi Shavit, eds. 2014. *The Challenges of Diaspora Migration: Interdisciplinary Perspectives on Israel and Germany*. Surrey, UK: Ashgate.

Silverstein, Paul. 2005. "Immigrant Racialization and the New Savage Slot: Race, Migration, and Immigration in the New Europe." *Annual Review of Anthropology* 34: 363–384.

Smith, Laurajane. 2006. *Uses of Heritage*. New York: Routledge.

Smith, Robert. 2003. "Diasporic Memberships in Historical Perspective: Comparative Insights from the Mexican, Italian, and Polish Cases." *International Migration Review* 37 (3): 724–759.

———. 2006. *Mexican New York: Transnational Lives of New Immigrants*. Berkeley: University of California Press.

Sofield, Trevor. 2003. *Empowerment for Sustainable Tourism Development*. Boston: Pergamon.

Spickard, Paul. 1996. *Japanese Americans: The Formation and Transformations of an Ethnic Group*. London: Prentice Hall International.

———. 1989. *Mixed Blood: Intermarriage and Ethnic Identity in Twentieth-Century America*. Madison: University of Wisconsin Press.

Steiner, Carol, and Yvette Reisinger. 2006. "Understanding Existential Authenticity." *Annals of Tourism Research* 33 (2): 299–318.

Stevenson, Nick. 2003. "Cultural Citizenship in the 'Cultural' Society: A Cosmopolitan Approach." *Citizenship Studies* 7 (3): 331–348.

Takahashi, Jere. 1982. "Japanese American Responses to Race Relations: The Formation of Nisei Perspectives." *Amerasia* 9 (1): 29–57.

———. 1997. *Nisei/Sansei: Shifting Japanese American Identities and Politics*. Philadelphia: Temple University Press.

Takamori, Ayako. 2010. "Rethinking Japanese American 'Heritage' in the Homeland." *Critical Asian Studies* 42 (2): 217–238.

———. 2011. "Native Foreigners: Japanese Americans in Japan." Ph.D. diss., New York University.

Takeda, Atsushi. 2012. "Emotional Transnationalism and Emotional Flows: Japanese Women in Australia." *Women's Studies International Forum* 35: 22–28.

Takenaka, Ayumi. 2009. "How Diasporic Ties Emerge: Pan-American Nikkei Communities and the Japanese State." *Ethnic and Racial Studies* 32 (8): 1325–1345.

Takezawa, Yasuko. 1995. *Breaking the Silence: Redress and Japanese American Ethnicity.* Ithaca, NY: Cornell University Press.

Tambiah, Stanley. 2000. "Transnational Movements, Diaspora, and Multiple Modernities." *Daedalus* 129 (1): 163–194.

Tamura, Eileen. 1994. *Americanization, Acculturation, and Ethnic Identity: The Nisei Generation in Hawaii.* Urbana-Champaign: University of Illinois Press.

Taylor, John. 2001. "Authenticity and Sincerity in Tourism." *Annals of Tourism Research* 28 (1): 7–26.

Terada, Yoshitaka. 2001. "Shifting Identities of Taiko Music in North America." In *Transcending Boundaries: Asian Musics in North America*, edited by Yoshitaka Terada. Osaka: Japan: National Museum of Ethnology, 37–59.

Thai, Hung. 2002. "The Formation of Ethnic Identities among Second-Generation Vietnam Americans." In *Second Generation: Ethnic Identity among Asian Americans*, edited by Pyong Gap Min. Walnut Creek, CA: Altamira Press, 53–84.

Tölölyan, Khachig. 1996. "Rethinking Diaspora(s): Stateless Power in the Transnational Moment." *Diaspora: A Journal of Transnational Studies* 5 (1): 3–36.

Tsuda, Takeyuki. 2001. "When Identities Become Modern: Japanese Immigrants in Brazil and the Global Contextualization of Identity." *Ethnic and Racial Studies* 24 (3): 412–432.

———. 2003. *Strangers in the Ethnic Homeland: Japanese Brazilian Return Migration in Transnational Perspective.* New York: Columbia University Press

———, ed. 2009a. *Diasporic Homecomings: Ethnic Return Migration in Comparative Perspective.* Stanford, CA: Stanford University Press.

———. 2009b. "Global Inequities and Diasporic Return: Japanese American and Brazilian Encounters with the Ethnic Homeland." In *Diasporic Homecomings: Ethnic Return Migration in Comparative Perspective*, edited by Takeyuki Tsuda. Stanford, CA: Stanford University Press, 227–259.

———. 2009c. "Introduction: Diasporic Return and Migration Studies." In *Diasporic Homecomings: Ethnic Return Migration in Comparative Perspective*, edited by Takeyuki Tsuda. Stanford, UK: Stanford University Press, 1–18.

———. 2009d. "Conclusion: Diasporic Homecomings and Ambivalent Encounters with the Ethnic Homeland." In *Diasporic Homecomings: Ethnic Return Migration in Comparative Perspective*, edited by Takeyuki Tsuda. Stanford, CA: Stanford University Press, 325–350.

———. 2012a. "Diasporas without a Consciousness: Japanese Americans and the Lack of a Nikkei Identity." *Regions and Cohesion* 2 (2): 83–104.

———. 2012b. "Disconnected from the 'Diaspora': Japanese Americans and the Lack of Transnational Ethnic Networks." *Journal of Anthropological Research* 68 (2): 95–116.

———. 2012c. "Whatever Happened to Simultaneity? Transnational Migration Theory and Dual Engagement in Sending and Receiving Countries." *Journal of Ethnic and Migration Studies* 38 (4): 631–649.

———. 2014. "'I'm American, Not Japanese!': The Struggle for Racial Citizenship Among Later-Generation Japanese Americans." *Ethnic and Racial Studies* 37 (3): 405–424.

———. 2015. "Is Native Anthropology Really Possible?" *Anthropology Today* 31 (3): 14–17.

Tsuda, Takeyuki, Maria Tapias, and Xavier Escandell. 2014. "Locating the Global in Transnational Ethnography." *Journal of Contemporary Ethnography* 43 (2): 123–147.

Tuan, Mia. 2001. *Forever Foreigners or Honorary Whites? The Asian Ethnic Experience Today.* New Brunswick, NJ: Rutgers University Press.

Turner, Terence. 1993. "Anthropology and Multiculturalism: What Is Anthropology that Multiculturalists Should Be Mindful of It?" *Cultural Anthropology* 8 (4): 411–429.

Tusler, Mark. 2003. "Sounds and Sights of Power: Ensemble Taiko Drumming (*kumi daiko*) Pedagogy in California and the Conceptualization of Power." Ph.D. diss., University of California, Santa Barbara.

Ueda, Reed. 2002. "An Early Transnationalism? The Japanese American Second Generation of Hawaii in the Interwar Years." In *The Changing Face of Home: The Transnational Lives of the Second Generation,* edited by Peggy Levitt and Mary Waters. New York: Russell Sage Foundation, 33–42.

Umezawa Duus, Masayo. 1987. *Unlikely Liberators: The Men of the 100th and 442nd.* Honolulu: University of Hawaii Press.

Van Hear, Nicholas. 1998. *New Diasporas: The Mass Exodus, Dispersal and Regrouping of Migrant Communities.* Seattle: University of Washington Press.

Van Niekerk, Mies. 2007. "Second-Generation Caribbeans in the Netherlands: Different Migration Histories, Diverging Trajectories." *Journal of Ethnic and Migration Studies* 33 (7): 1063–1081.

Vertovec, Steven. 2004. "Migrant Transnationalism and Modes of Transformation." *International Migration Review* 38 (3): 970–1001.

Waitt, Gordon. 2000. "Consuming Heritage: Perceived Historical Authenticity." *Annals of Tourism Research* 27 (4): 835–862.

Wang, Nina. 1999. "Rethinking Authenticity in Tourism Experience." *Annals of Tourism Research* 26 (2): 349–370.

Waters, Mary. 1990. *Ethnic Options: Choosing Identities in America.* Berkeley: University of California Press.

———. 1999. *Black Identities: West Indian Immigrant Dreams and American Realities.* Cambridge, MA: Harvard University Press.

Waters, Mary, and Tomás Jiménez. 2005. "Assessing Immigrant Assimilation: New Empirical and Theoretical Challenges." *Annual Review of Sociology* 31: 105–125.

Waterton, Emma, and Steve Watson, eds. 2011. *Heritage and Community Development: Collaboration or Contestation?* New York: Routledge.

Wei, William. 2004. "A Commentary on Young Asian American Activists from the 1960s to the Present." In *Asian American Youth: Culture, Identity, and Ethnicity,* edited by Min Zhou and Jennifer Lee. London: Routledge, 299–312.

Werbner, Richard. 2000. "The Reach of the Postcolonial State: Development, Empowerment/Disempowerment and Technocracy." In *The Anthropology of Power: Empowerment and Disempowerment in Changing Structures,* edited by Angela Cheater. London: Routledge, 57–72.

White, Paul. 2003. "The Japanese in Latin America: On the Uses of Diaspora." *International Journal of Population Geography* 9: 309–322.

Williams, Jay. 2013. "Cultural Performance: The Personal and Collective Negotiation of Ethnic Identity through Powwow and Taiko Drumming in Chicago." Ph.D. diss., University of Chicago.

Wong, Deborah. 2000. "Taiko and the Asian/American Body: Drums, *Rising Sun*, and the Question of Gender." *World of Music* 42 (3): 67–78.

———. 2005. "Noisy Intersection: Ethnicity, Authenticity, and Ownership in Asian American Taiko." In *Diasporas and Interculturalism in Asian Performing Arts: Translating Traditions*, edited by Hae-kyung Um. London: RoutledgeCurzon, 75–90.

Wong, Sau-Ling. 1995. "Denationalization Reconsidered: Asian American Cultural Criticism at a Theoretical Crossroads." *Amerasia Journal* 21 (1): 1–27.

Wooden, Wayne, Joseph Leon, and Michelle Toshima. 1988. "Ethnic Identity among Sansei and Yonsei Church-Affiliated Youth in Los Angeles and Honolulu." *Psychological Reports* 62 (1): 268–270.

Woodrum, Eric. 1981. "An Assessment of Japanese American Assimilation, Pluralism, and Subordination." *American Journal of Sociology* 87 (1): 157–169.

Wu, Jean, Yu-wen Shen, and Min Song. 2000. "Introduction." In *Asian American Studies: A Reader*, edited by Jean Wu, Yu-wen Shen, and Min Song. New Brunswick, NJ: Rutgers University Press, xiii–xxiv.

Yamashiro, Jane. 2008. "Transnational Racial and Ethnic Identity Formation among Japanese Americans in Global Tokyo." Ph.D. diss., University of Hawaii, Manoa.

———. 2011. "Racialized National Identity Construction in the Ancestral Homeland: Japanese American Migrants in Japan." *Ethnic and Racial Studies* 34 (9): 1502–1521.

Yanagisako, Sylvia. 1985. *Transforming the Past: Tradition and Kinship among Japanese Americans*. Stanford, CA: Stanford University Press.

Yenne, Bill. 2007. *Rising Sons: The Japanese American GIs Who Fought for the United States in World War II*. New York: St. Martin's Press.

Yoo, David. 2000. *Growing Up Nisei: Race, Generation, and Culture among Japanese Americans of California, 1924–49*. Urbana-Champaign: University of Illinois Press.

Yoon, Paul Jong-Chul. 2001. "'She's Really Become Japanese Now!': Taiko Drumming and Asian American Identifications." *American Music* 19 (4): 417–438.

Zhou, Min. 2004. "Are Asian Americans Becoming 'White?'" *Contexts* 3 (1): 29–37.

Zhou, Min, and James Gatewood. 2000. "Introduction: Revisiting Contemporary Asian America." In *Contemporary Asian America: A Multidisciplinary Reader*, edited by Min Zhou and James Gatewood. New York: New York University Press, 1–46.

Zhou, Min, and Jennifer Lee. 2004. "Introduction: The Making of Culture, Identity, and Ethnicity among Asian American Youth." In *Asian American Youth: Culture, Identity, and Ethnicity*, edited by Min Zhou and Jennifer Lee. London: Routledge, 1–30.

Zimmerman, Marc. 2000. "Empowerment Theory: Psychological, Organizational, and Community Levels of Analysis." In *Handbook of Community Psychology*, edited by Julian Rappaport and Edward Seidman. New York: Kluwer Academic, 43–63.

# INDEX

activism. *See* Asian American movement; ethnic activism

African Americans, 134, 175, 198. *See also* blacks

age: diasporicity and, 260–261, 269–270; ethnic heritage and, 106–107, 117, 119, 276–277, 293n3; generation and, 11, 111

agency, 145, 148, 248; 219–221; taiko and, 222, 223, 231, 235–236

ancestry. *See* ethnic heritage

Asian American movement, 24, 40, 87, 112, 117–120, 123, 131, 183–184, 203, 259, 279, 294n4

Asian Americans, 9, 106, 117, 135, 164, 211, 245–246, 250–251, 274, 295n2; population of, 7, 75, 133–134; racialization of, 145, 151, 154–155, 162, 167; stereotypes of, 41, 85, 226, 235, 236, 237–238, 244, 245, 281. *See also* Japanese Americans: Asian Americans and

Asian American Studies, 6–7, 25, 118, 135, 141, 157, 158, 162, 184, 251, 294n2

assimilation, 13, 21, 136–137, 157; diaspora and, 251, 253, 254, 258, 260, 263, 269–270; discrimination and, 7, 52, 54, 61–63, 275; ethnic heritage and, 16–20, 22, 41, 49, 54, 68–69, 88, 116–117, 123, 157, 160, 168–170, 178, 180, 191, 192, 193, 273, 280; transnationalism and, 20–21, 22, 273. *See also* Japanese Americans: assimilation of

authenticity, 226–228; defined, 226; homeland and, 14, 183, 191, 225, 226, 228–229, 231, 232, 247, 273, 296n1; modernity and, 227, 232, 234, 248; performative,

41, 226, 231–234, 235, 236, 239, 240, 248; taiko and, 225–226, 228–231, 232–234, 236, 239, 240, 247, 248

bilingualism/biculturalism, 2–3, 19, 33, 39, 50, 71, 88–89, 90, 92, 100–101

biracial. *See* Japanese Americans: biracial

blacks, 24, 54, 82, 84, 102, 141, 294n4, 294n6. *See also* African Americans

Bourdieu, Pierre, 219–220

Butler, Judith, 221, 235–236

Caucasians. *See* whites

citizenship, 135–138. *See also* cultural citizenship; racial citizenship; social citizenship

Cohen, Robin, 252

colorblindness, 27–28, 158, 176

concentration camps. *See* internment of Japanese Americans

cultural citizenship, 136–137

cultural heritage. *See* ethnic heritage

Day of Remembrance, 45–48, 56

diasporas, 42, 200, 222, 225, 228, 231, 232, 240, 248, 250–270; assimilation and, 251, 253, 254, 258, 260, 263, 269–270; definitions of, 251–253, 268–269; generations and, 257–260 261; historicity and, 257–259; and homelands and, 253, 256, 256–261; newer and older, 256, 261, 270; transnationalism and, 42, 251, 253–254, 256, 257, 259, 261–263, 266–268, 269. *See also* Japanese Americans: Japanese diaspora and; Japanese diaspora

## ABOUT THE AUTHOR

Takeyuki (Gaku) Tsuda is Professor of Anthropology in the School of Human Evolution and Social Change at Arizona State University. His primary academic interests include international migration, diasporas, ethnic minorities, ethnic and national identity, transnationalism and globalization, ethnic return migrants, and the Japanese diaspora in the Americas.